Institutional Advancement

Philanthropy and Education

Series Editor

Marybeth Gasman, Professor of Higher Education, Graduate School of Education, University of Pennsylvania, USA

This series highlights first-rate scholarship related to education and philanthropy, attracting the top authors writing in the field. Philanthropy is broadly defined to include time, talent, and treasure. In addition to traditional forms and definitions of philanthropy, the series highlights philanthropy in communities of color as well as philanthropy among women and LGBT communities. Books in the series focus on fundraising as it is an integral part of increasing philanthropy and has an ever-increasing market.

Philanthropy in Black Education: A Fateful Hour Creating the Atlanta University System
  By Vida L. Avery

Saving Black Colleges: Leading Change in a Complex Organization
  By Alvin J. Schexnider

Philanthropy and American Higher Education
  By John R. Thelin and Richard W. Trollinger

Institutional Advancement: What We Know
  By Eve Proper and Timothy C. Caboni

Institutional Advancement

What We Know

Eve Proper

and

Timothy C. Caboni

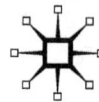

INSTITUTIONAL ADVANCEMENT
Copyright © Eve Proper and Timothy C. Caboni, 2014.
All rights reserved.

First published in 2014 by
PALGRAVE MACMILLAN®
in the United States—a division of St. Martin's Press LLC,
175 Fifth Avenue, New York, NY 10010.

Where this book is distributed in the UK, Europe and the rest of the world, this is by Palgrave Macmillan, a division of Macmillan Publishers Limited, registered in England, company number 785998, of Houndmills, Basingstoke, Hampshire RG21 6XS.

Palgrave Macmillan is the global academic imprint of the above companies and has companies and representatives throughout the world.

Palgrave® and Macmillan® are registered trademarks in the United States, the United Kingdom, Europe and other countries.

ISBN: 978–1–137–37930–6

Library of Congress Cataloging-in-Publication Data

Proper, Eve.
    Institutional advancement : what we know / Eve Proper, Timothy C. Caboni.
       pages cm.—(Philanthropy and education)
    Includes bibliographical references and index.
    ISBN 978–1–137–37930–6 (hardback)
     1. Educational fund raising. 2. Education, Higher—Administration.
I. Caboni, Timothy C. II. Title.
LB2335.95.P76 2014
379.1'3—dc23   2014025150

A catalogue record of the book is available from the British Library.

Design by Newgen Knowledge Works (P) Ltd., Chennai, India.

First edition: December 2014

10 9 8 7 6 5 4 3 2 1

Contents

List of Tables and Figures	vii
Series Introduction	ix
Foreword	xi
Acknowledgments	xv

Part I Introduction

1 Introduction — 3

Part II Review of the Literature

2 Research on Institutional Advancement Outside of Fundraising — 17
3 Research on Fundraising — 25
4 Hidden Research: Dissertations — 33

Part III Major Questions and Answers

5 Why Donors Give — 49
6 *The Campus Green* Update — 55
7 Trends in Research — 61

Part IV The Future of Advancement Research

8 Suggestions for Research — 67

Appendix	77
Notes	253
References	255
Index	259

Tables and Figures

Tables

1.1	Taxonomy of advancement literature	11
4.1	Universities producing the highest number of advancement dissertations	35
4.2	Number of advancement dissertations by department/program	36
4.3	Taxonomy of advancement dissertations	40

Figures

4.1	Most popular dissertation topics	42
7.1	Dissertations and publications, 1991–2013	62

Series Introduction

When I was in graduate school, I was given a copy of *The Campus Green* by Barbara Brittingham and Thomas Pezzullo. It was this book that started my interest in fundraising in higher education. The book was tiny and presented an overview of research related to fundraising within the college and university setting. Over the years, I looked for additional books that had this focus, but there were none.

When I began thinking about a series on philanthropy and fundraising in higher education for Palgrave Press, I immediately thought about *The Campus Green* and how in the nearly 25 years since I was given the book, no one had updated it or delved into the literature.

I am so pleased that Eve Proper and Tim Caboni, two of the most skilled researchers in the area of fundraising, agreed to write *Institutional Advancement: What We Know*—a new book that I consider the twenty-first-century update to *The Campus Green*.

Institutional Advancement is the answer for so many students and faculty—not to mention fundraisers —that are interested in fundraising within the college setting. Proper and Caboni have scoured the literature, updated it, and interpreted it for the reader. For those interested in conducting future research this book offers a roadmap and for those interested in the practice of fundraising it offers information on the best practices as identified by the field and empirical research.

Proper and Caboni's work complements new work by Noah Drezner on diversity in fundraising and my own work with Nelson Bowman on fundraising in communities of color. It draws the literature together in a comprehensive way and helps us to understand future directors in fundraising within the higher education setting.

MARYBETH GASMAN
Series Editor

Foreword

Many of us who consider ourselves scholars of philanthropy in higher education cut our academic teeth on Brittingham and Pezzullo's *The Campus Green: Fund Raising in Higher Education.* It was a map to the literature and a guide to what we needed to try to accomplish as academic researchers and practitioners. Proper and Caboni's *What We Know About Institutional Advancement* is in many respects a report card of the progress of research in the field. It reflects upon a set of goals established in 1991 and whether or not we accomplished those things. At a different level, it also benchmarks fundamental changes in the field of advancement since *The Campus Green* was published in 1990.

This new volume encompasses literature published between 1991 and 2013. Two contexts are important in viewing this work and the body of research it discusses. The first is the pervasive infusion of Internet-based information during this period. To begin with, Proper and Caboni had online tools to research this volume that Brittingham and Pezzullo could not have even imagined. The proliferation of easy access web-based information fundamentally changed the world of research. More work became available, it became available more quickly, and it was available to more students, researchers, and practitioners. Data sources such as the *Voluntary Support of Education Data Miner* (Council for Aid to Education) now provide desktop access to researchers with institutional subscriptions. Online full-text reports and documents through ERIC have largely replaced microfiche and print. The availability of e-books and e-journals has put research in all fields into a state of fast forward.

The Internet also fundamentally changed what there is about higher education advancement that can be researched—marketing of online learning, fundraising in the virtual environment, and alumni who are constantly connected via social media to name only three. With these changes have come new opportunities for cutting-edge methods of inquiry such as Internet ethnography, historical inquiry using digital collections, and online survey instruments.

To what extent can we see these changes reflected in the literature of higher education advancement? Are the changes in research quantity, quality, breadth, and depth commensurate with the proliferation of information resources that are now available—or are we lagging behind? The taxonomy that Proper and Caboni developed for their analysis reflects significant diversification of research and the growing complexity of the advancement field. It both documents change and provides a strong benchmark for future analysis.

The second notable context is the emergence and growth of the interdisciplinary field of philanthropic/nonprofit studies. The Nonprofit Academic Centers Council currently lists 47 research centers internationally that are engaged in research in the field. Higher education advancement and philanthropic/nonprofit studies share many common research goals including understanding donative behavior from multiple perspectives, development of theory and practice in fundraising and marketing, and inquiry into governance and organizational effectiveness. The body of literature, information assets, and theory development that support nonprofit/philanthropic studies have grown and matured rapidly during this same period. But have they had any impact on higher education advancement research and practice? Why do two interdisciplinary fields that have so much in common—including the ongoing conversation about professionalization in fundraising and advancement—apparently share so little in terms of research? If we truly want research in the field of advancement to grow and mature, we must consider the value in wandering into neighboring academic backyards. Just as educational pedagogy has drawn upon psychology, advancement scholars and professionals need to learn to draw more heavily and more skillfully on the work of other fields and disciplines including philanthropic/nonprofit studies.

In the same way that my generation embraced *The Campus Green*, a new crop of researchers will embrace this extensive compilation of literature and its suggestions for paths they might take in their work. They in turn will build on the taxonomy and, hopefully, fulfill their promise as researchers and research-based practitioners. For those of us who have been around awhile, *Institutional*

Advancement: What We Know is an opportunity to pause and take stock of how far we have come, quietly celebrate our successes, and consider thoughtfully what needs to be done. Then we need to get back to work.

FRANCES HUEHLS
Joseph & Matthew Payton Philanthropic Studies Library
Indiana University-Purdue University Indianapolis

Acknowledgments

This book is the culmination of a decade of work by the two authors, but many other people have helped along the way.

This project could not have been completed without the librarians and staff at the Peabody Library at Vanderbilt University and Newman Library at Baruch College. Special thanks are also due to Fran Huehls at the Indiana University's Joseph and Matthew Philanthropic Studies Library, Kim Nehls, Gen Shaker, Noah Drezner, Susan Baxter, and Diane Fahr, all of who aided in the search for sources. Thanks also to Sarah Zabrenksi, for assistance with formatting.

I

Introduction

1
Introduction

Consider the following news stories from 2012 and 2013:

- In 2013, donors gave $34 billion to North American colleges, the most ever raised in one year (Rivard 2014).
- Fourteen American colleges and universities have dropped the use of Native American terms or imagery from their athletics since 2005, thanks to public pressure (Rogers 2013).
- Vanderbilt University reduced average student indebtedness by over $5,000, thanks to a $108 million campaign to raise money for financial aid (Kiley 2013).
- The University of Delaware considered adding a PhD financed by JPMorgan Chase, which would include student aid, faculty salaries, and campus renovations; the bank would be involved with dissertation committees, among other areas (Rivard 2013).
- The University of Hawaii spent "hundreds of thousands of dollars" in damage control after attempting to hire Stevie Wonder for a concert but instead paying money to a sham talent agency (Stripling 2012).
- Two Koch brothers' foundations donated $12.7 million to colleges and universities in 2012, funding initiatives such as programs as the "moral imperatives of free markets and individual liberty" (Levinthal 2014).

Each of these stories is about the field of higher education administration known as institutional advancement, a field that includes fundraising, alumni relations, public relations, and marketing. Also called "development," this is the branch of the administrative apparatus responsible for communicating with its publics and raising support (both financial and attitudinal) from those publics.

Unfortunately, it is also known, both to critics and some practitioners, by pejoratives such as "rattling the tin cup" or by boosterish phrases such as "friend-raising," indicating the discomfort many feel with the presence of an activity that seems to have more in common with Madison Avenue than the ivory tower. One of the earliest expressions of general distrust of institutional advancement's role in higher education comes from the articulately outraged Veblen in *The Higher Learning in America:*

> The American university is not an eleemosynary institution; it does not plead indigence, except in that Pickwickian sense in which indigence without shame be avowed in polite circles; nor does it put its trust in donations of that sparseness and modesty which the gifts of charity commonly have. Its recourse necessarily is that substantial and dignified class of gifts that are not given thriftly on compunction of charity, but out of the fulness of the purse...Donations to university funds have something of the character of an investment in good fame. (pp. 113–14)

This statement is actually rather mild by Veblen's standards. Veblen was a veteran of Cornell University, the University of Chicago, Stanford University, and the University of Missouri by that point in his peripatetic career; one wonders what he would make of these universities' fundraising operations today with staffs of dozens and budgets sufficient to run a small college of his day.

Advancement itself is not a core function of the academy; it neither teaches students nor produces new knowledge. In business terms, all parts of advancement are staff functions rather than line functions, something necessary to the functioning of the organization rather than central to its mission. Fundraisers are not unlike accountants or janitors in that respect. Indeed, while alumni relations is specific, if not to higher education, at least to education, fundraisers often have backgrounds in fundraising at other sorts of nonprofit institutions, such as museums and hospitals. This alone may account for why the scholarly literature on it is rather small compared to the literature on the student experience or academic careers. (On the other hand, certainly more has been written about advancement than about collegiate janitorial services.) Scholars writing about advancement have been told by reviewers that their work is not important enough to merit inclusion in conferences or journals.

Nevertheless, this is a book on institutional advancement.

It is a cliché to note that "fundraising has been an important part of American higher education since Harvard first raised money in 1693," but historical importance does not guarantee present-day relevance. Most ancient European universities were founded on donations, yet today they are almost exclusively state supported. If this was the only rationale scholars could offer for our interest, we could leave the topic exclusively to our colleagues doing excellent work with historical approaches.

But advancement has advanced since the days of the colonial college, and today it is, if not a profession (Caboni 2010), still an important role in most institutions of higher education. Naturally, it is important to the men and women who work in the field. Like most nonprofit professionals, they are dedicated to their jobs and to the causes they work for. If no one else, we should expect fundraisers, alumni relations officers, public affairs practitioners, and others in the fold of "institutional advancement" to be interested in advancing their profession. Evidence suggests they are: both the Association of Fundraising Professionals conference and the Council for the Advancement and Support of Education offer an array of local, national, and training conferences and events every year.

It is the size of the field—and its continued growth—that provides another reason for studying advancement. All the functions of advancement, but most notably fundraising, have become increasingly important for *all* institutions of US higher education, including sectors that traditionally did not conduct advancement activities. Public universities have long practiced alumni relations; today, they are engaged in billion-dollar capital campaigns. Community colleges have traditionally not engaged in any form of advancement other than public affairs; today, they raise funds from alumni, foundations, and corporations. At most institutions, the percentage of the budget that comes from direct donations is still small but rising. For example, in 2008–2009, gifts accounted for 21 percent of revenues at private, not-for-profit four-year institutions, and almost 4 percent at public four-year institutions, according to data from the Integrated Postsecondary Education Data System.

What does this change in funding source mean for the institutions that engage in it, beyond the simple fact of a larger corps of advancement officers? Typically, the institutions themselves represent it in two ways. First, donations and endowments provide a "margin of excellence," enabling institutions to offer programs and services (including scholarships) they otherwise could not. This benefit is particularly stressed by professionals in the course of their work. Second, this income provides "freedom" for public institutions. Unlike (dwindling) public funds, donative income tends not to be based on state-mandated institutional measures such as performance funding or enrollment. Of course, many donations come with restrictions, but the restrictions tend to be of a different nature. In states such as Virginia, the more prestigious (read: successful at resource gathering) institutions have recognized that demands for increased state accountability ironically come at a time when state funding provides a smaller percentage of the budget than ever before, and that has provided leverage for attenuating the state link (McLendon and Mokher 2009).

Advancement does more than buy excellence and independence, though. Aside from typically unrestricted annual fund dollars, most fundraising income comes with its own set of restrictions. According to the Council for Aid to Education's Voluntary Support of Education 2011 survey, 86 percent of current operations gifts are restricted, and 90 percent of capital gifts are restricted. Historical research has shown that fundraising has often shaped institutional spending patterns, as institutions adjust their behavior to what donors are willing to contribute to (Neuman 2007) or even give up their own institutional identity under pressure from those holding the purse strings (Avery 2013). Most gifts do not have this kind of transformative power, but philanthropic giving can be a powerful force. Foundation spending is assumed to have the ability to reshape institutions. Witness the effect of the Northern philanthropy in pushing vocational education at HBCUs (Brown II, Ricard, and Donahoo 2004) or the role of the Carnegie Foundation for the Advancement of Teaching retirement plans in secularizing small colleges (Lagemann 1999).

Corporate fundraising, too, has been criticized, and not only from the direction of free-market economists such as Milton Friedman who believe that corporations have no business (pun intended) conducting philanthropy (Friedman 2008). Observers such as Derek Bok have noted the pernicious effects that some corporate donations have had on academic freedom (Bok 2003). Cases such as the Berkeley-Novartis case continue to scandalize academia by their chilling effects on academic freedom (Slaughter 2011).

Even private donations influence institutional choices. Small annual fund donors tend not to restrict their gifts, but major donors have a long history of making gifts for specific causes such as starting a new school or degree program. Many a college or university is saddled with endowed funds for scholarships that no longer make sense but cannot be spent elsewhere. Today, much of the criticism and debate comes from donations to athletics. Phil Knight's $100 million gift to the University of Oregon (Di Mento 2007) was met with a chorus to the effect that the money would be better directed to the university's academic programs. Despite the efforts by advancement officers to find common ground between institutional and donor interests, donors can rarely be swayed far beyond their original area of interest. The University of Oregon very likely faced a choice between a gift to athletics and no gift at all. And far from providing "excellence," some colleges, such as Fisk University, believe that donations are mandatory to merely remain in the good graces of accreditors (Fisk University 2011).

While fundraising has the most obvious effects on reshaping institutional priorities, other forms of advancement are not immune. Creating a cadre of interested, involved alumni may provide not only a source of support (not solely fiscal) for an institution, but also an oftentimes reactionary set of stakeholders. The more sophisticated public relations become, the more institutions become indistinguishable from for-profit corporations, at least in the eyes of some. Municipalities are increasingly seeking payments in lieu of taxes from not-for-profit colleges (Fischer 2010), institutions are depicted as "real-estate tycoons" (van der Werf 2006), and commenters on stories about campus amenities suggest colleges do not deserve tax-exempt status (Carlson 2013).

Ironically, too, some of the drivers of increased advancement activities are simultaneously sowing the seeds of reaction. Higher tuition and student loan debt lead some alumni to say, "Why should I give you *more* money?" Alumni in low-paying professions may be cynical that their small donations could be meaningful as anything except as numbers in *U.S. News and World Report* rankings. Increasingly, students are more likely to transfer and to attend graduate or professional school, meaning that donors have more institutions making claims on their interest and their wallets. In years when endowments perform well, critics clamor to mandate higher endowment spending; in years when endowments perform poorly, colleges and universities struggle to balance budgets. The success of a few elite institutions, in an era when $5 billion capital campaigns make the headlines, has obscured the fact that most institutions have far fewer resources.

Surely, advancement is not the only factor in these conversations. Philosophies such as Milton Friedman's and shifts in public opinion to regarding higher education as a private good are important, but they are part of the same national conversation. Advancement is both cause and effect of institutional change.

So why *this* book?

The majority of published work on fundraising is directed at practitioners—which is surely logical—who aim to improve their own institution's practice. Most of it is based upon a lifetime of experience, rather than on research. Some of it is based upon institutional research. It is difficult to evaluate the quality of this work, which has not been peer reviewed, because the authors typically do not explain their methodology in depth. A small but dedicated cadre of scholars has dedicated itself to the study of advancement; however, the majority of work continues to be produced by reflective practitioners rather than full-time scholars. One result of this has been that the field is fragmented. Many studies are never published. Other research is conducted by faculty in areas such as economics or business, and the resulting work is published in journals that many among their potential audience would not think to read. Some scholars find that the study of advancement is not seen as central to higher education, which has the effect of encouraging them to pursue other careers or to refocus their research. As a result, the literature is scattered. This fragmentation makes it difficult for newcomers to come up to speed in the field. It leads to reproduction of work. It makes obtaining large-scale funding difficult.

By contrast, only a few works in the field tend to be considered comprehensive. The first is Michael Worth's *New Strategies for Educational Fundraising* (Worth 2002). This book does not claim to be a literature review or meta-analysis, but it covers the major areas of interest within fundraising from the perspective of the reflective practitioner and is frequently used as an introduction to the subject. The second is *The Campus Green: Fund Raising in Higher Education* (Brittingham and Pezzullo 1990), to which this book is in many ways indebted. Its focus was strictly on fundraising, not on advancement writ large. *The Campus Green* was published as an ASHE-ERIC Higher Education report in 1990. Like the rest of the series, it focuses on what the authors believe are the most important ideas in the field. Brittingham and Pezzullo begin with a brief history of US higher education fundraising before discussing how fundraising is organized and what it costs; how donors behave and what motivates them; the role of ethics; and suggestions for researchers, institutions, and related organizations, all based on the previous two decades of research. Both of these books, despite their fine qualities, suffer from one common issue: They are slowly growing out of date. *The Campus Green* is now over two decades old. More recently, Drezner's *Philanthropy and Fundraising in American Higher Education* (2011) provides an excellent overview of the main research findings and theories in fundraising (again, not advancement as a whole); in many ways, it is the modern successor to where *The Campus Green* left off. His book serves as an excellent introduction to education fundraising for the newcomer.

We, the authors, started with a simple goal: update *The Campus Green* with literature published since then. Along the way we found that some new areas of scholarship had opened up, and that it made sense to parse the literature in ways differently than Brittingham and Pezzullo did. We also expanded our scope to include advancement activities outside of fundraising. Colleges and universities have rolled fundraising into larger departments with names such as "development and alumni relations" or "university advancement." Today, fundraising is often seen as one component in a larger project, just as admissions is only one part of enrollment management.

We have several hopes for this volume. First, it is intended to provide an introduction to research in this area for students, practitioners, and scholars new to the area. We hope that it will give the erudite reader an overview of advancement research. Second, although related to the first, we hope that it is comprehensive. In this sense, it is designed to be more similar to Pascarella and Terenzini's opus, *How College Affects Students* (Pascarella and Terenzini 2005) than to ASHE reports, which focus on the highlights. While we call for more research in questions of advancement, the smaller size of our field is a relative advantage here, and the result is many pages shorter than Pascarella and Terenzini's magnificent omnibus. Third, we hope to call attention to the body of research that tends to slip through the cracks including dissertations and articles published in journals outside the usual suspects. We encourage our readers to find and read the originals for themselves.

This book covers literature from 1991 to 2013, or 23 years. We started with 1991 as that was the year after *The Campus Green* was published. We chose 2013 as a delimiter recognizing that it would be impossible to avoid being slightly out of date by the time the book appeared no matter what.

We found relevant dissertations by searching *Dissertation Abstracts International*, which is a comprehensive database of theses. We used keywords such as *fundraising, institutional advancement,* and *donors,* as well as combinations such as *public relations* and *colleges,* then eliminated results that were clearly outside of our scope.

These ranged from tangentially related articles on nonprofit but not educational fundraising to those where the keywords were used in an entirely different sense, such as those on organ *donors*. Dissertations were the easiest sources of research to comprehensively access, thanks to the DAI database.

Books were similarly easy but for a different reason: Academia is a small world, and most of the researchers in institutional advancement know each other. There are simply very few scholarly books published on the subject. Many have been reviewed in the pages of the *International Journal of Educational Advancement* or the major higher education journals. Here, the authors started with their own knowledge, scanned the book reviews, searched WorldCat and Amazon.com, and asked our colleagues to recommend what we had missed. Interestingly, the number of books was quite small. We did not include many interesting topical books that were manuals for practitioners rather than reports on scholarly research, which narrowed our findings considerably.

Articles appear in the most diffuse sources. We began with inventorying the *International Journal of Educational Advancement*, the only journal devoted solely to the topic. Next, we examined the tables of contents for nearly all of the higher education journals and nonprofit management journals. We also did keyword searches in journal databases to find articles in journals from the disciplines such as economics. In many of these journals, only one article appeared in our 23-year span. As a check, we examined the reference list in some of the articles. Finally, we relied on the kindness of colleagues to point out anything we may have missed.

All of the works we found were cataloged, acquired, and taxonomized. For unpublished data, we tabulated data on several dimensions, such as quantitative/qualitative, data source, and theoretical framework. We also classified the works by topic (more on this follows). Initially, both authors did this cataloging, until we had established interrater reliability.

The taxonomy began as attempt to list the subjects of articles we expected to find, before we began formal analysis. As the project progressed, it became evident that there were topics we had missed and, in rare cases, that should be collapsed. A list of these codes is included as table 1.1. The numbering system is a shortened form of reference, and no significance should be attached to whether a given topic has a high or low number. A review of this list will show what we felt was within the purview of institutional advancement for higher education and what was outside of it. One of the most obvious omissions is research on fundraising for causes other than higher education. Much of this literature may be applicable to higher education, but we felt that including this would expand the project exponentially as well as introduce complicated calculations of utility. For example, scholarship on fundraising for independent schools seems very relevant, but what about fundraising for small social services organizations?

Beginning with this catalog, we attempted to make sense of the literature. Some natural topics suggested themselves. In the end, it made sense to view the research both by its sources—dissertations are significantly different from journal articles in many ways—and in some cases by its subject. Despite the quantitative trend in higher education, we were unable to use techniques such as meta-analysis, even for evergreen questions as, "Which alumni will give?" Studies simply varied too much both in technique and in rigor. We do use some descriptive statistics to describe the literature, but none are methodologically sophisticated.

Table 1.1 Taxonomy of advancement literature

1. Fundraising
    1.0 Literature review
    1.1 Organization/process
    1.2 Motivation and individual predictors of giving (for alumni, see 4.3)
    1.3 Managing/effectiveness and institutional predictors of giving
    1.4 Professionalization
    1.5 Planned giving
    1.6 Case studies
    1.7 Stewardship
    1.8 Internal perceptions
    1.9 Rhetorical analysis
    1.10 Ethics
    1.11 Grants
    1.12 Corporate or foundation giving
    1.13 Econometric models
    1.14 Benchmarking
    1.15 Effects of fundraising
    1.16 Government policy and its effects
    1.17 Online giving
2. Public relations
    2.1 Benchmarking and best practices
    2.2 Integrated communications management
    2.3 Media relations

continued

Table 1.1 Continued

- 2.4 Government relations
- 2.5 Community relations
- 2.6 Crisis communications
3. Marketing
    - 3.1 Electronic communications and social media
    - 3.2 Integrated communications management
    - 3.3 Image creation/branding
    - 3.4 University rankings
    - 3.5 Cause-related marketing
4. Alumni relations
    - 4.1 Benchmarking
    - 4.2 Case studies
    - 4.3 Alumni giving
    - 4.4 Associations
    - 4.5 Predictors of alumni involvement
    - 4.6 Alumni satisfaction
    - 4.7 Other alumni programming
5. International institutions
    - 5.1 Canada
    - 5.2 United Kingdom
    - 5.3 Asia
    - 5.4 Australia and New Zealand
    - 5.5 Africa
    - 5.6 Other
6. Leadership
    - 6.1 Presidents
    - 6.2 Trustees
    - 6.3 Vice presidents, provosts, and chief development officers
    - 6.4 Managers
    - 6.5 Staffing (career trajectories, perceptions, turnover, etc.)
    - 6.6 Deans
    - 6.7 Volunteers
    - 6.8 Faculty (including giving by faculty/staff)
7. History
    - 7.1 History of fundraising/PR
    - 7.2 Institutional history
    - 7.3 Biography
8. Institutional types and causes
    - 8.1 HBCUs
    - 8.2 Community colleges
    - 8.3 Graduate and professional units
    - 8.4 Athletics (including effect of athletics on giving)
    - 8.5 Student affairs
    - 8.6 Non-HBCU MSIs
    - 8.7 Other specific causes or units
    - 8.8 Religious institutions

The rest of the book is organized into several sections. Part II focuses on the sources of scholarly literature on educational fundraising: chapters 2 and 3 focus on books and journal articles, while chapter 4 examines doctoral dissertations.

Chapter 2 analyzes journal articles and books on all aspects of institutional advancement *except* fundraising. This includes literature on public relations, alumni relations, marketing, institutional leadership of advancement, and advancement office structure. In chapter 3 we turn to articles and books on fundraising, which comprise the lion's share of advancement scholarship. In both chapters, the literature comes from a variety of disciples and publications, most notably higher education, nonprofit management, human resources, and economics. The majority of the literature is focused on improving practice rather than developing theory. We turn a critical eye to this body of work, looking for trends and probing rigor.

In chapter 4, we examine doctoral dissertations. A great deal of the academic research on advancement is conducted by graduate students, many of whom are full-time practitioners who value scholarship but are not planning to dedicate their careers to producing it. Moreover, few dissertation committee members are up-to-date on the relevant literature. Most of the resulting work is not published, leading to a vicious cycle where researchers declare there is little or no research on their topic, but their own work is subsequently "lost." This chapter attempts to make this literature accessible.

Part III turns away from the sources of literature to the questions it answers. Chapter 5 focuses on what is the most heavily researched question in the field: Why do people give? This chapter is a systematic review of the research on the considerable body of work examining what makes individuals into donors. This is not a formal meta-analysis, as the body of literature is not suitable for formal quantitative review. Most research in this area consists of single-institutional studies asking what distinguishes undergraduate alumni donors from nondonors. In this question, we focus on individual donors rather than foundations or corporations, and we separate studies of alumni from studies of all donors or nonalumni donors. We focus on individual giving simply because there is so much more work in this area; only 27 of the works we examined dealt with either corporate or foundation giving.

In chapter 6, we return to the book that is in many ways this book's inspiration: *The Campus Green*. At the close of *The Campus Green*, the authors recommend that scholar pursue particularly questions more vigorously and that they devote less attention to others. Have these recommendations been followed? Do we have more answers (or substantive insight) into questions they said were of pressing importance?

In chapter 7, we examine emerging questions in the discipline. In the past two decades, new methods have been brought to bear on advancement research, and researchers have turned to questions that previously went unasked. Here we look at the topics and questions that are starting to gain traction among scholars and the new data sources and methods that researchers are using.

In part IV, chapter 8, we sum up the state of the field and where it is headed. Based on the previous chapters, where is more work needed? What kind of data should researchers, including organizations that conduct major surveys in higher education, be collecting to enable this research? Are there any questions we can definitively put to rest?

Finally, in appendix, we provide a complete list of the nearly 1,000 journal articles, books, and dissertations that we gathered for this project. Each book is identified by one or more label from our taxonomy. While a reference list of this sort is not compelling reading on its own, we suspect it may be one of the most useful parts of the text. Scholars interested in, for example, community colleges can look for the 92 entries tagged with "8.2."

We hope this volume will be of use to both scholars and practitioners, to both novices and the experienced. We hope that you will seek out some of the research we discuss. And we hope that you will be encouraged to contribute your own work to the field.

II

Review of the Literature

2

Research on Institutional Advancement Outside of Fundraising

While the majority of inquiry in advancement is devoted to fundraising, other areas have received limited attention from scholars since 1990. These include public relations, marketing, and alumni relations. The focus of this chapter will be to explore these disparate areas of study and describe the evolution in each during the previous two decades. The continuing challenges of this area of inquiry are then discussed.

Public Relations

The most prominent area of public relations research explored the relationship between various public relations frameworks as they related to the encroachment upon the public relations function by fundraising (Kelly 1991, 1993, 1998) and the assertion that fundraising actual should be considered a subset of public relations. Kelly (1991, 1993, 1998) grounds the practice of fundraising both historically and as a function within the domain of public relations.

Benchmarking and Best Practices

Within university leadership, one of the challenges facing higher education is the slow adoption of public relations professionals at the highest levels of administration (Peyronel 2000). The lack of a strategic communication perspective leaves many institutions vulnerable to external forces and issues that might be alleviated with professional public relations counsel (Peyronel 2000).

This is in contrast to the typical corporate/business model with a vice president for public relations reporting to the CEO (Hall and

Baker 2003). Much of what has been written on university public relations has focused upon how institutions might compare themselves to corporate organizations of similar size and function (Hall and Baker 2003), or more specifically, how universities might benchmark their activities to increase organizational effectiveness (Mahoney 2000; Kessels and Ruijgers 2003).

Integrated Communications

One of the modern tenets of public relations is that it revolves around the relationship between an organization and its various publics and that integrating efforts across various functional areas produces the most ideal outcomes (Volkmann 1994; Chapleo 2006). Bruning (2002) suggests that internal communication may serve as a retention strategy for universities operating in this mode.

Media Relations

Historically the outcome of public relations offices was measured by stories placed or number of column inches covering a specific institution. More recently the scholarly literature has been focused on the more general media coverage of colleges and universities and how postsecondary education is viewed as an industry (Dennis and LaMay 1993; Peyronel 2004) or those topics that appeared most frequently in the coverage of higher education (Stone 2005; Gasman 2007a). Studies also continued to examine the specific tactics employed to generate media coverage (Stone 2005; Carringer 2013).

Government Relations

At state institutions, the relationship between state legislatures and universities became ever more important as the percentage of institutional support from state general fund dollars shrank during the 1990s and 2000s (Hovey 1999, Rollwagen 2010). The use and functions of institutional lobbyists and how they compare with the lobbying work in other industries also received attention in the literature (Ferrin 2005) as institutions struggled to diversify their various revenue streams.

Community Relations

The relationship between universities and the communities in which they are situated or "town-gown" relationships attracted some attention from those interested in university public relations. The studies vary from case studies focused on single institutions and their work to enhance or repair relationships with their local communities (Benson, Harkavy, and Puckett 2000; Harasta 2008, Swanson 2008) to an evaluation of this kind of community building from a broader perspective (Narum 1999; Maurasse 2002). One of the most interesting developments in the community relations literature is the notion that measuring public engagement by alumni and others affiliated with an institution as a measurable outcome of a university education adds value to a community in similar fashion that giving adds value (Scott 2007; Weerts, Cabrera, and Sanford 2010).

Crisis Communications

The most apparent areas of public relations activity in higher education are the myriad institutional responses to difficult situations that put at risk the very brands and institutional missions of those colleges and universities. Not surprisingly these tend to be single-institutional analyses focused on specific instances and evaluating institutional responses to the crises at hand (Murphree and Rogers 2004; Collins 2005; Brune 2010; Isaacson 2012).

Marketing

The landscape of marketing in higher education has matured and become more intensely competitive since 1990. An important development in this maturation was the publishing of *Strategic Marketing for Education Institutions* (Kotler and Fox 1985) coauthored by one of the leading figures in the field of marketing, Phillip Kotler, who applied his general principles of marketing to colleges and universities. The text is used widely and is a handbook for those interested in how to market their institutions. The book followed several smaller papers related to bringing marketing concepts to university activities (Hyre 1991; Stewart 1991) and preceded scholars addressing how marketing might be adopted effectively and used ethically (Caruanam, Ramaseshan, and Ewing 1998; Toma 1999; Gibbs and Murphy 2009).

Electronic Communications and Social Media

When Brittingham and Pezzullo authored *The Campus Green*, email on university campuses was in its infancy, and the World Wide Web and social media did not exist. In the 20 years since, the electronic marketing and communication channels available to university marketers and PR professional have grown exponentially. The examination of how institutions make use of the web to create two-way symmetrical communication (Shadinger 2010; McAllister 2013; Shadinger 2013) how websites might be evaluated for usability (Coloma 2012), the organizational constraints on how electronic communication is used (McAllister and Taylor 2012), and how university narratives and reputations are built using websites (Ridley, Mateev, and Cuevas 2005), all helped to inform our understanding of the use of electronic means to communicate the university. A more recent area of inquiry is the advent of social media as marketing tool available to university administrators (Alkhas 2011; Palmer 2013).

Integrated Marketing/Communications Management

Sevier (1998) suggests that marketing functions in higher education should not be "siloed" in various suborganizations across the institution, but rather those disparate functions should be centralized and combined in a single organization or at least operate in close coordination with each other to ensure a common effort and voice for the university being represented.

Several studies examine the efficacy of these integrated efforts with single-institution or multisite examinations or case studies (Lauer 2000; Simpson and Hossler 2001; Morris 2003; Edmiston-Strasser 2009; Lineberger 2009; Sciple 2010; Broussard 2011; Franklin 2012; Tolbert 2013). The rest of the articles on integrated marketing tend to describe the concept and make recommendations for implementation or describe the advantages versus other more disparate models (Liu 1998; Joyce, Lambert, and Spotts 2000; Liao and Sargeant 2000; Chapleo 2003; O'Neil 2003).

Image Creation/Branding

Out of the acceptance of marketing as a common institutional administrative function came an increased willingness within higher education institutions to apply marketing concepts typically reserved for products or service providing corporations with a large number of articles focused on the creation, enhancement, or changing of institutional brand (Sevier 2000, 2004).

Beginning with an examination of how an institution's brand creates a position within a competitive marketplace (Drea and McNally

1997; Heyes and Liston-Heyes 2004; Clark 2005; Tobolowsky and Lowert 2006; Blanton 2007; Owston 2007) to examinations of how a brand orientation may be used to create or reflect organizational change (Terkla and Pagano 1993; Toma, Dubrow, and Hartley 2005; Stensaker 2007), how branding might be used to increase voluntary support (Bennett 1998; McAlexander, Koenig, and Schouten 2006; McAlexander and Koenig 2012; Stephenson 2013), and how successful institutions have been at implementing the tactic (Chapleo 2002, 2005, 2008; Schofield 2013), there is a robust examination of what on its surface would appear a narrow area of the broader marketing landscape.

University Rankings

The emergence of *U.S. News and World Report* ranking of universities as a driver of university activity came to the forefront of university activities during the past two decades. In addition, the relationship between rankings and a variety of institutional outcomes and inputs began to receive serious attention from scholars of higher education (McDonough, Antonio, Walpole, and Perez 1998; Baughman and Goldman 1999; Keith 1999; Trainer and Sapp 2000; Porter 2000; Larsen 2003; Meredith 2004; Schubert 2009; Nardone 2009). Of specific interest in the literature are the relationships between rankings and student applications and admissions (Coles 2007; Griffith and Rask 2007; Somers 2007; Hou, Morse, and Yueh-jen 2012; Stoltz 2012), reputation and prestige (Sweitzer 2008; Bowman and Bastedo 2009; Gernhart 2009; Sweitzer and Volkwein 2009; Bowmen and Bastedo 2011), institutional responses and strategies (Walleri and Moss 1995; Ehrenberg 2003; Ridley, Cuevas, and Matveev 2003; Head 2005; Fogerty 2008; O'Connell 2013), and intercollegiate athletics (Fisher 2007, 2009). Finally, several studies evaluated and critiqued the validity and methodology of the rankings themselves (Dill and Soo 2005; Hazelkorn 2007; Nardone 2009; Tofallis 2012; Pusser and Marginson 2013).

Alumni Relations

The relationship between an institution and its graduates is the foundation of modern institutional advancement, with alumni secretaries serving as the first administrative officers focused on external relations and the continued engagement of former students in the life of an institution. By far the most expansive area of the literature included in our analyses was alumni relations, comprising more than 20 percent of the books and articles we examined. We detail those factors and examine the articles related to alumni giving in chapter 5. Here we deal with the remainder of the studies that do not involve philanthropic giving.

Benchmarking

Alumni relations as a functional area of advancement is challenged by its lack of a clear and simply understood outcomes of its activities (unlike fundraising that can be measured bluntly with dollars raised). Lacking a universally accepted set of metrics, practitioners and researchers focused on alumni relations during the past 20 years have striven to create data that might allow for cross-institutional comparisons of programmatic and tactical effectiveness (McNamara 1998; Pettit and Litten 1999; Andrade, Ingle, and Diaz-Rios 2002; McDoo 2012).

Associations and Involvement

With the remarkable diversity of institutional types in the higher education system, there are endless organizational arrangements designed to engage graduates, including career placement efforts (Chiavacci 2005), programs designed for specific alumni demographics (Daniels 1999), and variation between associations based upon institutional function and purpose (Marshall 2009; Newman 2009; Newman and Petrosko 2011). Scholars have examined both the efficacy of programming and those activities and characteristics of what created an active and engaged alumnus (Mael and Ashforth 1992; Johnson and Eckel 1997; Mulugetta, Nash, and Murphy 1999; Baker 2004; Johnson 2004; Ingram, Haynes, Davidson-Shivers, and Irvin 2005; Barnes 2007; Kelleher 2011; Maynard 2011; Specter 2012; Starace 2012).

Satisfaction

With limited outcomes of alumni relations beyond involvement and the relationship between programming and giving, the alumni relations profession has turned to how satisfied their alumni are with the collegiate experience and extending that satisfaction throughout the lifespan of a large percentage of the alumni population (Scarborough 1991; Hartman and Schmidt 1995; McLaughlin 2002; Pung 2013).

Challenges

One of the significant critiques of the institutional advancement literature leveled in *The Campus Green* was the prevalence of single-site studies without broad generalizability. The issue for the topical area of study continues with the majority of articles we reviewed examining only one or a few institutions. In addition, while there is a rich variety of institutional types available for study, the literature still focuses as a whole on large majority white universities. It appears that this continues to be driven by convenience with many authors studying their home institutions or others within geographic proximity.

Another significant challenge, especially for alumni relations, is the absence of a set of national benchmarks or repository for alumni relations data. Fundraising scholars have access to IPEDS data and the Voluntary Support of Education annual report of institutional performance. No similar collection exists for the nondevelopment areas of advancement, which makes large-scale studies exceedingly difficult to conduct. In addition, the lack of agreed upon measures that are collected by all colleges and universities makes comparisons between institutional performance or effectiveness near impossible.

The peer-reviewed articles included in this volume come from a wide variety of journals (save the now defunct *International Journal of Educational Advancement*), making the collection and synthesis of the literature more difficult than if there were an accepted outlet to which many advancement oriented articles might be submitted for review. This is compounded by the number of studies that are the sole (or almost only) published piece of scholarship by an author. While there are some university faculty who take the study of advancement issues as one of their primary research strands, the literature continues to suffer from a lack of sustained inquiry that builds upon previous studies over an extended period of time.

3

Research on Fundraising

Fully three-quarters of the research we examined fell under the category of "fundraising," dwarfing the amount of research on alumni relations, public relations, or marketing in higher education. What exactly is all this research about?

The lion's share of fundraising research focuses on questions of effectiveness and donor motivation, examining institutional factors that make fundraising successful and individual characteristics that increase the propensity of making or increasing donations. This research is discussed in depth in chapter 5.

The remaining research can be grouped in three major areas:

- Fundraising as a profession and staffing issues
- The role of leadership in fundraising
- The history of fundraising

This chapter will discuss each of these three areas.

In addition, this research ranges across a wide variety of institutional types and causes. Historically, most research has been conducted on general-purpose giving (giving across the annual fund, campaigns, and major gifts) to predominantly white, four-year institutions in the United States. We will explore the extent to which researchers have focused on other institutional types, such as Minority-Serving Institutions and community colleges, and specific units within institutions, such as giving to athletics and student affairs.

It is worth mentioning a few articles and books in a category of their own: the literature reviews. Within the time frame of our review, these include only a handful of volumes (Lindahl and Conley 2002; Akin 2005; Drezner 2011; Walton and Gasman 2012). Some of these focus on a particular niche (Akin on community colleges; Walton and Gasman on women in philanthropy), while others focus on the best of extant research (Drezner 2011). Lindahl and Conley circumscribe the literature on nonprofit fundraising, rather than limiting themselves to only higher education.

Fundraising as a Profession

The ongoing professionalization of fundraising and advancement, as well as concerns as to whether or not it is a distinct profession, has been the topic of some scholars (Kelly 1991; Caboni 2001, 2003, 2010, 2012; Bloland 2002), while others have focused on career paths (Lamm 1991; Carnes 1996; Duronio and Tempel 1997; Cleveland 2003; Meisenbach 2004). Other research has looked at behaviors (Ryan 2006) and professional spaces (Breazeale 1999).

Managerial issues, such as turnover (Sanders 1997; Iarrobino 2006; Oliver 2007; Thomas 2010), race (Borum 1991; Pettey and Wagner 2007; Bowman III 2010b) and gender (Carnes 1996; Cleveland 2003; Titus-Becker 2007; Owen 2009), knowledge acquisition (Lepke 1991; Strmiska 1998; Lanning 2007; Peet et al. 2010), and recruitment (Wright 2001; Winter and Wright 2003) also have a significant body of literature.

The Role of Leadership

There is a rich literature on the role of various institutional leaders in institutional fundraising, including presidents, boards of trustees, academic leaders, chief development officers, volunteers, and faculty—in addition to fundraising staff. Of all the work we reviewed, nearly 10 percent dealt with these issues, too many to list comprehensively here. The majority of these dealt with the role of the president in fundraising (Schulze 1991; Walter 1993; Cook 1994, 1997; Janney 1994; Spangler 1994; Glass and Jackson 1998a; Mathis 1998a, 1998b; Eldredge 1999; Cockrum 2004; McGee 2003; Satterwhite 2004; Stovall 2004; Satterwhite and Cedja 2005; Whitaker 2005; Stewart 2006; Nicholson 2006; Sturgis 2006; Hall 2007; Nehls 2007, 2008; Wesley 2007; Boyd 2008; Goddard 2009; Saunders 2009; Besikof 2010; Hodson 2010; Ballinger 2012; Thompson 2012; Strickland 2013). In general, researchers have found that presidents have a significant impact on institutional fundraising.

The History of fundraising

There is growing interest in studying the history of fundraising, including studies of specific institutions (Olsen 2000; Upton and de Rovzar 2002; Gaier 2003; Beilke 2004; Watts 2004; Drezner 2005a; Black 2008; Gasman and Drezner 2010; Courtney 2011; Foster 2012; Avery 2013), consortia (Tucker 2002; Wells 1993; Gasman 2007b, 2007d; Drezner 2008; Gasman and Drezner 2009), and individuals (Williams 1991; Gasman 2001, 2002b, 2002c; Keene 2001; Walton 2001; Drezner 2005b; Williams 2012; Davis 2013), as well as trends in higher education development more broadly.

In particular, there is a robust work around Historically Black Colleges and Universities and Predominantly Black Institutions (Brazzell 1992; Waddell 1992; Anderson and Moss 1999; Gasman 2001, 2002b, 2002c, 2007a, 2007b, 2007d; Gasman and Epstein 2004; Drezner 2005b, 2008; Gasman and Drezner 2008, 2009, 2010; Freeman 2010; Leak and Reid 2010; Tucker 2002; Avery 2013). Given the predominance of research universities in effectiveness and motivation studies, it is surprising how little research there is on the history of fundraising at universities (Cash 2000; Cash 2003; Hancock 2004; Black 2008; Kimball and Johnson 2012; Avery 2013). Some studies examine the history of education broadly (Oliver 1999; Thelin 2000; Walton 2000; Strickland 2007; Kimball and Johnson 2012). In addition, many institutional histories of varying quality discuss fundraising, although they are beyond the scope of this review.

Giving to HBCUs and MSIs

There has been a surge in research on Historically Black Colleges and Universities and, to a lesser extent, other Minority-Serving Institutions since the turn of the century, in large part due to the work of Marybeth Gasman and Noah Drezner.

In addition to the above-mentioned historical research, research on present-day giving to HBCUs often focuses on donor motivation. Studies that take as their subject institutional practices (Boyce 1992; Williams 1992; Hunter 1997; Rowland 1997; Hunter, Jones, and Boger 1999; Scott 2001; Wells 2001; Harris-Vasser 2003; Stovall 2004; Gasman 2005; Wells et al. 2005; Cohen 2006a, 2006b; Tindall 2007, 2009; Berry 2008; Bowman III 2010b; Coupet and Barnum 2010; Cox 2010; Drezner and Gupta 2012; Baldwin 2013; Bowen 2013; Schexnider 2013). Because of the slippage between descriptive and prescriptive research, undoubtedly more works could be included in this category with less strict parameters for inclusion.

There has been much less research on other Minority-Serving Institutions. Of course, some multi-institutional studies may include, for example, Hispanic-Serving Institutions, but this status is treated as incidental. Regarding tribal colleges and related institutions, there is some work on an institution that formerly served Native Americans but is not a tribal college (Neuman 2002, 2007) and on the American Indian College Fund, a fundraising consortium to support tribal colleges and Native American students (Wells 1993). Three studies have focused on Hispanic Serving Institutions (Mulnix, Bowden, and Lopez 2002, 2004; Arriola 2005). Drezner (2005a) has also written about deaf-serving Gallaudet University as a minority-serving institution. We found no work on Asian American and Native American Pacific Islander-serving institutions (it's a formal gov't designation). Of all these MSI-related articles, only one was published before 2000, suggesting that interest in this topic is slowly growing.

Giving to Community Colleges

There is a robust research community around two-year public institutions. Donor motivation is discussed in chapter 5, but the majority of research is focused on institutional characteristics and practices rather than donors.

General research includes literature reviews, overviews of trends, and advice (Brumbach and Bumphus 1993; Adams, Keener, and McGee 1994; Riggs and Heleg 1996; Jackson 1997; Jackson and Glass 2000; Jackson and Keener 2002; Keener, Carrier, and Meaders 2002; Babitz 2003; Bass 2003; Carlsen 2003; Milliron, de los Santos, and Browning 2003; Ryan 2003; Errett 2004; Akin 2005; LaBeouf 2005; Beard 2008; Garcia 2009; Wagoner and Besikof 2010). Research on the effects of fundraising includes Dowd and Grant (2007).

Descriptive research on practice documents current fundraising practice (Gatewood 1994; Miller 1994; Shaw 1997; Jenkins and Glass 1999; Katsinas 1999; Young 2002; Herbkersman and Hibbert-Jones 2003; Hull 2004; Kenton et al. 2005; McWherter 2005; Bristow 2013). There is some degree of overlap with research that attempts to identify successful tactics: Research focused on institutional factors that affect fundraising success includes everything from multi-institutional quantitative analyses to single-institution case studies (Ironfield

1991; Mitzel 1991; Dye 1992; Roney 1993; Koelkebeck 1994; Johnsen 1995; McCormick 1995; Gilmore 1996; Miller 1997; Pichon 1999; Stevenson 2001; Carrier 2002, 2004; Hall 2002a; Anderson 2003; Tisdale 2003; Fife 2004; Morgan 2005; Jones 2007; Shuford 2007; Sanders 2008; Warren 2008; Grant 2009). There is also a good bit of research on the role of the president (Schulze 1991; Walter 1993; Glass and Jackson 1998a; Boyd 2008; Karns 2008; Gentile 2009; Saunders 2009; Besikof 2010; Pinchback 2011; Brunen 2012; Carringer 2013), as well as some on on fundraising staff (Ciampa 2009) and on trustees (Graham 1994; Nielsen, Newton, and Mitvalsky 2003).

There is virtually no historical research on community college giving with a study by Brazzell being the exception (Brazzell 1992). Some case studies, however, do discuss institutional history; nevertheless, this is no substitute for research that takes history as its purpose and method.

Giving to Religious Institutions

While multi-institutional studies may include colleges and universities with religious ties of varying strength, these ties are generally ignored or treated in a cursory fashion. However, some studies intentionally focus on institutions with religious ties.

Some of these are case studies of individual institutions (Smith 1998; Boswell 2003; Lineberger 2009; Boal 2011; Rugano 2011; Song 2011; Williams 2012). Other research compares institutions within a denominational association. Groups of institutions studied include members of the Association for Biblical Higher Education (formerly the American Association of Bible Colleges) (Brown 1992; Meadows 1999) and the Council for Christian Colleges and Universities (formerly the Christian College Coalition) (McCown 2000; Bee 2001; Cockrum 2004; Gardner 2010; Curry, Rodin, and Carlson 2012). Denominations studied include Baptist colleges (Melton 1996), Roman Catholic institutions (Cristantello 1992; Hopkins 1998; Wesley 2007), and Seventh-Day Adventist institutions (Gustavsson 2000). Other studies used multiple institutions but did not reflect membership in a particular organization (Dillon 1990; Jones 1991; Lawrence 1991; Smith 1993; Fincher 2003; Cohu 2012).

There are some notable gaps in this literature. First, there is no research on any Jewish institutions, nor is there any research on graduate seminaries or rabbinical schools. While some of the studies include institutions that have seminaries, it is likely that fundraising is quite different for graduate-only institutions. Moreover, the focus on similar institutions makes it difficult to tease out the effects of organizational affiliation. Catholic colleges are typically affiliated with individual religious orders; mainline Protestant colleges are affiliated with denominations; and many evangelical colleges are not affiliated with only denominations, although they are allied with a particular religious culture. How might these ties—as well as cultural shifts in the popularity of various religious organizations—affect giving to related colleges?

Giving Abroad

It is perhaps unsurprising that much of the English language research focuses on American institutions, which have the strongest tradition of fundraising. (While our study was limited to dissertations from Canada and the United States, our examination of journals drew from global English language journals.) Nevertheless, there is some research on institutions in Canada (Page 1995; Shaw 1997; Caton 1999), the United Kingdom (Rosenberg 2000; Keene 2001; Weir 2003; Hancock 2004; Proper 2009; Daly 2013); Asia (Smith 1992; Liu 2007b; Onishi 2007; Lin 2009; Sulaiman, Adnan, and Nor 2009; Tang 2010); Africa (Bongila 2001; Nkoane 2006; Mokopakgosi 2008; Niwagaba 2012); and Europe outside the United Kingdom (Boswell 2003; Liu 2007b; James and Wiepking 2008; Rollwagen 2010). In addition, some research reaches donors worldwide (Muller 2004). Surprisingly, we found no research on fundraising —or advancement more broadly—in any South or Central American countries.

As more countries begin to wrestle with the costs of providing higher education for the masses on one hand and economic challenges on the other, we can expect to see increased pressure on institutions to institute or ramp up fundraising programs. As this occurs, we can hope that scholars will turn their attention to fundraising as an international phenomenon.

Giving to Athletics and Influenced by Athletics

The ability of institutions to convert athletic success into fundraising success for either academics or athletics is a hot topic. Much of the research in this area is in programs and journals devoted to sports management rather than higher education. Related areas include giving by alumni who were involved in athletics, discussed in chapter 5. Studies that examine the effect of winning tend to focus on revenue-generating sports such as basketball and football and on Division I institutions, although there is also some research on other athletic divisions (Parker 1995; Baade and Sundberg 1996; Rhoads and Gerking 2000; Stinson 2005; Humphreys and Mondello 2007; Stinson and Howard 2008; Meer and Rosen 2009b; Mesisca 2009; Cohen; Whisenant; and Walsh 2011; Anderson 2012; Stewart 2012). Given the more prominent role of college athletics at Division I institutions, this focus is to be expected.

Giving to Student Affairs

Another nonacademic institutional unit that has been examined for fundraising success is student affairs. Nearly all of this work examines how advancement and student affairs divisions work together (Kroll 1991; Fygetakis 1992; Hendrix-Kral 1995; Kellogg 1996; Hillman 2002; Rovig 2009; Puma 2013) with a few exceptions that focus on fundraising success (Schoenecke 2005, Sonn 2009) or fundraising for diversity (Lang 2008).

Giving to Other Units within Institutions

Finally, there is a body of work on giving to academic divisions within institutions—schools, colleges, or majors—and to divisions such as libraries and museums. Some of this work compares similar units across institutions (Palmer 1992; Shealy 1992; Heyns 1994; Latour 1995; McGraw 1996; Bloomfield and Kuhl 2007; Chive 2007; Lorenzen 2009; Barascout 2012). While alumni major is often used as a predictor variable in studies of likely donors, it is not the primary focus of any studies.

Conclusion

In addition to the research explicitly cited in this chapter, additional work on fundraising for higher education is listed in appendix. However, this chapter demonstrates the breadth of topics that scholars have explored. In some areas, there is a substantial body of work. In others, there are significant gaps. One surprising lacuna concerns work on the effects of fundraising: How does it change institutions?

Aside from historical explorations, there is very little work in this area. The notable exceptions include work on the effects of venture philanthropy (Boverini 2005, 2006); the role of fundraising in financial turnarounds (Carey 2013); and analyses of where fundraising dollars are spent—or saved (Ehrenberg and Smith 2003; Maniaci 2003; Maniaci, Poole, and Wilson 2003; Flabiano 2013). As institutions and policymakers extol the virtues of fundraising, whether to make up for lost revenues or to ensure excellence, it is disappointing that so few scholars have examined whether fundraising is capable of fulfilling these purposes.

4

Hidden Research: Dissertations

One of the primary sources of research articles focused on fundraising are doctoral theses that authors subsequently submit for peer review and publication, yet many more dissertations are never published in a form beyond the thesis. From 1991 to 2013, an average of 20 dissertations a year on some aspect of advancement was published. The production of research by doctoral students is problematic for the profession for several reasons. First, most doctoral dissertations that take fundraising as their focus are written by practitioners pursuing a terminal degree primarily as a credential to advance their administrative careers (Kelly 1998). Second, the faculty guiding those dissertations have limited experience with fundraising or related research. As a result, much of the work is repetitive and focused on single institutions and donor characteristics (Kelly 1998). Finally, Kelly (1998) suggests that much of what is written in theses dissertations never makes it to journal publication because of the limited professional utility for the authors of having a published manuscript. These problems are not limited to fundraising, however. Public administration, a profession in a similar position to fundraising, trains both practitioners and researchers in doctoral programs, and doctoral research in public administration has repeatedly found to be weak (McCurdy and Cleary 1984). A recent review of business dissertations found that only 18.4 percent of dissertations written in traditional business programs were published, where "traditional" programs were those that required a long-term residency (Hahn, Bowlin, and Britt 2007). In this sense, fundraising does not represent a unique problem but a case typical of the practitioner-heavy fields.

However, the introduction of a journal focused entirely on institutional advancement and fundraising in higher education in 2000

(*International Journal of Educational Advancement*) and the creation of research awards designed to reward and incentivize outstanding doctoral research on fundraising, raises the question, "What is the current quality, rigor, and publication rate of doctoral dissertations focused on fundraising?"

Because one of the main sources for new knowledge is research that is conducted within the doctoral training process, we ask the following questions related to fundraising dissertations:

1. What percentages of doctoral dissertations focused on fundraising use national data sets and have results that are generalizable beyond a single institution?
2. What percentages of dissertations are produced in education departments versus those in other fields?
3. What theoretical frameworks are used to ground the research questions addressed in the study?
4. What percentages are practically oriented versus those focused on building theory?
5. How many (what percentages of) dissertation authors have become full-time faculty members?
6. Of the dissertations, how many have been published in a peer-reviewed scholarly journal?

Dissertation Abstracts International was searched for key words likely to appear in doctoral dissertations in institutional advancement between 1991 and 2013; results were examined to ensure they were in fact on appropriate topics, producing 348 relevant dissertations. The resulting dissertations were read and coded by the researchers. Initially, dissertations were double coded to ensure interrater reliability.

Dissertations were coded on multiple dimensions, which included the following:

- Department of origin
- Theoretical framework (e.g., sociology)
- Methodology (quantitative vs. qualitative)
- Data source (whether the dataset was from a single or multiple sites, whether the dissertator either studied or worked at that site, and the name of the extant dataset used, if appropriate)
- Focus of dissertation (theory-building or practically focused)
- If there was a causal relationship tested, and if so, what the dependent variable(s) were

In addition, a database of fundraising articles (created by the researchers) tracked whether the article had also been printed as a book or article(s), whether the dissertator had been or was a practicing fundraiser, and whether the dissertation subsequently worked as a tenure-track faculty member at a research university. The year, advisor, and abstract were culled from the dissertations. The results were tracked and analyzed using Excel.

Three hundred forty-seven dissertations were found during this time period. One hundred eighty-eight, or 54.3 percent, were written by PhDs; 153, or 44.2 percent, were written by EdDs. The remaining five were produced by a DSM, DMgt, DA, DMin, and DPA.

Where Do They Come From?

The universities producing the majority of dissertations in advancement are, unsurprisingly, ones with larger programs in educational administration. Table 4.1 lists all institutions that produced at least five dissertations over the period of study. However, not all large programs are on this list: Teachers College, for example, only produced three. Two were completed at the US Sports Academy and one at Asbury Theological Seminary, the only two highly specialized institutions to appear in the list.

Table 4.1 Universities producing the highest number of advancement dissertations

University	Dissertations
University of Pennsylvania	15
University of Virginia	10
Vanderbilt University	10
University of Alabama	9
University of Michigan	9
Indiana State University	8
University of Missouri-Columbia	8
University of Nevada-Lincoln	8
University of Texas-Austin	8
Michigan State University	7
North Carolina State University	7
SUNY Buffalo	7
Union Institute	7
College of William and Mary	6
Florida State University	6
University of Northern Colorado	6
George Washington University	5
Southern Illinois University-Carbondale	5
University of Central Florida	5
University of Southern Mississippi	5

The vast majority were completed in schools of education, although specific program and department names vary widely. Eighteen theses were not identified by department or program name, but 85 percent of identifiable dissertations came from schools of education. Unexpectedly, 11 came out of programs in kinesiology, sports management, or physical education—these tended to be on athletic fundraising. Nine were in business programs with other disciplines having only a handful. Aside from two in theology, none were in traditional disciplines such as economics, anthropology, or sociology. Rather, the applied disciplines dominate the list. This is reflected in the topics chosen, which will be discussed further at another point. Surprisingly, none of the theses came out of nonprofit management programs, even though nonprofit management journals were a significant sources of publications—11 articles in *New Directions for Philanthropic Fundraising*, eight each in *Nonprofit and Voluntary Sector Marketing* and *Nonprofit and Voluntary Sector Quarterly*, nine in *Nonprofit Management and Leadership*, and a handful in other public sector journals.

The majority of dissertations were supervised by professors who, at least during the time under study, did not supervise any other dissertations in the subject, with several notable exceptions. (In addition, 14 dissertations were not labeled either in DAI or within the dissertation itself with a director's name.) Marybeth Gasman of the University of Pennsylvania in particular has directed seven dissertations (all but one EdDs), and as a mid-career academic is likely to direct many more. Marvin Peterson, now emeritus at the University of Michigan, directed six, all PhDs. Irvin Cockriel, now emeritus at the University of Missouri-Columbia, and Ronald Stein, recently retired vice president of advancement at SUNY Buffalo, each directed five PhD dissertations. Five faculty members directed three each: John Braxton,

Table 4.2 Number of advancement dissertations by department/program

Program	Dissertations
Education	281
Sports management	11
Business	9
Communications	2
Library science and informatics	2
Philanthropy	2
Theology	2
Human Resources	1
Marketing	1

Vanderbilt University; Fred Dressel, Ohio University; Annette Gibbs, University of Virginia; Timothy Letzring, the University of Arizona; and Arthur Southerland, University of Southern Mississippi. In addition, 26 faculty members (or pairs of faculty) directed two dissertations each.[1]

Caution should be used in making inferences about any particular faculty member's expertise in fundraising based solely a small number of dissertations directed—for example, fundraising scholar Robert Carbone only directed one dissertation. A faculty member may have retired in 1993, or only begun his or her career in 2006. In addition, a scholar's institutional type may provide him or her with access or more or fewer doctoral students.

What Methodological Approaches Do They Use?

The authors of this book believe that a robust mix of methods is desirable to advance the field. Both quantitative and qualitative approaches add to the body of knowledge; we need historians and economists, anthropologists and human resources experts. That said, we believe anything worth doing is worth doing well and that claims of generalizability should be appropriate to the work those claims are based on. Therefore, we ask: What methods are being used, and are they being used well?

One hundred thirty-six of the dissertations examined used qualitative methods, 174 used quantitative methods, and 36 used mixed methods. These are broad categories; the qualitative methods ranged from history to textual analysis, and the quantitative methods ranged from simple descriptive statistics based on surveys to sophisticated regression analyses from extant datasets. The majority of quantitative and mixed-methods dissertators relied on data they collected themselves rather than on preexisting datasets, such as IPEDS or VSE. Only 29 relied primarily on data from a dataset. Two dissertations, both of which were highly theoretical, did not use data from any source, but the remainder (and majority) used author-collected data. By far the most popular data source was VSE used in 16 dissertations. *US News and World Report* rankings data were used by five; IPEDS by five; institutional databases by four. Surprisingly, only one made extensive use of IRS Form 990s. Other researchers may have drawn on some of these sources to create lists of potential subjects, or to fill in missing/control variables, but here we tally only those for whom the dataset was a major or primary source.

We found a surprising number of single-institutional studies. In some cases, of course, this is the appropriate choice, as it may be in a history or an ethnography. In others, it suggested convenience or a research project more suited to a capstone format than a thesis. Of the qualitative dissertations, 44 were single-site, 90 were multiple-site, and for 2 this was not applicable. (An example of the last is Frank Oliver's *Fellow Beggars: The History of Fundraising Campaigning in United States Higher Education*, where analysis was at the level of the field rather than the institution.) Of the quantitative dissertations, 106 were single-site, 99 were multiple-site, and for 4 this was not applicable. And of the mixed-methods dissertations, 6 were single-site and 30 were multiple-site. For the quantitative dissertations in particular, the result was surprising; one of the strengths of good quantitative analysis is the generalizability it offers, which is foregone with a convenience sample of one. These efforts may be useful for the institutions themselves in decision-making, but they do little to forward the state of disciplinary knowledge.

Another potential source of concern is "insider research." In at least 46 studies, the researcher was an insider—that is, they either worked or were currently a student at an institution they examined (and in some cases, this was the same place). We say "at least" because some single-institutional studies with anonymized subjects did not provide sufficient identifying detail to discern whether the researcher was otherwise affiliated with that institution.[2] Our figure of 13 percent, therefore, is likely lower than the actual percentage. Toma, Hartley, and Montoto asked graduates of a higher education doctoral program aimed at practitioners about their attitudes toward using one's own workplaces for a dissertation (2008). While some graduates had used their own workplace and found it to be a positive experience, others felt that they were pressured to report only positive findings, were worried about pressuring employees, did not learn as much as they could have, and had some trouble separating their "work" selves from their "research" selves. Within the 13 percent, we saw a wide variation in how close the researcher was to the subject. In many cases, they did their research within their own department—even interviewing their subordinates.

One of the most important questions regarding methodology is what theoretical framework the dissertators used. Unlike the disciplines, the field of education does not have a standard research methodology of its own. Researchers employ concepts and methods from economics, history, sociology, anthropology, political science, and even literary analysis. The framework used delimits what kind of questions can be asked as well as what kind of answers can be found. What we discovered in our review was a startling lack of explicitly deployed conceptual or theoretical frameworks. At base, of course, *every* piece of research has a theory of how the world works behind it, even if it is not explicitly stated. A common pattern in these dissertations was a literature review on the topic under investigation and a declaration that the researcher was used quantitative (or qualitative methods), but no referral to any theory to bolster why the particular question or hypothesis was chosen. If anything, it was often, "We know X influences y at another type of college—does it do so here?" or "Factors A, B, C, and E have been shown to influence Y, but no one has investigated D's influence." A small subset of dissertations stated they were using "constructivist paradigms" or Lincoln and Guba's naturalistic inquiry; this was done with varying degrees of fidelity.

Among those dissertations that not only mentioned a theory but also actually used it to guide their research, the most common conceptual frameworks came from organization theory (32). Three more disciplines comprised a second tier: psychology and social psychology (12); sociology, primarily social capital (12); and branding/marketing (10). Communications, history, economics, human resources, and public relations each had a handful. There were a few outliers: dissertations using theology, gender studies, or rhetorical analysis, but the majority of the remainder—252 theses—were not avowedly guided by any conceptual framework. Most of these fell into the positivist or postpositivist traditions; their literature reviews focused on literature in either higher education or fundraising, but no theoretical model connected their literature review to their methodology. It should come as no surprise below to find out that most of these dissertations do not use their findings to build theory, either.

What Topics Do They Address?

Next, we turn to the topics addressed by the dissertations. Are they concerned with building theory or improving practice? What topics are most addressed? What kind of postsecondary institutions are described?

We begin with the question of theory: Is a dissertation primarily concerned with improving advancement practice, or is the focus on building theory? For our purposes, the theories could either be general (e.g., the nature of professions or the role of boundary spanning in organizations) or specific to the field (e.g., the development of a grand unified theory of why donors give). We were less interested in what authors *stated* their goal to be than what they actually *wrote* in their discussions, conclusions, and implications. Sixty-six of the dissertations made concerted attempts at building theory, not unexpected for a field that is practitioner-oriented.

More specifically, precisely what topics are addressed? To answer this question, we used the taxonomy mentioned in Chapter 1. Each dissertation was coded with one or more codes. Most commonly, when more than one code was used, the second code referred to the institutional type. For example, David Fincher Bradford's *Characteristics and Strategies of Bible College Fund-Raising Letters* was coded as 1.9 (rhetorical analysis) and 8.8 (religious institutions). Only seven dissertations were coded with other multiple topic codes, such as Steven Dale German's *Nonprofit Relationship Marketing: The Role of Identification*, which was coded as both 4.3 (alumni giving) and 4.5 (predictors of alumni involvement). Every effort was made to categorize dissertations with a more specific subcategory (i.e., 1.0, fundraising literature review) rather than a top-level general category (i.e., 1, fundraising), although this was not always possible. For example, Rebecca G. Beard's *The Money Tree—Alternative Revenues for Community Colleges* did not fit under any of the fundraising subcategories. Table 4.3 shows the results of this classification.

Table 4.3 Taxonomy of advancement dissertations

Topic		Theses	Topic		Theses
1.	Fundraising	0	1.12	Corporate or foundation giving	12
1.0	Literature review	0	1.13	Econometric models	1
1.1	Organization/process	60	1.14	Benchmarking	0
1.2	Motivation and individual predictors of giving (for alumni, see 4.3)	33	1.15	Effects of fundraising	6
			1.16	Government policy and its effects	5
1.3	Managing/effectiveness and institutional predictors of giving	61	1.17	Online giving	5
			Total fundraising		**232**
1.4	Professionalization	7	2.	Public relations	
1.5	Planned giving	5	2.1	Benchmarking and best practices	0
1.6	Case studies	14			
1.7	Stewardship	6	2.2	Integrated communications management	2
1.8	Internal perceptions	6			
1.9	Rhetorical analysis	9			
1.10	Ethics	2	2.3	Media relations	1
1.11	Grants	0	2.4	Government relations	0

continued

Table 4.3 Continued

Topic	Theses	Topic	Theses
2.5 Community relations	3	6. Leadership	
2.6 Crisis communications	1	6.1 Presidents	30
Total public relations	**7**	6.2 Trustees	5
3. Marketing		6.3 Vice presidents, provosts, and chief development officers	9
3.1 Electronic communications and social media	1		
3.2 Integrated communications management	5	6.4 Managers	1
		6.5 Staffing (career trajectories, perceptions, turnover)	14
3.3 Image creation/branding	2		
3.4 University rankings	9		
3.5 Cause-related marketing	0	6.6 Deans	3
		6.7 Volunteers	0
Total marketing	**17**	6.8 Faculty (including giving by faculty/staff)	2
4. Alumni relations			
4.1 Benchmarking	1	**Total leadership**	**64**
4.2 Case studies	0	7. History	
4.3 Alumni giving	81	7.1 History of fundraising/PR	3
4.4 Associations	3	7.2 Institutional history	2
4.5 Predictors of alumni involvement	3	7.3 Biography	0
		Total history	**5**
4.6 Alumni satisfaction	4	8. Institutional types and causes	
4.7 Other alumni programming	3		
Total alumni	**95**	8.1 HBCUs	12
5. International institutions		8.2 Community colleges	49
5.1 Canada	1	8.3 Graduate and professional units	7
5.2 United Kingdom	2		
5.3 Asia	3	8.4 Athletics (including effect of athletics on giving)	26
5.4 Australia and New Zealand	0		
		8.5 Student affairs	8
5.5 Africa	1	8.6 Non-HBCU MSIs	2
5.6 Other	2	8.7 Other specific causes or units	11
Total international	**9**		
		8.8 Religious institutions	17

Note: Many theses fall into more than one category, so totals add up to more than the total number of theses.

What does Table 4.3 tell us? First, over two-thirds of dissertations are about fundraising —either in general (167) or alumni (82). Moreover, the majority of these are focused on process and effectiveness. Figure 4.1 shows the most common subcategories. The first three alone comprise nearly half of the total dissertations; all three

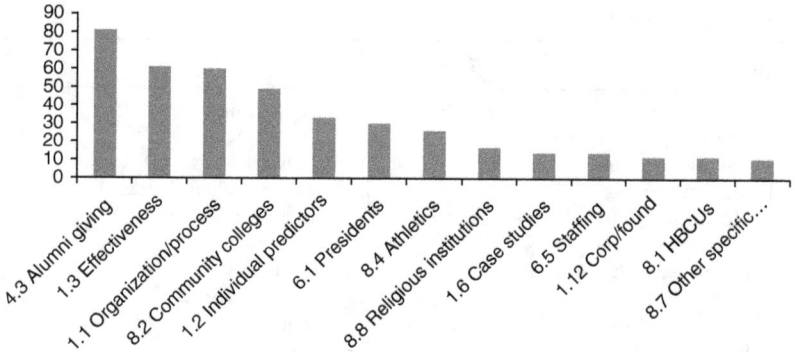

Figure 4.1 Most popular dissertation topics.

categories are focused on the question, "How can we increase individual donations to institutions?"

What about the types of institutions studied? The vast majority of dissertations focused on US institutions, not surprising given that the dissertations were drawn from DAI and were limited to degrees granted at US and Canadian universities. While advancement is becoming increasingly important worldwide, the higher education marketplace (and the study of it) remains highly nationalized. We also looked at institutional type, focusing on types that have been understudied in the past.[3] Notably, research on community colleges comprised a significant share of the theses with 48 dissertations. The two-year college is no longer being ignored in advancement research. Surprisingly, only 12 dissertations addressed HBCUs, and only 1, Rolando S. Arriola's *The Utilization of a Market-Driven Strategy for Fundraising at a Hispanic Serving University*, addressed non-HBCU MSIs. Another institutional type receiving scant attention was the graduate institution. This category included stand-alone institutions that only serve postbaccalaureates, such as seminaries, as well as graduate-only units within universities, such as law schools: there were 12 dissertations in this area. More popular than any of these were dissertations focused on religious institutions, of which there were 15. In some cases, these focused on the colleges affiliated with a particular denomination or order. Other dissertations focused on giving to specific programs. Most popular was athletics, with 19 dissertations, and student affairs, with 18. Another 8 focused on a variety of other programs. These included libraries, museums, diversity programs, and colleges of engineering and education.

How Have They Been Shared?

The final question we were interested in was how the knowledge gained in these dissertations had been shared. All, of course, were available through the libraries of the graduating institutions, although in many cases this was limited to a single physical copy. The newer dissertations tended to be available electronically—a terrific advance over microfilm or hardback and one that increases the likelihood of it being read. However, at most institutions, electronic distribution is limited to DAI, which only some universities and few colleges have access to. For example, among the City University of New York institutions, only the CUNY Graduate Center library has DAI access. In addition, some of the dissertations may have been shared on the job or with the institutions being examined, although we have no way of tracking this. What we can track is which dissertations, in whole or in part, were also published as peer-reviewed articles or books. The number was disappointingly small. None were published in any major educational journals such as *Research in Higher Education* or *The Journal of Higher Education*. None were published in the nonprofit research journals, such as *The Nonprofit and Voluntary Sector Quarterly*, either. Seventeen were published in the *International Journal of Educational Advancement*, the only journal devoted solely to the topic. The *Community College Journal of Research and Practice* publishes much more on fundraising than does any other major journal: Linnie Carter's dissertation on "The Philanthropic Motivations of Community College Donors: A Study of the Educational Foundation of a Mid-Sized, Multi-Campus Community College in Virginia" is at the heart of a subsequent article in that publication (Carter and Duggan 2010). Work based on portions of Kyle V. Sweitzer's *The Correlates of Changes in Prestige Among American Colleges and Universities* appeared in *New Directions in Higher Education*; however, it was based on nonadvancement portions of the dissertation. Two practitioner-focused articles appeared in nonacademic publications based on Frank C. Dickerson's *Writing the Voice of Philanthropy: How to Raise Money with Words*. Just two were published as books—Fygetakis's dissertation was published under the *New Directions for Student Services* imprint as *The Relationship between Student Affairs and Institutional*

Advancement Offices in Educational Fundraising and Cascione's dissertation was published by Routledge as *Philanthropists in Higher Education* (coauthored by Jon C. Dalton, her chair at Florida State University).

Our findings have critical implications for the development of the knowledge-base undergirding university fundraising. In the 24 years since Brittingham and Pezzullo's call for a more focused research agenda, it appears that little progress has been made to increase the quality of research focused on fundraising. The majority of the dissertations examined were of marginal quality and a scant few made it into the research literature.

Of the 241 dissertations examined, 43 focused on institutional characteristics that led to successful fundraising. These include variables such as institutional age and prestige and more specific research foci such as board, consortium, and foundation characteristics. Another 83 dissertations examined donor characteristics and motivations for giving. This does not include theses that examined "alumni loyalty" abstractly or only nondonative participation; it does include theses that were concerned with donations to a subunit of the university, such as to athletics.

Many of these were replications of motivational-type studies that appeared in Brittingham and Pezzullo's (1990) review of the literature. Kelly (1998) describes these types of studies as "magic button" research—as researchers look for the magical combination of demographic variables that will explain giving for a particular institution. She suggests that there is limited utility to these works and that they frequently are executed in a vacuum, paying little attention to previous studies that might inform the research (Kelly 1998).

Most dissertation chairs were faculty members who do not study fundraising themselves, as were committee members. This meant they were unable to guide their dissertators to the work that had been previously been done, which mostly consists of unpublished dissertations. Many dissertations contained words to the effect of, "There has been limited research published about the characteristics of alumni donors in higher education," for example, while in fact there was a plethora of literature on the topic. Because the works remained unpublished, they were not readily visible to the next set of researchers.

This issue may be tied to a larger concern about the blurring of purposes between EdD and PhD training. At the national level, there have been calls to reevaluate and redesign the EdD to differentiate it significantly from the PhD (Shulman et al. 2006). The results of this study demonstrate no differences in either the conceptual framework of the dissertation or the eventual career of the dissertator between those receiving a PhD and those receiving an EdD degree. If we are certifying individuals as administrative practitioners, this raises the question: What is the utility of having individuals produce original research that will not extend or revise significantly what we know about fundraising?

Of those dissertations that were published in a research journal, none were included in the three core higher education journals, *Research in Higher Education*, *The Review of Higher Education*, and *The Journal of Higher Education*. This has important implications for the study of higher education. At private institutions, which is the modal institutional type, 21 percent of university funds come from fundraising, suggesting the field's understanding of an essential part of the mechanisms of colleges and universities is woefully underdeveloped. For researchers interesting in higher education, this is substantial blind spot in the conceptualization of university functioning and postsecondary education financing.

Perhaps the lack of published inquiry in core journals is tied to faculty reluctance to engage in research addressing issues of fundraising because of the perception that that type of work is unseemly (Payton 1987). It also may be a function of those receiving doctorates returning to practice instead of pursuing faculty positions, whether by choice or because their research is less attractive to hiring institutions. For practicing fund raisers, there is virtually no incentive to publish original scholarship, and in some cases it may prove detrimental to one's career.

With so few individuals pursuing fundraising research as an extension of their doctoral training joining the professorate, little is done to resolve the issue of faculty with limited understanding of college and university advancement guiding and mentoring the next generation researchers interested in fundraising. This perpetuates the cycle of the unfamiliar mentoring those with interest in the area.

Finally, this study also suggests that the creation of a robust body of knowledge that informs professional practice continues to prove problematic for the fundraising profession as it moves toward professionalization. While other criteria are likely candidates for advancement's claims to professional status, the knowledge base is still not sufficiently well developed, nor does the research being conducted systematically address major issues confronting fund raisers and their institutions.

For fundraising to move along the continuum of professions and for the study of higher education to begin to develop a more robust understanding of a critical and underexamined function, this is an issue that must be addressed.

III

Major Questions and Answers

5
Why Donors Give

The question asked most frequently in advancement research is, "How can we predict which prospects will become donors?" To that end, we study the characteristics of institutions and try to measure best practices. We study theories of donor motivation. But most of all, we segment prospects by demographic and attitudinal characteristics to determine who are likely donors and, of those donors, who is likely to give large gifts. Perhaps this is not surprising. After all, a young, technically oriented community college in an urban area is not likely to turn into an old, private research university in a small town, so knowing that the latter can more easily garner support does not help fundraisers at the community college do their jobs.

Scholars have been critical of this focus. Kelly comments that, "there are few, if any studies on basic research or theory building" (1991, 114) in the literature of the profession. The research that does exist is limited, fragmented, and of marginal quality (Brittingham and Pezzullo 1990). As discussed in Chapter 4, much of the research has only been published in dissertations, which fewer practitioners (and scholars) have access to. This has resulted in a duplication of effort, as well as a plethora of single-institutional studies that are difficult to compare with each other. Nevertheless, it is important to try to synthesize this work.

In this chapter, we leave aside questions of institutional characteristics and practices and focus on the donors themselves. What characteristics of alumni and other potential donors increase their likelihood of giving, and of giving large gifts? We will first discuss what factors affect alumni giving, and then giving by all donors.

Factors Influencing Alumni Giving

One-fifth of the articles, books, and dissertations we examined were about alumni giving, either all or in part. Some of these studies focused on giving to particular units, while others focused on particular segments of the alumni population.

We examined this literature. There were 172 unique pieces of research (while dissertations were included, theses that were subsequently published in another form were dropped from this analysis). Of these 172, 60 were peer-reviewed, published articles; 5 were editorially reviewed book chapters; and 98 were unpublished dissertations.

Fully 114 of these studies were single-institutional; only 29 used more than 30 institutions. Most of the quantitative single-institutional studies used individual alumni as the unit of analysis, while the multiple-institutional studies typically used the institution as the unit of analysis. The majority of studies contained a quantitative element, 141 all told. Of those 141, 5 used factor analysis, 2 used structural equation modeling, and 126 used some flavor of regression (logit, tobit, and multiple regression being the most common). The majority of the remainder used descriptive statistics, correlations, discriminant analysis, or ANOVA. Almost none used a sophisticated method of dealing with missing data, despite the fact that how missing data is treated can have big impacts on the regression results (Cox et al. 2014).

The qualitative studies relied primarily on interviews, although surveys, data sets, focus groups, and documents were also used. The quantitative studies used institutional data (35), survey data (73), and data sets (16). The most common data set used was the Council for Aid to Education's Voluntary Survey of Education, although the Integrated Postsecondary Education Data System, *U.S. News & World Report*, the National Collegiate Athletic Association, College & Beyond, and various college guides also served as sources.

Studies used a range of institutions, including public and private, colleges and universities, prestigious and comprehensive institutions, religious and secular institutions. One institutional type, however, was notably absent: Only two studies looked at community college alumni giving. In his book on community college fundraising, Klingaman says, "Assertions have been made—'Alumni don't give to community colleges'—that don't hold water....In the end, we must conclude that if donors aren't giving, it is because they aren't being asked" (2012, 259) Better data is clearly needed to determine the scope of alumni donations to two-year institutions. Are two-year colleges with successful alumni fundraising programs lucky aberrations, or are less successful institutions undervaluing the willingness of alumni to be donors?

Studies varied in whether they looked at social and economic factors, institutional characteristics, or individual alumni characteristics. Only five quantitative studies tried to measure the effects of the economy or society at large, and of these, only one was multi-institutional (Dos Santos 2013).

Among the studies that try to distinguish institutional factors that result in improved fundraising using a large number of institutions, the dependent variable is typically the percentage of alumni that give or total alumni giving; most of these studies are based on data sources such as VSE that only contain institutional-level records. A surprising number of studies try to measure institutional-level factors with only one institution. These single-case studies use variability over time, such as won-loss records in athletics at a single institution (Holmes, Meditz, and Sommers 2008; Meer and Rosen 2009b); vary the conditions under which the ask is made (Meer 2011); or measure the effect of a major institutional change (Okunade, Wunnava, and Walsh 1994). Others are case studies or perceptual studies.

By far the largest area of interest was the characteristics of individual alumni. This focus has been criticized by scholars such as Kelly, who calls it "the theory of magic buttons," in which researchers search for the perfect likely donor based on demographics and beliefs (1998, 352). Nevertheless, interest in this area continues, particularly among scholar-practitioners who are interested in improving practice. In our review, the individual characteristics studied include demographic, college experience, and socio-economic traits as well as alumni perceptions. Because these studies used individual data, giving is measured in the individual rather than the aggregate: donor status as a binary variable, giving levels, total dollars (over a period of time or lifetime), number of gifts made, and intent to give. Methodological complexity varies widely, ranging from comparing two alumni groups based solely on N and percents (Johnson 2013) to structural equation modeling (Mosser 1993; Conner 2005).

The studies examined use a wide range of theories to explain donor behavior. These include, but are not limited to, resource dependence (Wright and Bocarnea 2007), crowding-out and crowding-in

(Gottfried 2008), social identity theory (Stephenson 2013), Bekkers and Wiepking's eight-factor model of donor giving (Metcalf 2013), Volkwein's four-construct model of alumni giving (Diehl 2007), self-interest (Metcalf 2013), serial reciprocity (Ebersole 2011), social exchange theory (Skari 2011), and symbolic interactionism (McDearmon 2013). However, many more studies have no discernable theoretical basis, citing findings from many previous studies without committing to any particular framework. Other research deliberately tests practitioner beliefs (Meer 2013).

Factors Influencing General Donors

While alumni are a natural fundraising constituency for colleges, they are not their only donors. Other individual gifts come from parents, community members, and athletic fans, all of which might have very different motives for giving. Moreover, some studies utilize giving data that may include alumni but are not limited to them. Sixty-three unique publications and dissertations looked at motivations for giving among nonalumni or mixed populations.

Of these studies, 11 looked at women as donors, 4 looked at faculty and/or staff giving, 12 looked at donors to athletics, and 8 looked at major donors (one of which looked at major donors to athletics). Most of the remainder examined a variety of general donor characteristics. Interestingly, no study focused on why members of local communities or parents gave—the one study on parent giving looked at the institutional factors affecting program success, not the parents themselves.

Institutional Factors Influencing Fundraising Success

Nearly 100 studies during this time period looked at institutional factors that influence fundraising success, with one-fifth of those focusing on community colleges. These include four distinct types of factors:

- Those that are immutable or very hard to change (relative age, institutional type)
- Those that are changeable but not by advancement (athletic success)
- The role of the president, trustees, and/or foundation
- Factors under the control of advancement (program structure, direct mail strategy)

Challenges

There are several challenges to this line of research.

First, among alumni, it is relatively easy to compare donors to nondonors, as the population is clearly bounded. Among nonalumni, who should be considered potential donors? It is impractical, to say the least, to compare all nonalumni donors to all nonalumni nondonors in the state, country, or world. This is a methodological challenge often worked around by comparing donors/nondonors among faculty or season ticket holders, or by comparing this year's donors to those who gave in a previous year but have ceased making donations. Scholars may wish to consider naturally bounded populations, such as parents, event attendees, local businesses, and so on, rather than "all potential donors."

Second, the chestnut of "correlation is not causation" applies as well to this research as to any other. Sometimes, findings seem intuitively obvious; if wealthy alumni give more than poor alumni, we might reasonably speculate that wealth increases the probability of being able to make a donation and, therefore, of making one. But what if we find giving varies by race, gender, or other personal demographic characteristic? Can we confidently assert that men are more generous, or is it possible that institutions have done a better job of soliciting donations from men? Likewise, it is risky to compare giving across academic units when one unit has an older, more robust fundraising program, or when alumni wages vary by student major.

Third, good data is hard to come by. Many researchers have worked with data pulled from a college or university that has generously shared it, but aside from a very few categories, such as gender, it is likely not comparable across institutions. Researchers sometimes turn to national data sets. Unfortunately, IPEDS data does not ask detailed questions on fundraising. Income is categorized as gift income versus other sources such as tuition, but it is not parsed any finer. The strength of IPEDS, though, is that nearly every institution of higher education in the United States is included, and the data is regarded as reliable. One other major source, the Voluntary Survey of Education conducted annually by the Council for Aid to Education, contains fine-grained detail, but it is unfortunately not all colleges and universities participate. There is reason to believe that institutions with more robust fundraising programs are more likely to respond—after all, they have the personnel and data resources to do so. Other periodic surveys, conducted by individual researchers or organizations such as the Council of Independent Colleges, generally promise participating institutions anonymity, which means the data cannot be widely shared nor can findings be replicated.

Conclusion

In addition to considering whether a research question is truly novel, scholars ought to pay closer attention to methodology. There is a need for more methodological consistency in research on predictors of giving. While there is not "one true way," researchers should hew to best practices, whether using qualitative or quantitative work. Claims of generalizability should be tempered to the data and method, and missing data should be dealt with rather than ignored. Finally, work needs to be done on bringing together theories and extending them, rather than testing common sense but atheoretical propositions.

6

The Campus Green Update

In *The Campus Green,* Brittingham and Pezzullo offered suggestions for advancement research, based on their literature review. They included the following areas:

- Consistency of college mission
- Spending and effectiveness of fundraising
- Roles of governance and trustees
- Attitudes of alumni
- Evaluation
- Segmented markets
- Broader questions/methodology (Brittingham and Pezzullo 1990, 87–91)

How have these areas of research fared in the over two decades since these recommendations were made?

Consistency of College Mission

Brittingham and Pezzullo recommended this area of research based on a study by the Coalition of Women' Colleges. Colleges' missions have changed over time as institutions moved from single-sex education to coeducation, attenuated church affiliations, and responded to economic, political, and cultural forces.

Today, research on this topic remains rare. Scholars have looked at mission statements (Ayers 2005; Morphew and Hartley 2006); why changes in mission occur (Gallagher 1997; Morphew 2002); and the immediate effects of institutions deliberately changing missions (Gonzales 2013), but this work rarely explores effects of mission change on advancement.

One exception to this is a dissertation on the effect of a women's college becoming coeducational (Clarke 2011). Clarke examined student and alumnae opposition to coeducation at a women's college in the South. Her dissertation explores a multitude of effects, including on fundraising.

Another exception is Neuman's dissertation and subsequent article on Bacone College, a Baptist college that educated Native American students until becoming a primarily white institution in the mid-twentieth century. Because Bacone raised much of its funds from Native Americans, it emphasized the values of Indian culture in addition to white culture, unlike most schools that educated Native Americans. After suffering financially during World War II, the college opened enrollment to white students and become a two-year institution (Neuman 2002, 2007).

Despite these two counterexamples, Brittingham and Pezzullo's charge remains unanswered. Many institutions are undergoing great change, in some cases voluntarily but in many other cases a result of political pressure or mission creep, and the effects of these changes on fundraising and alumni attitudes has not been explored.

Spending and Effectiveness of Fundraising

How should institutions allocate their fundraising dollars? At first glance, there seems to be a great deal of research on this question—over one hundred pieces of research were tagged as "managing/effectiveness," and even more were devoted to donor motivation and rhetorical analysis. Yet few of these studies rigorously examine expenditures rather than best practices. Far more studies examine the impact of donor-side variables and institutional characteristics that are either immutable (such as relative age and sector) or outside the control of the advancement department (such as athletic success).

One important work is Rooney's "A better method of analyzing the costs and benefits of fundraising at universities" (1999). His article does not evaluate different fundraising tactics, but it does provide an improved framework for institutions to conduct cost-benefit analyses.

Unfortunately, institutions rarely undertake anything like scientific trials of methods. Most of the studies that examine effectiveness do so by comparing institutions against each other; few compare "the returns under reasonably comparable institutional types" (Brittingham and Pezzullo 1990, 88). However, a few do. Simmel and Berger use a nested design to compare the effects of various statements in telephone fundraising (Simmel and Berger 2000, Simmel et al. 2002). Harrison et al. look at the effect of overall fundraising expenditures (Harrison, Mitchell, and Peterson 1995).

The challenge in this area is one routinely faced in the social sciences; it is difficult, and in some cases unethical, to convince practitioners to use randomized trials and similar research methods. While nonprofits may test several variations on a fundraising letter, they are unlikely to try strategies that stray far from accepted practice.

Roles of Governance and Trustees

Brittingham and Pezzullo suggest that, in particular, the roles of governance and trustees in *public* institutions should be explored including both institutional and foundation trustees. Here, a few answers have appeared in the intervening years. Examination of foundation trustees includes work by Fraser (2006). Examination of institutional trustees includes works by Graham (1994), Green (2000), and Nielsen, Newton, and Mitvalsky (2003). Notably, both Graham's and Neilson et al.'s research focuses on community colleges.

Other research on effective fundraising does not focus on trustees, but includes some aspect of trusteeship as a factor. Today, as when *The Campus Green* was written, there is much more literature on the role of trustees at private colleges and universities.

Attitudes of Alumni

While there is some research on alumni satisfaction (Hartman and Schmidt 1995; Terry 2010; Dobson 2013; Pung 2013), the authors of *The Campus Green* in particular are interested more specifically in linking alumni attitudes to fundraising. As they point out, there is a robust literature on alumni characteristics, but less on the impact of attitudes of donor behavior.

Of nearly two hundred pieces of research on alumni giving, a significant portion of them include some component of attitude. This includes both qualitative and quantitative works, interviews, and surveys. However, much of this research was conducted only among donors making it difficult to contrast them to nondonors; presumably, donors have more positive attitudes toward their alma maters than do nondonors. There is a robust literature that includes both donors and nondonors (Burgess-Getts 1992; Cristantello 1992; Martin 1993; Snyder 1993; Ashcraft 1995; Nirschel 1997; Baker 1998; Belanger 1999; Hanson 2000; Higgins 2000; Patouillet 2001; Teich 2001; Filardo 2003; Gonzalez 2003; Pumphrey 2004; Caboni and Eiseman 2005; Conner 2005; Gaier 2005; McDearmon and Shirley 2009; Drew-Branch 2011; King 2011; Rugano 2011; McDearmon 2013; Stephenson 2013). In addition, there is a small body of research focusing on nondonors, most of it quite recent (Wastyn 2008; McDearmon 2010; Foxx 2013).

In this area, Brittingham and Pezzullo's charge has been taken up and addressed by scholars. While this line of research has not been played out—and demographic and economic changes suggest that future alumni may have different attitudes than previous generations—this is no longer an area of neglect.

Evaluation as Research

Here, more than any other area, the *Campus Green* authors' call has been answered. They posit a need for "[m]iniresearch projects, designed to test [something] in a single institution" (Brittingham and Pezzullo 1990, 90). Thanks to the applied nature of education research, many doctoral students are interested in producing a piece of work that is useful to their employing institution, and as a result many dissertations are evaluations of single colleges and universities or a comparison of a small number of programs. In fact, there are too many to list here; readers are encouraged to consult the Appendix. Unfortunately, many of these research products are unpublished dissertations.

Segmented Markets

While some scholars, such as Kelly (1998), suggest that the search for donors who are most likely to give has been overemphasized, Brittingham and Pezzullo call for more research of this type, albeit more smartly conducted. Rather than see if students of a particular graduating year are most likely to give, they suggest that researchers should segment donors into cohorts. Scholars have amply addressed this question, as discussed in chapter 3. The advance in readily available statistical software may be partially responsible for this; it is easier for scholars to conduct quantitative analyses today than when *The Campus Green* was published.

Broadened Questions and Methodology

Finally, the authors note that most research uses surveys for data collection and econometric models to analyze it. They call for "theories and techniques derived from anthropology, organizational theory, communication theory, and linguistic analysis" (Brittingham and Pezzullo 1990, 91) noting that these theories were little used in advancement research but have much to offer it.

While there has been a greater diversity in data collection methods—such as case studies, Delphi techniques, and focus groups—unfortunately, most research in the area of advancement continues to use the same theories. Much of the research is atheoretical, drawing on previous findings that only loosely connect to any theory (Carbone 1986; Kelly 1998). Among the theories specifically mentioned, anthropology has been the least adopted. One of the few exceptions is Neuman's work on Bacone College (Neuman 2002, 2007); Neuman herself is a practicing archeologist. Linguistic and rhetorical analyses have been applied to fundraising appeals and speeches (Howard 1993; Simmel and Berger 2000; Hubbard 2001; Ncube 2002; Simmel et al. 2002; Fincher 2003; Gasman 2004; Dickerson 2009a, 2009b). Communication theory has also been used (Simmel and Berger 2000; Bongila 2001). Organization theory has been the most widely adopted used as a theoretical foundation in too many studies to list here.

Other theoretical bases include psychology, public relations, marketing, and nonprofit management. Of these, the nonprofit management literature is most frequently drawn upon, although much of the literature in nonprofit management has the same atheoretical nature as higher education. There is certainly room for scholars to bring new theoretical approaches to the field, as well as for scholars to more rigorously use, apply, and modify the theories currently in use.

Conclusion

Some significant progress has been made since the publication of *The Campus Green* over 20 years ago, but some of their requests have gone largely unheeded. These include research on consistency of mission, research on spending and effectiveness of fundraising, and the use of broader questions/methodology across the board. Notably, these are some of the more difficult areas to do work in. Consistency of mission likely requires extensive data collection and qualitative methods;

spending and effectiveness requires detailed budgeting information from multiple institutions. Broader methodological approaches can only come from those scholars trained in them, which in many cases means scholars outside colleges of education, or education scholars working in collaboration with outsiders.

7
Trends in Research

What topics and questions are starting to gain traction? What new data sources or methods are researchers using? Our research suggests two trends: overall growth, and a larger volume of research by economists or researchers using econometric methods. There is clear evidence of growth or decline only in two areas, online giving and faculty giving.

Overall Increase in Research

The amount of research in the field of advancement, both published and unpublished, has increased over time. Beginning in 1999, there was an uptick in the number of dissertations, with an increase in the number of publications a few years later. It is unwise to draw precise conclusions (e.g., the dip in 2006 is likely a random fluctuation rather than a meaningful number), but evidence suggests there was an increase in fundraising interest around the turn of the century. The *CASE Journal of Institutional Advancement* launched in 2000, for example. (After three volumes, it was renamed the *International Journal of Institutional Advancement*. It ceased publication in 2011.) Interestingly, we have not seen a significant decline in the number of dissertations and publications since its demise.

Given the overall increase in the number of both dissertations and publications over time, we would expect to see a rise in most subareas of research. The growth of many areas, such as research on HBCUs and community colleges, is partially a reflection of overall growth, as the increase in the number of these works over the time of our study does not outpace general growth in advancement research. In some topics, such as non-US advancement, we see growth above and

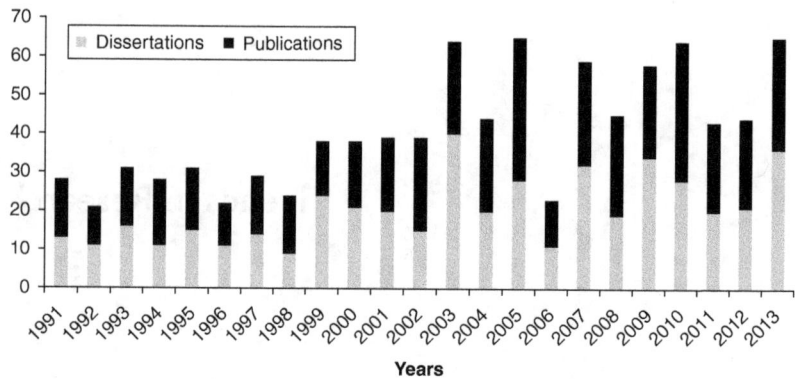

Figure 7.1 Dissertations and publications, 1991–2013.

beyond the general increase, although the numbers are typically not large enough to confirm that the trend is nonspurious. One counterexample is research on online giving; all five dissertations on the topic appeared 2003–2007, which makes sense given the growth of the Internet during this time frame.

Of course, the number of articles over time by particularly productive scholars has waxed and waned depending on where they are in their careers. For example, there are 19 journal articles or book chapters by Marybeth Gasman in our dataset, with the earliest dating to 2001; she earned her PhD in 2000. At the other end of the career spectrum, Marvin W. Peterson oversaw five dissertations in fundraising during our time span, with the last completed in 2003; as a recent professor emeritus, he would not be expected to chair dissertations any longer. No scholars in our data were productive throughout the entire period, at least within the area of advancement.

Publication Patterns

One interesting nontrend is that the journals that scholars are publishing in have changed little over time with the obvious exception of the *International Journal of Educational Advancement*—or any other journal that began or ceased publication during our 23-year time frame.

We see a very slight increase over time that mirrors the increase in total publications and dissertations, but overall little change. The noticeable exception occurs in 2003, when a special issue of *New Directions for Community Colleges* focused on fundraising.

In order for research to be published, several things need to occur:

1. The research needs to be conducted. This may be by scholars hoping to publish, graduate students completing a thesis, an institution producing knowledge to guide its own behavior, or a professional organization trying to bring attention to a particular area. We know this research is being conducted, and in the case of dissertations, we know it has increased over time.
2. The research needs to be submitted for publication. We hypothesize that faculty are more likely to submit their research to journals than are graduate students or practitioners. It is unlikely, however, that the relevant journals have thorough enough records going back to 1991 about what has been submitted to them to hazard a guess about submission rates. Book chapters and submissions to the various *New Directions* series are likely to have more submissions by students and practitioners, as their editors seek out research. While we know how many dissertations become publications, how many other projects are only submitted to conferences or not submitted at all?
3. The research must be accepted for publication. Any particular study may be rejected because it is outside of the scope of the journal, it is deemed less important than other submissions, or because its quality is less than that of other submissions.

While we know that more research in advancement is being published, too many variables are missing to hazard a guess as to whether research was being published at a higher *rate* in 2013 than in 1991. We do not know how many studies are being conducted and never submitted (or only submitted to a conference), or how many studies have been submitted for publication and rejected. We also do not know whether studies are being rejected for being "not important enough" versus "not done well." In other words, it is not clear if work is not being published because it is not being done, because it is not being submitted, because it is low quality, or because it is being rejected by gatekeepers for other reasons.

Types of Research

Gibbons (1998) distinguishes between two types of research, what he calls Mode 1 and Mode 2. Mode 1 is traditional, discipline-based research; Mode 2 is "produced in a context of application," is transdisciplinary, uses a variety of methods and skills, and is of interest to more users, including practitioners (Gibbons 1998, 5). It should be evident that the vast majority of advancement falls into Mode 2. Higher education, after all, is a field of study rather than a discipline, drawing from many disciplines. During the time we examined, there was little change in this.

Topics of Research

One emerging area of research is giving by employees, particularly faculty (Holland 1997; Schneider 2000; March 2005; Nesbit, Christensen, and Gossett 2012; Leslie, Snyder, and Glomb 2013; Loveday 2013; Shaker 2013a, 2013b), and the role of faculty in soliciting donations (Gasman 2005). The other area of relative growth, as mentioned earlier, is the role of the Internet in soliciting donations. While the number of articles in this area is few, we do feel confident in speculating that the number of articles and dissertations that explored the role of online giving prior to 1991 was small, and thus the increase is real. However, as the Internet becomes a part of life for most Americans, the questions asked about are likely to change. Donors have grown more comfortable with online giving and with receiving information online. Future research is likely to focus on effective use of technology, rather than its novelty.

Conclusion

Overall, there was surprisingly little change in the subjects researchers chose to examine over our time period, given the social changes that have occurred over this time period, as well as the new quantitative tools available to researchers. We are nevertheless heartened to see more scholars conducting and publishing research in advancement, of course, but believe it is time that some of that energy be turned to more neglected areas, which we will discuss in the final chapter.

IV

The Future of Advancement Research

8

Suggestions for Research

Over the past 22 years, the amount of research made available on institutional advancement has increased. As we saw in chapter 6, some of Brittingham and Pezzullo's calls for research have been amply answered, while others have not. In the interim, too, new issues have arisen, ranging from the technical (online giving) to the economic (how does fundraising fare in a recession?). Today, what are the areas of research needed by practitioners and scholars? What new approaches are available thanks to new data or new research tools?

The fact that few studies were found in some areas is not by itself a reason to call for further research. In some ways, higher education advancement is unique: The alumni/nonalumni donor distinction applies only here and in fundraising for private K-12 schools, although the "grateful patient" donor in health care philanthropy is similar. In other ways, the issues that higher education faces are not so unique. For example, questions about how donors have adapted to giving through the Internet likely have less to do with the specific cause than the medium. In some ways, the advancement function at a university is very similar to the advancement team at any other large nonprofit organization. By limiting this review to higher education advancement, we missed out on many studies of relevance to both scholars and practitioners in the field. While only five studies on online giving may not seem like a lot, there is a significant body of work on that topic in the nonprofit management literature that obviates the need for further higher education-specific studies.

Research is needed is six areas: why donors give, the effects of fundraising, ethics, the role of leadership in advancement, history, and public relations. Each of these is explored more fully as follows.

In addition, two additional recommendations are made, one for supervision of theses and directors of graduate programs, and one for better data.

Why Donors Give

The literature is replete with analyses of the characteristics of donors versus nondonors, especially alumni. While it might seem hard to justify new work in this general area, there are some significant lacunae in this work. In particular, we need more studies of nontraditional donors, quantitatively sophisticated multi-institutional analyses, and analyses of neglected institutional types or units that might have different donative patterns or donor motivation.

Nontraditional donors: In its search for the most likely set of donors, philanthropy has targeted the wealthy, the white, and the male. According to Drezner:

> A better understanding of how to engage nontraditional donors is needed.... Having a better understanding, from practice to research, of how alumni of color, women, and members of the lesbian, day, bisexual, transgender, queer, questioning, and intersex communities think about their support of higher education is important. (2011, 87)

In some contexts, the nontraditional donor might even be a white male with wealth: As we saw in chapter 5, there is almost no work on community college alumni as donors, or on parents and community members as donors. In the two-year context, *all* alumni count as nontraditional donors. Of course, quantitative methods may be appropriate for some populations, but qualitative methods and case studies may be equally appropriate, especially for researching donor motivation and perceptions.

Quantitatively sophisticated multi-institutional analyses: Improved statistical software, including user-friendly programs such as SPSS, means that researchers can more easily do methodologically sophisticated research. Descriptive statistics and tests such as ANOVA and chi-squared should be starting points rather than end points for quantitative researchers. In particular, researchers should apply multilevel models to fundraising, taking into account both individual and institutional characteristics. Other potential methodologies include time-series regressions, as much extant work is cross-sectional; event history analysis to model donor behavior; meta-analysis, where possible, to aggregate findings; and structural equation modeling. In addition, quantitative researchers need to confront missing data problems. Even if modern techniques such as multiple imputation are not used, the implications of missing data should be discussed honestly.

Analyses of neglected institutional types or units: Scholarship on some institutional types is plentiful, such as research universities. Even some formerly underrepresented institutions, such as community colleges and Historically Black Colleges and Universities, now have robust literature bases. However, some institutional types remain neglected; there is, for example, *no* published research on Jewish colleges, rabbinical schools, or seminaries, and there is very little research on Christian seminaries. Seminaries in particular might be supposed to have different fundraising issues than even religious universities due to a potentially narrower base of donors and the shrinking of mainline denominations (Funk and Smith 2012; Nelson 2013). Yet the last work of research focusing on seminary fundraising is from 1990 (Dillon 1990). Minority-serving institutions, other than HBCUs, have also been relatively ignored. We might reasonably expect MSI fundraising to be different from HBCU fundraising, as Latina/o and Asian American-serving institutions are less likely to embrace their designation. Native-serving institutions and tribal colleges may be more like HBCUs from a fundraising perspective, but this has yet to be explored.

In addition, some units within institutions have only been cursorily examined, such as museums. As institutions such as Fisk University and Randolph College struggle with the costs of maintaining art museums (Kennedy 2012; Jaschik 2014), institutions could benefit from understanding potential revenue sources.

The Effects of Fundraising

How does fundraising affect the institutions it purports to serve? Do donors lead institutions into projects they would not otherwise undertake? This includes consistency of college mission, as Brittingham and Pezzullo termed it. It might also include the impact of having the institution associated with a donor or cause that has a negative public image. For example, Vanderbilt University tried to change the name of Confederate Memorial Hall, and more recently Duke and the University of North Carolina have struggled with renaming buildings named after white supremacists (Jaschik 2005; Weinberg 2014). Not all the effects of fundraising are negative, of course: Vanderbilt University reduced average student indebtedness by over $5,000, in part due a $108 million campaign to raise funds for financial aid (Kiley 2013).

This would also include historical work. While there has been a growth in the historical study of fundraising, much work remains to be done. Of course, many institutional histories, both hagiographic and critical, discuss fundraising endeavors, but they rarely are given center stage. An ambitious historian could make his or her mark by taking up where Curti and Nash's (1965) history of higher education philanthropy left off, not only bringing us farther into the present but also adopting a fresh perspective. How many institutions have survived extinction only by a well-timed fortuitous gift? How have their missions been shaped, particularly during times of impecuniousness, by awareness of what donors are interested in funding? In addition to traditional historical methods, quantitative techniques such as historical-comparative methods might be useful for examining cultural changes such as the rise of fundraising in public institutions worldwide.

Ethics

We only found five studies that addressed ethical issues in fundraising, yet surely there are important ethical issues in advancement. Some of these include the aforementioned problems of naming rights. Other questions include those of honoring donor intent, such as the selling off of donated art or using funds more broadly than intended, as Princeton University has been accused of doing (The Chronicle of Higher Education 2002).

The process of raising funds also generates ethical questions. One study looked at the attitude of donors toward prospect research (Gerstle 1995), and more work in this area would be valuable. In May 2014, a heated discussion appeared on the ARNOVA-L listserv about the appropriateness of nonprofit staff members volunteering and donating to their employers (Sowa 2014). How might an ethical framework tackle the issue of faculty and staff giving to their college and university employers? Another possible area is the extent of donor control—can a donor of an endowed chair choose the individual faculty member to occupy it, for example?

There are also ethical stances taken by the Council for the Advancement and Support of Education and the Association of Fundraising Professionals that may be worth examining. Both organizations, for example, state in their codes of conduct that fundraisers should not work based on commission (CASE Board of Trustees 2005; Association of Fundraising Professionals 2007). Do any institutions use commission-based fundraising? What happens when, even without commissions, fundraisers divert donor resources toward themselves? What other conflicts of interest might occur when large sums of money are involved?

Ethical problems are not limited to fundraising; they may also arise in marketing and crisis communications. While our review of marketing materials did not address marketing to potential students, it can be difficult to determine who the target market is for many marketing materials, particularly those online. For example, institutions have been caught blatantly adding students of color to mostly white scenes, or of exaggerating the percentage of minority students on their campuses (Jaschik 2008). Crisis communications also has the potential for ethical issues to arise, as institutions struggle with how much information to share and worry about protecting their images.

Leadership

The role of leadership in fundraising—including chief development officers, trustees, and particularly presidents—has been the subject of many studies. Research explores what these leaders in fact do, what others expect them to do, and how they perceive their role. However, most of this work is perceptual or second-hand. Documenting the actual practices of fundraisers and other institutional leaders involved in fundraising would give us a better picture of how their work is conducted.

One potential approach would be time-diary studies. While this requires a larger commitment from research subjects than filling out a survey, it likely gives a more accurate picture of how their time is spent. Time-diary studies have been successful in other areas including the study of faculty (Milem, Berger, and Dey 2000; Flaherty 2014). Another possible approach—although hardly used at present in any facet of the study of higher education—is ethnographic approaches. Ethnography is possible within higher education, as demonstrated by the work of Bill Tierney (1987). Observational studies in fundraising present challenges, particularly as major donors may be reluctant to be observed in what otherwise might be private meetings. Such research would require strong relationship-building skills and a commitment to privacy and thoughtful disclosure.

History

No doubt, there is some excellent work being done in historical research, particularly as regards fundraising. However, most of it focuses on one institution, one donor, or one organization. We already mentioned that there is a need for more work on the effects of fundraising over time, but there is also a need for a descriptive, field-level approach. How has fundraising changed throughout time? One obvious answer is that there is simply more of it today; fundraising has gone from an activity conducted by private colleges and universities to one conducted by all institutions, even by a few for-profit institutions through related 501(c)3 foundations.

This work might also address fundraising as a profession. Today, many fundraisers have earned degrees in nonprofit management or related fields, something that was unheard of a century ago. While there is work that addresses fundraising as a profession (Lamm 1991; Bloland 2002; Caboni 2003; Daly 2013) most of it addresses fundraising as it currently is, rather than taking a historical approach. Notable themes to address might be the feminization of a formerly male occupation, the increased educational requirements, the advent of credentials such as CFRE, the rise of professional organizations, and whether the involvement of top administration has changed over time.

Finally, technological changes should be addressed. Computers have revolutionized advancement, just as they have changed all higher education administration. Donor records were moved from paper to spreadsheets to purpose-built databases such as Raiser's Edge; prospect research was revolutionized by the Internet. Donors can now give through the web and via text. Crisis communications was radically altered by the ability to immediately update websites and to send out emergency alert text messages. Alumni relations and public relations rely on email, not just the US Postal Service, to get their messages out. Overall, the rise of social media has increased the preponderance of two-way communication over one-way communication.

Public Relations

In the realm of public relations and marketing, some areas are scantily addressed. While the subject of "town-gown" relations is in the news often, it rarely makes it into the research. Questions of eminent domain, quality of neighborhood life, and the degree to which institutions are viewed as resources or adversaries by their surrounding neighborhoods are questions that we have little data on. In addition, we found that, in many single-site case studies, there was a relative deficit of multi-institutional comparative work in public relations. Institutions represented in these case studies tend to be either outliers or institutions chosen for convenience (e.g., the researcher's home institution). High quality multi-institutional research would likely require a significant financial commitment, however, to do well.

Data We Need

One challenge for researchers has been to find data beyond the level of the individual institution. The two major sources for this are IPEDS and VSE, but both have drawbacks. Beyond that, periodic surveys provide varying levels of access to researchers.

The Integrated Postsecondary Education Data System is collected by the federal government in two waves each year. In its favor, it includes nearly every postsecondary institution in the United States and its outlying territories. (Institutions that eschew federal funding, such as Hillsdale College, are excluded, but they are few in number.) The data is carefully checked before being made available to the public. It is also freely available to all. However, it has one major drawback: few details on fundraising. The finance survey component of IPEDS includes two items of interest: "gifts, including contributions from affiliated organizations" and "investment income." Gifts cannot be broken down by source (individual, foundation, or corporation) or by cause (annual fund, capital campaign, or endowment). Even the number of donations is not available.

The Voluntary Support of Education survey, conducted annually by the Council for Aid to Education, is another prime source of data. Data is available for a fee (much lower for institutions that participate). Unlike IPEDS, the VSE also collects data from private K-12 institutions. Given its more narrow purpose, it delves much deeper into the details of institutional fundraising than IPEDS does. Data includes information on pledges and bequests, enrollment and endowment, advancement expenditures, donations by source (alumni, parents, individuals, religious organizations, foundations, consortia, and corporations) and purpose, deferred gifts, and capital campaigns. Despite this level of detail, the VSE cannot serve all purposes. Not all institutions participate; those that do may not answer every question or participate every year. Researchers should be particularly cautious about trying to use VSE data longitudinally. (For researchers only interested in the percentage of alumni who give, this data is also available from the *U.S. News and World Report* higher education rankings.)

Other, periodic surveys are also conducted. The Council of Independent Colleges, in conjunction with CASE, for example, has conducted five advancement surveys (covering more than just fundraising) of its members going back to 1976. While their results are useful, their disaggregated data is typically not available to researchers. And just like with the VSE, not all CIC members participate.

One drawback to all of these surveys is that they are institutional level, not individual level. We might use VSE to test whether institutional age affects the percentage of alumni who give, but we cannot test whether an individual alumna is more likely to give if she joined a sorority during her college years. Gathering this information across institutions takes considerable time and effort. One project currently underway is the National LGBT Alumni Survey, headed by Jason Garvey at the University of Alabama. These kinds of surveys can provide detailed insight into donor behavior, but they require financial support that secondary data analysis doesn't.

We encourage organizations that conduct these surveys to consider making their data more readily available, rather than just publishing aggregated results. Also, institutions should consider funding projects such at the National LGBT Alumni Survey. However, our greatest wish would be for more detailed questions in IPEDS. While IPEDS is unlikely to ever be as detailed as VSE, a good start would be disaggregating gifts by source. One worthwhile project would be for a consortium or university system to consider a multi-institutional survey that would contain both institutional-level and individual-level data.

Recommendations for Research Supervisors

One persistent problem over the two decades has been the variable quality of theses. While variation in quality will never be eliminated, part of the problem stems from requiring students who have no desire to be researchers to do a research project to earn their doctorate. While this has often been framed as a matter of clearly separating research-based PhD programs from practitioner-based EdD programs, in practice these two degrees are often not differentiated. Whatever an institution calls its doctoral programs, the work required ought to be useful for the students engaged in it. Some institutions have successfully implemented real-world capstone programs for EdD students (Caboni and Proper 2009). While this is not the only possible model, it does make sense for students in administrative careers (or preparing for them) to do work that has a more tangible benefit than the traditional theory-driven "original research" inherent in dissertations. Directors of graduate study and other program architects should seriously consider what their program is to students, and offer an alternative format if appropriate. For dissertation writers and supervisors required to use the traditional model, it makes sense to consider work that is practice-based as far as possible—but caution should be exercised in claims of generalizability.

Conclusion

Like observers before us, we recognize that there is more work to be done.

Appendix: Annotated Bibliography of Higher Education Advancement Literature, 1991–2013

This appendix includes all scholarly publications related to higher education advancement, 1991–2013. It does not include white papers, reports, or conference presentations. The focus is on research, rather than on advice for practitioners, although in some cases work straddles both. For example, Worth's *New Strategies for Educational Fundraising* is aimed at practitioners but has a scholarly base.

Each publication is given one or more numerical codes as well as abstracted. While abbreviations are kept to a minimum for clarity, some acronyms that are common in higher education are used to save space (e.g., IPEDS or HBCU). In some cases institutional names are abbreviated if the citation itself makes the abbreviation intelligible. The conventions of each paper's author(s) are followed for racial and other demographic characteristics, such as "black" versus "African American."

1. Fundraising
    1.0 Literature review
    1.1 Organization/process
    1.2 Motivation and individual predictors of giving (for alumni, see 4.3)
    1.3 Managing/effectiveness and institutional predictors of giving
    1.4 Professionalization
    1.5 Planned giving
    1.6 Case studies
    1.7 Stewardship
    1.8 Internal perceptions
    1.9 Rhetorical analysis
    1.10 Ethics
    1.11 Grants
    1.12 Corporate or foundation giving

  1.13 Econometric models
  1.14 Benchmarking
  1.15 Effects of fundraising
  1.16 Government policy and its effects
  1.17 Online giving
2. Public relations
  2.1 Benchmarking and best practices
  2.2 Integrated communications management
  2.3 Media relations
  2.4 Government relations
  2.5 Community relations
  2.6 Crisis communications
3. Marketing
  3.1 Electronic communications and social media
  3.2 Integrated communications management
  3.3 Image creation/branding
  3.4 University rankings
  3.5 Cause-related marketing
4. Alumni relations
  4.1 Benchmarking
  4.2 Case studies
  4.3 Alumni giving
  4.4 Associations
  4.5 Predictors of alumni involvement
  4.6 Alumni satisfaction
  4.7 Other alumni programming
5. International institutions
  5.1 Canada
  5.2 United Kingdom
  5.3 Asia
  5.4 Australia and New Zealand
  5.5 Africa
  5.6 Others
6. Leadership
  6.1 Presidents
  6.2 Trustees
  6.3 Vice presidents, provosts, and chief development officers
  6.4 Managers
  6.5 Staffing (career trajectories, perceptions, turnover, etc.)
  6.6 Deans
  6.7 Volunteers
  6.8 Faculty (including giving by faculty/staff)
7. History
  7.1 History of fundraising/PR
  7.2 Institutional history

7.3 Biography
8. Institutional types and causes
   8.1 HBCUs
   8.2 Community colleges
   8.3 Graduate and professional units
   8.4 Athletics (including effect of athletics on giving)
   8.5 Student affairs
   8.6 Non-HBCU MSIs
   8.7 Other specific causes or units
   8.8 Religious institutions

Abelman, Robert, and Amy Dalessandro. "The Institutional Vision of Community Colleges: Assessing Style as Well as Substance." *Community College Review* 35 no. 4 (2008): 306–35. 3.3, 8.2.

The authors conducted a content analysis of mission/vision statements using a stratified sample of 240 institutions and content analysis software. They found that mission statements and vision statements served different purposes. Community colleges had visions more shared and observable than other public institutions; their mission statements were more shared, complex, and observable and had higher relative advantage, but were less clear and compelling.

Absher, Keith, and Gerald Crawford. "Marketing the Community College Starts with Understanding Students' Perspectives." *Community College Review* 23 no. 4 (1996): 59–68. 3.3, 8.2.

This study surveyed students at four Alabama community colleges about factors influencing their choice of college and used factor analysis to group students into segments: Advice-Seekers, Joe College, Goodtimers, Warm Friendlies, and Practical-Minded (the largest group at 58%). Quality, academic reputation, faculty, and safety mattered to the last group.

Abzug, Jody, and Rikki Abzug. "The Old College Try: Volunteers in Fundraising Efforts for Small Liberal Arts Colleges." *New Directions for Philanthropic Fundraising* 39 (2003): 105–18. 4.3, 6.7.

The authors surveyed directors of development/alumni relations at top-ranked liberal arts colleges regarding volunteers. Alumni volunteers were used to solicit alumni for annual gifts; 90 percent used student volunteers. The number of class agents positively correlated with the percentage of alumni that donated.

Acebo, Kayla K. "The Ties That Blind: The Perceived Influence of Organizational Culture and Self Efficacy on Leadership Success for Women Fundraisers." PhD, University of Oklahoma, 2008. 6.3.

Using qualitative interviews and a survey of development officers, and drawing on attribution theory, the author examined why a majority female profession is male dominated at top levels. Female respondents reported negative impacts of workplace culture and work/life balance.

Adams, J., B. Keener, and E. A. McGee. "Going Public with Private Fund-Raising: Community Colleges Garner Fair Share of Support." *Community College Journal* 65 (1994): 39–42. 8.2.

A National Resource Development Council study of community college fundraising found that more successful foundations were older, were more likely to have dedicated staff, relied more on corporations than affiliated individuals, and used techniques such as annual campaigns and endowments. Enrollment did not affect success.

Agypt, Brett, Robert K. Christensen, and Rebecca Nesbit. "A Tale of Two Charitable Campaigns: Longitudinal Analysis of Employee Giving at a Public University." *Nonprofit and Voluntary Sector Quarterly* 41 no. 5 (2012): 802–25. 1.2, 6.8.

This study used HLM to measure the effect of individual factors on employee giving in two annual campaigns to community nonprofits (2001–8) at a public university. Salary positively predicted giving but sex and age did not; the effects of tenure and length of service were mixed.

Akin, S. Reneo. "Institutional Advancement and Community Colleges: A Review of the Literature." *International Journal of Educational Advancement* 6 no. 1 (2005): 65–75. 1.0, 8.2.

This literature review focused on effective community college fundraising. Findings were arranged topically to provide an overview of the state of knowledge; details of individual studies were not provided.

Alkhas, Adrenna B. "An Examination of Internet Social Media Marketing in Higher Education Institutions." EdD, California State University, 2011. 3.1.

This mixed-methods dissertation surveyed marketing professionals at the 23 CSU campuses about use of social media. Using agenda-setting theory for analysis, Alkhas found that, despite budget cuts, marketers try to continuously monitor several platforms, coordinate across the university, and have multiple goals.

Allen, David I. "Primary Motives and Giving Behavior of Athletic Donors at a Florida Division I-A University." EdD, United States Sports Academy, 2008. 1.2, 8.4.

This dissertation surveyed donors using Mahony, Gladden, and Funk's Donor Motivation Scale. Donors who gave for nonbenefit reasons (such as loyalty) gave at higher levels than donors who gave primarily for ticket benefits. Men and women had differences in motivation, although both had a mix of benefit and nonbenefit motivations.

Alsmeyer, Ann Marie. "An Analysis of Institutional Commitment among Older Alumni of Texas A&M University." PhD, Texas A&M University, 1994. 4.3.

Using interviews, this dissertation explored the motivation for giving in alumni who graduated from Texas A&M over 50 years previously. In addition to having the means to give, these alumni were influenced by individuals at the university, the college's military code, and the Great Depression and World War II.

Anctil, Eric. "Institutional Advancement and Spectator Sports: The Importance of Television." *New Directions for Higher Education* 148 (2009): 35–44. 8.4.

This theoretical paper explored the impact televising sporting events may have on donations and applications. This "advertisement" may increase institutional affiliation through both affective conditioning and mere exposure.

Anderson, Barbara. "Approaching Experience-Sharing Consultancies in Advancement, with Special Reference to Higher Education in Central and Eastern Europe: A Personal Perspective." *CASE International Journal of Educational Advancement* 3 no. 3 (2003). 1.1, 5.6.

The author explored the possibility of importing advancement techniques to universities in Bosnia and Herzegovina, particularly those of UK institutions.

Anderson, E., and A. A. Moss, Jr. *Dangerous Donations: Northern Philanthropy and Southern Black Education, 1902–1930*. Columbia: University of Missouri Press, 1999. 1.6, 7.1.

Drawing on the Rockefeller Archives, Southern Education Board correspondence, and UNC-Chapel Hill libraries, this history examined the Ogden Movement, where Northern white philanthropies funded Southern black colleges. It discussed the influences of philanthropists as well as the limits of that influence.

Anderson, Michael L. "The Benefits of College Athletic Success: An Application of the Propensity Score Design with Instrumental Variables." National Bureau of Economic Research Working Paper Series No. 18196, 2012. 1.3, 8.4.

This paper tested the effect of winning football games on donations in Division I institutions using a propensity score design to account for the probability of winning games. Winning had several effects including increasing donations to athletic programs, and was most prominent at Bowl Conference Series institutions.

Anderson, Spencer. "Fundraising Programs in Community Colleges: Factors That Contribute to Effectiveness." EdD, Texas A&M University—Commerce, 2003. 1.3, 8.2.

Using Delphi technique with fundraisers at large community colleges, the author found that 44 characteristics influence fundraising success; of these, marketing ranked third in importance.

Andrade, Sally J., Yolanda Rodriguez Ingle, and R. Leticia Diaz-Rios. "'First-Generation Alumni'—Improving Survey Research at a Commuter University." *CASE International Journal of Educational Advancement* 2, no. 3 (2002): 242–57. 4.1.

Based on the experience of the University of Texas at El Paso, methods of effective alumni survey research were discussed. This is particularly crucial at commuter institutions, as off-campus alumni have often not been regarded as being as engaged as those who lived on campus.

Andris, Mary Kate. "Motivation Through Circles: An Analysis of Women's Giving Circles on Philanthropy in Higher Education." Widener University, 2011. 1.2.

This case study of women's giving circles at two universities found that participation resulted in members giving larger amounts and volunteering more hours. Women were more likely to join when extended a personal invitation.

Anumatratchakit, Phongphat. "Perceptions of the University Presidents and Public Relations Officers of University Public Relations Officer in Private University in Thailand." EdD, University of Pittsburgh, 2002. 5.3, 6.1, 6.4.

University presidents and public relations officers at private Thai universities were surveyed regarding the responsibilities, skills, and activities of PR officers. The two groups ranked the importance of their activities differently, but not the necessary skills: presidents considered alumni relations to be more important than PR officers did.

Apsey, Gary Ronald. "Marketing Strategies by Higher Education for Corporation Fund-Raising." PhD, Michigan State University, 1993. 1.3.

Corporate fundraising officers at public and private Michigan institutions were surveyed as to the role of marketing in corporate fundraising. Companies were more likely to give to private institutions, those with programs that benefitted them, and those with a good reputation. Enrollment and program diversity also mattered.

Arnett, Dennis B., Steve D. German, and Shelby D. Hunt. "The Identity Salience of Relationship Marketing Success: The Case of Nonprofit Marketing." *Journal of Marketing* 67 no. 2 (2003): 89–105. 3.3.

The authors compared their identity salience model of marketing success against the satisfaction model using donor data and surveys from a large university. Using structural equation modeling, they found evidence for both models, but that identity salience was predictive of giving whereas satisfaction was not.

Arnold, Gertrude Lee. "Friend Raisers and Fund Raisers: Alumni Relations and Development in Large, Public Universities." PhD, University of Michigan, 2003. 4.3.

The author examined the structure of alumni relations and development at Research I universities, developed a classification scheme for their relationship, and conducted a case study on each of the five most common arrangements. As institutional and resource dependency predicted, the units cooperated to generate resources.

Arriola, Rolando S. "The Utilization of a Market-Driven Strategy for Fund Raising at a Hispanic Serving University." EdD, University of Pennsylvania, 2005. 1.12, 8.6.

This survey of community college presidents found that their involvement in fundraising varied widely. While 90 percent had no previous fundraising experience, they now spent 10–20 hours per week on it. Personal and institutional characteristics influenced time spent.

Ashcraft, Robert Frank. "An Analysis of Alumni Donation and Nondonation Related to Selected Personal, Involvement and Outcome Factors." PhD, Arizona State University, 1995. 4.3.

Donors and nondonors of ASU were compared using Pace's model of student development. Data was collected via survey and factor analysis conducted. Factors influencing giving included decade and school of graduation, gender, household income, cocurricular engagement, faculty attachment and peer relationships, analytical skills, attitudes and values, and job skills.

Avery, Vida L. *Philanthropy in Black Higher Education: A Fateful Hour Creating the Atlanta University System*. New York: Palgrave Macmillan, 2013. 1.15, 7.2.

This history of the affiliation between Morehouse and Spelman Colleges and Atlanta University foregrounded the role of John Hope, president of Morehouse and Atlanta, placing it within the context of philanthropic pressures on the area institutions.

Azzaro, James Anthony. "Understanding a High-Performance University Development Organization: Leadership and Best Practices." EdD, Ohio State University, 2005. 1.1, 6.3.

OSU development officers were surveyed and profiled based on Quinn's Competing Values Framework. The most important best practices were dedication to major gift cultivation, teamwork and collaboration, and commitment to the alignment of development objectives with academic priorities.

Baade, A., and J. O. Sundberg. "What Determines Alumni Generosity." *Economics of Education Review* 15 no. 1 (1996): 75–81. 4.3.

This paper used 2SLS econometric analysis to analyze alumni giving, controlling for institutional characteristics, at over 125 doctoral-granting and liberal arts colleges. Several factors were found to increase alumni gifts: higher tuition prices, higher student wealth, higher levels of selectivity, older age, private status, and higher levels of soliciting donations.

Baade, R. A., and J. S. Sundberg. "Fourth Down and Gold to Go? Assessing the Link between Athletics and Alumni Giving." *Social Science Quarterly* 77 no. 4 (1996): 789–803. 4.3, 8.4.

This paper estimated the effect of participating in football bowl games and men's basketball tournaments on alumni giving at doctoral universities and winning percentages in those sports at liberal arts colleges using time-series data. Bowl games positively correlated with giving, and tournament participation correlated with giving at public universities. Winning percentages correlated with higher levels of giving at liberal arts colleges.

Babitz, Brenda. "Strategies for Leveraging a Community College Foundation." *New Directions for Community Colleges* 2003 no. 124 (2003): 5–14. doi: 10.1002/cc.128. 8.2.

Babitz suggested that community colleges can gain support from corporations and foundations by emphasizing that their students are tomorrow's workforce. She discussed who should be involved and campaign types.

Baker, Jill C. "Impact of the Student Experience on Alumni Involvement." EdD, University of Central Florida, 2004. 4.5.

Using survey data from UCF, this thesis examined the impact of student involvement/satisfaction on alumni involvement, which was found to be positively correlated. Also correlated were alumni involvement and perception of university support thereof, and student involvement and satisfaction.

Baker, Mary Kacmarcik. "A Student Advancement Program Model for a Multicultural Nontraditional Institution of Higher Education." EdD, Pepperdine University, 1996. 4.3.

This thesis used the Delphi technique among experts on diverse, commuting, and metropolitan institutions to develop consensus on what student life programs would foster alumni donations. Of six areas of programming, the most important was career related. In addition, students should be exposed to alumni relations early in their college careers.

Baker, Paul C. "The Relationship of Selected Characteristics and Attitudes of Professional School Alumni to Financial Support within a Public Research University." PhD, State University of New York at Buffalo, 1998. 4.3, 8.3.

Graduate alumni of the schools of education, management, law, and medicine at were surveyed with questions based on Pace's student development theory, and donors and nondonors were compared. Emotional attachment was the strongest differentiator between the two groups; they also varied in participation, satisfaction, gender, and age.

Baldwin, Karen Meshad. "How Reciprocity Influences Alumni Giving: A Qualitative Study." EdD, University of Alabama, 2008. 1.5, 8.1.

Using interviews from alumni of a public flagship university, this thesis examined the role of reciprocity in motivating alumni donors. Positive support experiences as an undergraduate motivated giving among alumni.

Baldwin, Robin Lynn Brunty. "Dynamics of a Successful Planned Giving Program Utilizing Shared Leadership at Historically Black Colleges and Universities (HBCUs)." DEL, University of Charleston, 2013. 1.5, 8.1.

A survey of development officers examined planned giving programs at HBCUs, finding that 44 percent had them. Regression analyses conducted on the ten responses with programs found that development officers did not believe leadership practices influenced program success.

Ballinger, Marcia J. "Fundraising Behaviors and Presidential Background Characteristics of Community College Presidents." PhD, Walden University, 2012. 1.1, 6.1.

A survey of community college presidents was conducted to study relationships between presidential characteristics and fundraising behavior. The only relevant characteristics were last job before first presidency and last position before current presidency. A regression model accounted for 21 percent of variance in behavior.

Baluss, Kay Smith. "The Spirit of Innovation and the Soul of Tradition: Institutional Advancement and Organizational Culture at an Oxford

University College." EdD, Peabody College for Teachers of Vanderbilt University, 1995. 1.6, 5.2.

This case study examined the role of organizational culture and institutional advancement at a college of Cambridge University. Using and updating the advancement umbrella model, the author found six areas of potential cultural dissonance and reaffirmed that while image attracts outsiders, culture is the organizational glue that holds organizations together.

Barascout, Roger. "Gifts on a High Note: A Case Study of Major Donors to Music Programs in Higher Education." Temple University, 2012. 1.2, 8.7.

This case study of two university schools of music examined the decision-making patterns of major donors. Donors were motivated by a passion for music, rather than by receipt of benefits or by alumni status; they were not necessarily donors to the university as a whole.

Barnes, Amy Catherine. "What Predicts Alumni Satisfaction? The Impact of Investment, Involvement, and Post-College Outcomes." EdD, College of William and Mary, 2007. 4.5.

Using Astin's I-E-O model, this thesis examined alumni satisfaction by surveying three classes of alumni from a public university. Satisfaction with career and salary positively influenced alumni satisfaction; other variables were not significant.

Barrett, Susan E. "Corporate and Foundation Relations Officers' Perspectives on Job Performance Measures." EdD, Widener University, 2010. 6.3.

Based on interviews with corporate and foundation officers at private colleges/universities, this thesis examined how their goals were set and work was assessed. Goals were set by senior leadership. While assessment and satisfaction varied, officers saw their work as inherently linked to economic necessity.

Barrett, T. Gregory. "Institutional Culture, Life-Cycle Issues and Other Factors: Issues That Selected Alumnae Who Are Actively Involved in Spelman College Self-Report as Being Influential in Their Giving Decisions." *CASE International Journal of Educational Advancement* 2 no. 3 (2002): 259–78. 4.3, 4.5, 8.1.

Based on interviews with six Spelman alumnae, factors influencing alumnae donation were explored. Donors were motivated by a desire to help the next generation, a sense of rebuilding/repaying, and loyalty to Spelman. Life cycle also influenced donation decisions through affecting financial capacity.

Barrett, T. Gregory. "Stewardship as an Organizational Response: Understanding the Interaction of Institutional and Task Environments and Organizational

Contexts on Fund Raising in Professional Schools at the University of Michigan." PhD, University of Michigan, 2002. 1.7.

This thesis examined the effect of the environment on stewardship process at five professional schools within the University of Michigan using comparative case studies. External factors influencing stewardship included resource dependency, uncertainty, interconnectedness, legitimacy, efficiency, legal coercion, and norms; organizational factors also played a role.

Barrett, T. Gregory. "Stewardship as an Organizational Response: Understanding the Interaction of Institutional and Task Environments and Organizational Contexts on Fund Raising in Professional Schools and Colleges at the University of Michigan." *International Journal of Educational Advancement* 4 no. 3 (2004). 1.7.

This paper is based on Barrett's dissertation, above.

Bartlett, Robert Polk. "Institutional Determinants of Market Structure in Corporate Funding of United States Four-Year Colleges and Universities." PhD, Cornell University, 1992. 1.12.

This thesis examined the influence of institutional research, disciplinary focus, and production of outputs on corporate fundraising among doctoral and comprehensive universities and liberal arts colleges. Factors that increased support were scientific/management specialties, especially applied, and graduate/research productivity (with undergraduate studies influential among colleges). Private control, alumni executives, and doctoral status were also significant.

Bass, David. "From the Foundations Up: Contexts for Change in Community College Advancement." *New Directions for Community Colleges* 2003 no. 124 (2003): 15–26. doi: 10.1002/cc.129. 1.16, 8.2.

Community colleges have much smaller advancement staffs than public four-year institutions and may not be able to emulate their practices. However, there is no one universal model for them to adopt. Strategic planning and a separate foundation can help them find their own strengths.

Bass, David. "The Foundation-Institution Partnership: The Role of Institutionally Related Foundations in Public Higher Education." *New Directions for Higher Education* 149 (2010): 17–25. 1.1.

Most public institutions conduct fundraising through an affiliated 501(c)3 foundation and rely less on institutional presidents and trustees. Foundation board members can be recruited for specific skillsets as well as donations. Some degree of autonomy is necessary, but roles should be clarified through a memorandum of understanding.

Bass, Jordan R. "The Politics of Fundraising: An Organizational Ethnography of Intercollegiate Boosters." PhD, Florida State University, 2013. 1.1, 8.4.

This ethnography studied the booster organization of an athletics department at a university using the circuit model of culture. The department had an unusual model, more separate than at similar institutions, which created some tensions with athletics, although it worked well with the main fundraising department.

Baughman, James C., and Robert N. Goldman. "College Rankings and Faculty Publications: Are They Related?" *Change* 31 no. 2 (1999): 44–51. 3.4.

This article examined the connection between faculty publication productivity and selectivity rankings in *Barron's Profiles*, based on admissions rates. The authors found a strong correlation between the two, independent of institutional type.

Beard, Rebecca G. "The Money Tree-Alternative Revenues for Community Colleges." PhD, University of Nebraska—Lincoln, 2008. 1.16, 8.2.

Community colleges were surveyed to discover what revenue sources they were using beyond tax revenues and tuition. Ordered from most to least common, they used public grants/contracts, individual donors, investments, foundations, private grants/contracts, corporate charities, and alumni. Different sources gave to different causes: grants/contracts to current expenditures, and individuals to scholarships.

Bee, Richard Earl. "The Preparation of the Christian College President and Fund Raising Effectiveness." PhD, Talbot School of Theology, Biola University, 2001. 6.1, 8.8.

Using Council of Christian Colleges data, this thesis examined the effect of presidential training and experience on donated income as a percentage of total budget. Training/experience did not have an effect, but amount of time spent did. Presidents with less experience were more likely to use paid consultants.

Beeson, Melisa Jane Ellis. "Women's Giving Circles: A Case Study in Higher Education Philanthropy." EdD, Indiana University, 2006. 1.2.

This case study of a women's giving circle at public university used Shaw and Taylor's women's philanthropy framework. Support was found for create, change, collaborate, and connect, but not for commit and celebrate.

Beilke, Jayne R. "Building the Institutional Competence of Black Universities: The Role of Philanthropic Fellowship Programs, 1928–60." *International Journal of Educational Advancement* 4 no. 3 (2004). 1.15, 7.2, 8.1.

This article examined General Education Board and Julius Rosenwald Funds fellowship programs, which paid black leadership for advanced study.

85 percent of GEB fellows returned to the South as educational administrators, while Rosenwald fellows followed more diverse paths. These leaders were able to strengthen their institutions financially and academically.

Bekkers, Rene, and Pamala Wiepking. "A Literature Review of Empirical Studies of Philanthropy: Eight Mechanisms That Drive Charitable Giving." *Nonprofit and Voluntary Sector Quarterly* 40 no. 5 (2011): 924–73. 1.0.

This review of over 500 articles focused on why donors give. While not focused on higher education, it was included. The authors identified eight mechanisms that drive giving: awareness of need, solicitation, costs and benefits, altruism, reputation, psychological benefits, values, and efficiency.

Belanger, Judy M. "Motives and Characteristics of Gift-Giving at the University of Nevada, Las Vegas." EdD, University of Nevada, Las Vegas, 1999. 4.3.

The author built a model to predict whether UNLV alumni were nondonors, small donors, or large donors. Differences were few between the groups, although the model for large donors was moderately predictive, based on college of study, years between graduation and first gift, desire for tax benefits, amount given, giving to other educational institutions, and marital status.

Belfield, C. R., and A. P. Beney. "What Determines Alumni Generosity? Evidence for the UK." *Education Economics* 8 no. 1 (2000): 65–81. 4.3, 5.2.

The study examined the determinants of alumni giving at two UK universities in response to telephone solicitations. Female, single, and older alumni were more likely to give. Male, single, older alumni with higher incomes and honors degrees gave larger gifts. College campaigns were more successful than university campaigns.

Benson, Lee, Ira Harkavy, and John Puckett. "An Implementation Revolution as a Strategy for Fulfilling the Democratic Promise of University–Community Partnerships: Penn–West Philadelphia as an Experiment in Progress." *Nonprofit and Voluntary Sector Quarterly* 29 no. 1 (2000): 24–45. 2.5.

This article examined a university/community partnership that encouraged academic/practitioner collaboration, service learning and research, and action research. The authors argue the partnership was mutually beneficial.

Bent, Lauren G. "Young Alumni Giving: An Exploration of Institutional Strategies." EdD, Johnson & Wales University, 2012. 4.3

Using McMillan and Chavis' sense of community theory, this dissertation explored the strategies institutions use to increase young alumni giving. Data from interviews and other sources were analyzed into five findings: foster community, treat young alumni as partners, educate about philanthropy, solicit feedback, and use emotional connections.

Berger, Paul D., and Gerald E. Smith. "The Effect of Direct Mail Framing Strategies and Segmentation Variables on University Fundraising Performance." *Journal of Direct Marketing* 11 no. 1 (1997): 30–43. 1.3.

In empirical tests of direct mail framing strategies, the authors studied the size of suggested donation, negative/positive framing, and inclusion of reference information; recency, frequency, and monetary variables; and demographics on response rate and gift size. Among other findings, a lower suggested donation sizes led to a higher response rate.

Bernstein, Alison R. *Funding the Future: Philanthropy's Influence on American Higher Education*. Lanham, MD: R&L Education, 2013. 1.12, 7.1.

This book examined the role that twentieth-century foundations played in higher education and the roles they play today. These effects included worldwide stature, scholarly creativity, access for women and minorities, and increased corporatization.

Berry, John M. "Characteristics of Effective Philanthropic Fundraising at Historically Black Colleges and Universities: An Analysis of Endowment Development." PhD, Union Institute and University, 2008. 1.3, 8.1.

A survey of fundraising at HBCUs measured trustee participation, technology, staff size, capital campaign completion, and the use of trained volunteers. The last three variables were correlated with endowment size.

Besikof, Rudolph Joseph. "The Role of the Community College President in Fundraising: A Best Practices Study." EdD, University of California Los Angeles, 2010. 6.1, 8.2.

Case studies of three community colleges examined the role of their presidents in fundraising. Each devoted one-fifth of their time to it, although time devoted to asking for gifts varied. All attended foundation board meetings and fundraising events.

Billings, Meredith S. "Examining Young Alumni Giving Behavior: Every Dollar Matters." In *Expanding the Donor Base in Higher Education: Engaging Non-Traditional Donors*, edited by Noah D. Drezner, 102–20. New York: Routledge, 2013. 4.3.

Survey data from young alumni (graduated in the past 10 years) at one university was collected and a donor prediction model built. The model correctly predicted donor status with 72 percent accuracy, explaining

27 percent of variance. Nine significant predictors related to demographics, undergraduate experience, and alumni engagement.

Binkley, Paul Michael. "Relationship of Graduate Student Involvement to Graduate Alumni Donor Behavior." EdD, George Washington University, 2012. 4.3, 8.3.

Using national data from the Performance Enhancement Group and Astin's I-E-O model, this thesis examined the effect of demographic and involvement factors on graduate alumni donor status. Involvement in ethnic/cultural centers negatively impacted donations; relations with peers and faculty had no effect; professional/career related activities had a positive effect.

Black, Thomas L. "An Organizational History of the University of Mississippi Foundation: 1973–2005." PhD, University of Mississippi, 2008. 7.2.

This thesis followed the first 32 years of the Ole Miss foundation, examining changes in structure, leadership, and responsibilities of the foundation. It divided the history into three periods: the early years (1973–1983), the middle years beginning with Chancellor Gerald Turner (1984–1994), and a period of growth (1995–2005).

Blanton, Jay. "Engagement as a Brand Position in the Higher Education Marketplace." *International Journal of Educational Advancement* 7 no. 2 (2007): 143–54. 3.3.

This case study of the University of Kentucky's brand engagement efforts found that public engagement and branding were related and interdependent.

Bloland, Harland G. "No Longer Emerging, Fund Raising Is a Profession." *CASE International Journal of Educational Advancement* 3 no. 1 (2002): 7–19. 1.4.

Bloland argued that fundraising has become a full-fledged profession because it requires expertise, provides a high income, is important to organizations, and they act like managerial professionals, although fundraising still needs a stronger theoretical base.

Bloomfield, Victor A., and Michelle Wittcoff Kuhl. "Institutional Advancement and Public Engagement in the STEM and Health Science Disciplines." *International Journal of Educational Advancement* 7 no. 2 (2007): 131–42. 1.1, 8.7.

Using the University of Minnesota as a case study, this paper suggested a framework for advancement/STEM department collaboration to secure funding for community-based projects.

Boal, John R. "Influencing Factors of Alumni Giving in Religious Institutions of Higher Education." DSci, Robert Morris University, 2011. 1.6, 4.3, 8.8.

This thesis examined factors influencing alumni giving at Grace College and Seminary (Indiana), based on focus groups with alumni. Four recommendations emerged: Reinforce ties that alumni built with faculty as undergraduates, assure institutional commitment to the mission statement, emphasize the continuity of campus rituals, and communicate effectively with alumni.

Bogue, E. Grady. "Improvement versus Stewardship: Reconciling Collegiate and Civic Accountability Cultures." *CASE International Journal of Educational Advancement* 1 no. 3 (2001): 209–19. 1.7, 2.5.

The rise of accountability culture has introduced two competing cultures. One favors peer review, process, and improvement, while the other favors stewardship, evidence, and regulation. The author argued that these two cultures are not as irreconcilable as they may seem.

Bohna, Susan Elaine. "A Comparative Study of Alma Mater Support between First-Generation Alumni and Other Alumni." EdD, West Virginia University, 1997. 4.3.

Based on a survey of the WVU class of 1975, the support of first-generation alumni was compared to other alumni. Third-generation alumni gave most often. Regardless of professional characteristics, first-generation alumni did not give more.

Bongila, Jean-Pierre Kulemfuka. "Funding Strategies for Institutional Advancement of American Private Universities: Applications for Congolese/African Universities." EdD, University of San Francisco, 2001. 1.3, 5.5.

This thesis compared advancement programs at seven US universities and two Congolese universities, using Grunig's Four Models of Public Relations. Data came from surveys and interviews. The universities in the Congo had little experience with fundraising, and the author recommends adopting some American advancement strategies.

Borum, Regina Ann. "A Comparative Profile of African-American and Caucasian Institutional Advancement Professionals in Selected Influential Colleges and Universities in the United States." PhD, the Union Institute, 1991. 6.5.

A survey of white and African American advancement officers was designed to explore why the field has so few African Americans, based on questions about education, professional experience, personal activities, and personal data. T-tests and chi-squared tests revealed few differences, and African American officers were professionally satisfied and productive.

Boswell, Colin. "Fund Raising for a Belgian University." *CASE International Journal of Educational Advancement* 3 no. 3 (2003): 228–39. 1.6, 5.6, 8.8.

This case study of the Université Catholique de Louvain's first capital campaign described how it adopted fundraising methods from the United States. At publication time, it looked like the campaign would not meet its goal, but the institution did not regard this as a failure.

Bourgeois, Sheryl A. "The Relationship between Alumni Presence on the Governing Board and Institutional Support." PhD, Claremont Graduate University, 2012. 4.3, 6.2.

In this study of private comprehensive masters universities, the effect of the percentage of the board composed of alumni was tested on five financial variables, followed by five case studies. Alumni percentage positively affected alumni giving, unrestricted giving, and the percentage of support from alumni.

Bouse, Gary A. "Factors Related to Levels of Presidential Satisfaction with Fund Raising at Selected Colleges and Universities." EdD, Indiana University, 2001. 1.8, 6.1.

Presidents at research/doctoral universities were surveyed regarding their satisfaction with institutional fundraising. Presidents were moderately satisfied, and their satisfaction was related to their perception of fundraising staff and productivity.

Boverini, Luisa C. "When Venture Philanthropy Rocks the Ivory Tower." *International Journal of Educational Advancement* 6 no. 2 (2006): 84–106. 1.15, 4.3.

This article, based on the author's dissertation below, explored the rise of venture philanthropy in higher education and presents a case study of venture philanthropy at the University of Maryland. Venture philanthropists are highly involved with the institutions they give to, and the author makes several recommendations to institutions that work with them.

Boverini, Luisa C. "When Venture Philanthropy Rocks the Ivory Tower: An Examination of High Impact Donors and Their Potential for Higher Education Development." EdD, University of Pennsylvania, 2005. 1.15, 4.3.

See description of the article version of this dissertation above.

Bowen, Mya T. "An Examination of Institutional Advancement Vice Presidents' Reports at Four-Year Public and Private Historically Black Colleges and Universities Regarding Their Use of the Five Minds to Promote Stewardship." EdD, University of Hartford, 2013. 1.7, 6.3, 8.1.

This case study examined the use of reporting by advancement vice presidents at private HBCUs. Utilizing Gardner's five minds model, the author interviewed five vice presidents and found that they used their relational, leadership, and analytic capacities for stewardship.

Bowman III, Nelson. "Fundraising During an Economic Downturn within the Historically Black College and University Environment." *International Journal of Educational Advancement* 9 no. 4 (2010a): 266–72. 1.3, 8.1.

This article discussed strategies for HBCU fundraising during an economic downturn, drawing on literature as well as experiences at Prairie View A&M. Suggested strategies include using outcome-based appeals, developing alumni ambassadors, involving faculty, and communicating proactively.

Bowman III, Nelson. "Cultivating Future Fundraisers of Color at Historically Black Colleges and Universities." *International Journal of Educational Advancement* 10 no. 3 (2010b): 230–34. 6.5, 8.1.

Bowman offered suggestions on how to increase the number of minorities in fundraising from the then-current 11 percent. He suggested HBCUs cultivate their own fundraisers, including through education offerings, rather than hiring existing fundraisers.

Bowman, Nicholas A., and Michael N. Bastedo. "Getting on the Front Page: Organizational Reputation, Status Signals, and the Impact of 'U.S. News and World Report' on Student Decisions." *Research in Higher Education* 50 no. 5 (2009): 415–36. 3.4.

This study explored the effect of *U.S. News* rankings by examining the effects of moving from the second page to the first and the effects of moving within the top tier. Moving pages positively affected all admission measures in the next year. Moving within a tier affected universities; liberal arts colleges were more affected by prices.

Bowman, Nicholas A., and Michael N. Bastedo. "Anchoring Effects in World University Rankings: Exploring Biases in Reputation Scores." *Higher Education* 61 (2011): 431–44. 3.4.

The authors explored the effects of initial rankings on subsequent years' ranking in *Times Higher Education Supplement* rankings. Initial-year rankings influenced the peer assessment component of third-year rankings, but second-year rankings did not.

Boyce, M. Starita. "Fund-Raising and Marketing Effectiveness at Historically Black Colleges and Universities." EdD, State University of New York at Albany, 1992. 1.3, 8.1.

This study explored the effect of institutional characteristics on total funds raised, number of corporations solicited, total alumni contributions, and gift income from trustees at HBCUs. It concludes that institutional characteristics are responsible for much of the variability in outcomes.

Boyd, John Charles. "Presidential Fundraising in South Carolina's Two-Year Technical Colleges." PhD, Clemson University, 2008. 6.1, 8.2.

Based on IRS Form 990 information, survey data, and interviews, this thesis analyzed the effect of presidential characteristics on fundraising outcomes. Strategies influencing better outcomes included a higher level of presidential commitment to fundraising and a working foundation board with influential, affluent members.

Bradburd, Ralph M., and Duncan P. Mann. "Wealth in Higher Education Institutions." *Journal of Higher Education* 64 no. 4 (1993): 472–93. 1.14.

The authors proposed a new method of measuring institutional wealth that includes endowments as well as regular income flows, arguing this allows for more accurate comparisons between institutions. They compared the several components of this measure, finding that endowments were the most variable; gift income was less variable but more so than appropriations.

Brazzell, Johnnetta Cross. "Brick without Straw: Missionary-Sponsored Black Higher Education in the Post-Emancipation Era." *Journal of Higher Education* 63 no. 1 (1992): 26–49. 7.1, 8.2.

This article focused on Spelman as an example of Southern black higher education sponsored by Northern missionary societies. While paternalistic, racist, and evangelizing, these societies viewed education as a liberating force that would enable blacks to enter mainstream American life.

Breazeale, Sandra Elizabeth Clardy. "A Meeting of Minds: The ALUMNI-L Listserv®." PhD, University of South Carolina, 1999. 1.4.

This case study asked if administrator participation in the ALUMNI-L listserv during its first eight months produced a professional community with a distinct culture. Based on observation and surveys, the author found that a unique culture without status distinctions developed.

Bressi, Dorothy Elizabeth. "Women and Philanthropy: Making a Difference in Higher Education." PhD, University of Tennessee, 1999. 1.2.

Based on a survey of female donors to a public university, this study explored what factors are important to female donors and what types of recognition they prefer to receive.

Briechle, Peter. "Alumnae Supporting Higher Education." PhD, State University of New York at Buffalo, 2001. 4.3.

This dissertation served as the basis for the following author's paper.

Briechle, Peter. "Does Institutional Type Affect Alumnae Donating Patterns in the United States?" *International Journal of Educational Advancement* 4 no. 1 (2003): 19–28. 4.3.

This paper analyzed the effect of institutional type (public, religiously affiliated, private nonsectarian) on alumnae donations, using survey data gathered from alumnae donors at three institutions. Institutional type mattered in why alumnae gave as well as in the specific areas they directed donations to.

Bristol, Ralph, Jr. "How Much Will Alumni Give in the Future?" *Planning for Higher Education* 20 no. 2 (1991): 1–12. 4.3.

This paper estimated whether alumni giving would increase by 2010, based on the projected number of alumni, VSE alumni giving data, and economic data. He extrapolated an increase in giving of 1 percent per year and applied his model to Amherst College.

Bristow, W. Vance. "The Status of Planned Giving Programs in Community and Junior Colleges in the State of Mississippi." PhD, Mississippi State University, 2013. 1.5, 8.2.

The author surveyed development professionals at the 15 Mississippi community colleges regarding fundraising, obstacles to giving, and planned giving efforts. The colleges were not actively pursuing planned giving, and the colleges rated it a low priority.

Brookes, M. "Higher Education: Marketing in a Quasi-Commercial Service Industry." *International Journal of Nonprofit and Voluntary Sector Marketing* 8 no. 2 (2003): 132–34. 3.3, 5.2.

The author compared marketing in US and UK higher education and argued for new marketing approaches for UK institutions, based on interviews and press releases.

Broussard, Sharee LeBlanc. "Source-Message-Receiver in Integrated Marketing Communication: A Study of U.S. Institutional Advancement." PhD, University of Southern Mississippi, 2009. 3.2.

This dissertation was the basis for the paper below.

Broussard, Sharee LeBlanc. "Source-Message-Receiver in Integrated Marketing Communication." *International Journal of Educational Advancement* 10 no. 4 (2011): 139–62. 3.2.

This study explored whether integrated marketing communications was an appropriate model for studying advancement based on a survey of practitioners. Practitioners indicated they understood and used IMC.

The findings suggest advancement can be used to further build IMC theory.

Brown, Brian O'Neil. "An Exploratory Study of Fund Raising by Athletic Directors at Division I-A and Division I-AA Institutions." PhD, University of Missouri—Columbia, 2005. 1.3, 8.4.

This thesis examined the role of athletic directors in fundraising at D1 institutions. ADs identified mentors and personal contact with donors as important. African American ADs relied more heavily on fundraising books, periodicals, and coursework than their peers; they also raised more dollars.

Brown, David Alan. "The Role of the Bible College President as Fund-Raiser." EdD, University of Florida, 1992. 6.1, 8.8.

Presidents and their boards, administrators, and staff at American Association of Bible Colleges were surveyed about the role of the president as fundraiser. While levels of consensus varied in some areas, there was no evidence of role conflict.

Brown, David W. "NCPG, CASE, and the Present Value of Testamentary Commitments: Analysis, Conclusions, and Recommendations." *CASE International Journal of Educational Advancement* 3 no. 2 (2002). 1.5.

The author discussed two different approaches to calculating the present value of planned gifts, as both were under review at the time. He argued that a new standard was needed.

Brown, Jeffrey R., Stephen G. Dimmock, and Scott Weisbenner. "The Supply of and Demand for Charitable Donations to Higher Education." National Bureau of Economic Research Working Paper Series No. 18389, 2012. 1.13.

Using a panel data model and data from IPEDS, NACUBO, VSE, and other sources, the authors found that both supply and demand affect university donations. Supply characteristics include local income levels and housing prices; demand was specified as negative endowment shocks.

Bruggink, T. H., and K. Siddiqui. "An Econometric Model of Alumni Giving: A Case Study for a Liberal Arts College." *American Economist* 39 no. 2 (1995): 53–60. 4.3.

This paper estimated alumni giving at a formerly all-male liberal arts college using cross-sectional, time-series data. Larger donations were correlated with higher income, being female, fraternity/sorority membership, residing closer to the college, age, being single, majoring in engineering, and involvement in alumni activities. The 1987 stock market crash, which was hypothesized to negatively influence giving, did not.

Brumbach, Mary A., and Alice W. Villadsen. "At the Edge of Chaos: The Essentials of Resource Development for the Community's College." *Community College Journal of Research & Practice* 26 no. 1 (2002): 77–86. 1.6, 8.2.

Based on the model of Brookhaven College, the authors suggested that giving fundraising offices freedom with fewer operational responsibilities resulted in significant returns.

Brune, Michelle Lyn. "A Qualitative Study of a Native American Mascot at 'Public University.'" PhD, University of Missouri—St. Louis, 2010. 2.5.

This semiotic study examined meanings associated with a Native American athletic mascot, which had recently been changed. While not focused on advancement, this thesis discussed alumni and community perception.

Brunen, Meredith Noel. "Raising the Bar: The Modern Community College Presidency." EdD, University of Arkansas, 2012. 6.1, 8.2.

This case study focused on three presidents with fundraising backgrounds to explore how their background helped them engage with external constituents. Presidents reported that their previous experience was highly transferrable to the presidency.

Bruning, Stephen D. "Relationship Building as a Retention Strategy: Linking Relationship Attitudes and Satisfaction Evaluations to Behavioral Outcomes." *Public Relations Review* 28 no. 1 (2002): 39–48. 2.

This survey of students in an introductory communications course at a private university found that student-university relationship attitudes and satisfaction varied between students who returned for the fall semester and those who did not; those students who did not return were less satisfied.

Buchanan, Pauline W. "Variables Influencing Corporate Giving to Higher Education in Michigan." PhD, University of Michigan, 1991. 1.12.

This thesis surveyed directors of development at Michigan four-year institutions and corporate contribution managers in Michigan regarding factors influencing corporate giving. Development officers ranked personal contacts, corporate citizenship, and their offices' skills as important; corporate officers rated employment and recruitment of graduates, alumni as executives, employees taking courses, and stewardship as important.

Buchanan, Suzanne S. "The Difference in Alumni Support between Traditional and Nontraditional Students." PhD, University of North Carolina at Greensboro, 1998. 4.3.

A survey of alumni at a public university was combined with institutional data to compare traditional and nontraditional alumni on involvement, donations, and attitude. Nontraditional alumni were less involved and less enthusiastic but gave comparable gifts and had a higher participation rate than traditional alumni.

Buchanan, Walter W. "A Study of Predictor Variables for Alumni Giving in a School of Engineering and Technology Using a Phonathon as a Vehicle for Analysis." PhD, Indiana University, 1993. 4.3, 8.7.

A survey of class of 1991 alumni from the school of engineering at Purdue University (Indianapolis) to determine differences between participants and nonparticipants in a telethon. Three factors were predictive: attendance at alumni events, prior donations, and prior spousal donations. The two prior donation variables explained 73 percent of total variance.

Buckla, Robert J. "Organizational Culture and Alumni Annual Giving at Private Colleges and Universities." EdD, Peabody College for Teachers of Vanderbilt University, 2004. 4.3.

Private regional colleges and universities were examined to see if organizational culture impacted the percentage of alumni that donated, but the hypothesis was rejected. Four factors were found to influence culture: misalignment of leadership style and organizational characteristics, cultural bonding elements, local philanthropists, and advancement staff.

Bulotaite, Nijole. "University Heritage—An Institutional Tool for Branding and Marketing." *Higher Education in Europe* 28 no. 4 (2003): 449–54. 3.3, 5.6.

The University of Vilnius was used as a case study of an institution using symbolism and traditionalism for branding purposes. By far the oldest university in Lithuania, Vilnius has revived its heritage for promotion and branding, despite a move away from these traditions in the mid-twentieth century.

Burchette, Brett Michael. "Examining Factors That Influence Donor Motivation among Former Student-Athletes and NCAA DI Classification." EdD, Drexel University, 2013. 4.3, 8.4.

Former student-athletes at three institutions were surveyed regarding philanthropic motivations. Female alumni were on average younger, had less income, and gave less. Receipt of benefits was a not motivation for giving except for alumnae at one university; scholarship recipients were more likely to donate and saw giving back as important.

Burgess-Getts, Linda Faye. "Alumni as Givers: An Analysis of Donor-Nondonor Behavior at a Comprehensive I Institution." EdD, the College of William and Mary, 1992. 4.3.

Alumni were surveyed to determine what factors led alumni to be donors or nondonors. Important factors included income, graduation year, attendance of relatives, planned visits, identification with the institution, and designating gifts to the library.

Burkhardt, John C. "Transformational Giving and Its Relationship to the Emerging Roles of Public Colleges and Universities." *International Journal of Educational Advancement* 7 no. 2 (2007): 155–64. 1.15.

This paper explores the role of transformational giving and also serves as an introduction to a special issue of the journal. The author argues that today's donors are less interested in building institutions and more interested in transforming society, but we need to clarify our understanding of transformational change.

Butcher, Kristin F., Caitlin Kearns, and Patrick J. McEwan. "Giving Till It Helps? Alumnae Giving and Children's College Options." *Research in Higher Education* 54 (2013): 499–513. 4.3.

Using data from a women's college, this paper explores whether alumni are motivated by a desire to increase their children's chances of admission. Alumnae with teenaged daughters gave more than those with teenaged sons or those with children over 18. The same effect was not found for donations under $5,000.

Caboni, Timothy C. "The Normative Structure of College and University Fund Raising." PhD, Vanderbilt University, 2001. 1.4.

Based on a survey of fundraisers, this thesis examined what behaviors they consider inappropriate. Three inviolable norms emerged in factor analysis: misappropriation of gifts, institutional disregard, and exploitation of institutional resources. Six admonitory norms included donor manipulation, exaggeration of experience, dishonest solicitation, institutional mission abandonment, commission-based compensation, and unreasonable pledge enforcement.

Caboni, Timothy C. "Toward Professionalization: Fund Raising Norms and Their Implications for Practice." *International Journal of Educational Advancement* 4 no. 1 (2003): 77–91. 1.4.

This article was based on the previous dissertation, and discussed whether fundraising is truly a profession as described in the sociological literature.

Caboni, Timothy C. "The Normative Structure of College and University Fundraising Behaviors." *Journal of Higher Education* 81 no. 3 (2010): 339–65. 1.4.

This article was based on the aforementioned dissertation and contained a detailed description of methods and the behaviors prohibited by each norm.

Caboni, Timothy C. "College and University Codes of Conduct for Fund-Raising Professionals." *New Directions for Higher Education* 160 (2012): 41–48. 1.4.

Based on his previous research (see "The Normative Structure") as well as gaps in existing professional codes, the author made recommendations for institutional-based codes of conduct for fundraisers.

Caboni, Timothy C., and James S. Eiseman. "Organizational Identification and the Voluntary Support of Higher Education." *International Journal of Educational Advancement* 5 no. 3 (2005): 221–30. 4.3.

Based on a survey of alumni at a liberal arts college, a model was used to predict giving. Perceived organizational prestige and years since graduation influenced giving; involvement was found to have a negative effect. Organizational identification and educational effectiveness were not significant. Organizational identification, perceived organizational prestige, involvement, and years since graduation influenced willingness for one's child to attend the institution.

Cabrales, Jose E. "Conceptualizing Latina/o Philanthropy in Higher Education: A Study of Latina/o Undergraduate Alumni from a Predominantly White Jesuit Institution." PhD, Iowa State University, 2011. 4.3.

This thesis used Yosso's Community Cultural Wealth Model to explore how Latina/o alumni interact with their alma mater. Nine alumni of Mexican descent from Santa Clara University were interviewed. Madrina/padrino capital was particularly important. Alumni saw their alumni involvement as giving back to their community.

Cabrales, Jose E. "An Approach to Engaging Latina/o Alumni in Giving Initiatives: Madrinas y Padrinos." In *Expanding the Donor Base in Higher Education: Engaging Non-Traditional Donors*, edited by Noah D. Drezner, 26–39. New York: Routledge, 2013. 4.3.

This chapter is based on the author's dissertation, "Conceptualizing Latina/o Philanthropy in Higher Education."

Cahill, Donald Thomas. "Understanding and Influencing Fund Raising Leadership." EdD, University of Pennsylvania, 2003. 6.

This study examined 20 capital campaign leaders at Marian College, using transactional, transformational, situational, and contingency leadership models. Leaders recognized the need for both transactional and transformational leadership, although they mostly used the former.

Calvario, David Anthony. "College Experience, Satisfaction and Intent to Financially Support One's Alma Mater." PhD, University of Northern Colorado, 1996. 4.3.

Using surveys, seniors were queried about their satisfaction with their institution and their intent to donate as alumni. Discriminant analysis predicted donors with 79 percent accuracy and nondonors with 81 percent. Future nondonors were less satisfied with their experience.

Capobianco, Fausto D. "Reputation versus Reality: The Impact of US News and World Report Rankings and Education Branding on Hiring Decisions in the Job Market." EdD, Pepperdine University, 2009. 2.6.

This thesis explored the use of *U.S. News* ranking by human resources professionals in evaluating job applications. Graduating from a top-tier institution had little impact on hiring decisions compared to work experience, degree field, and employee referrals.

Cardona, Jose D. "The Emergence of the Educational Marketer as a Campus Leader." EdD, Rowan University, 2007. 3, 6.3.

The role of campus marketers was explored including their impact on campus planning. At nine campuses, a marketer, the chief academic officer, and faculty president senate were interviewed. All campuses embraced marketing, but marketing was not included in strategic planning; they were viewed as tacticians and specialists, not strategists.

Carey, Amy Bragg. "On the Edge: A Study of Small Private Colleges That Have Made a Successful Financial Turnaround." EdD, Azusa Pacific University, 2013. 1.15.

This case study examined two private universities that successfully transformed their finances from near-closure. Among other factors, the role of fundraising revenue and the fundraising staff was important. In addition to providing financial resources, fundraising was also a source of momentum.

Carlsen, Charles J. "Weaving the Foundation into the Culture of a Community College." *New Directions for Community Colleges* 2003 no. 124 (2003): 47–51. doi: 10.1002/cc.133. 1.1, 8.2.

Using Johnson County Community College (Kansas) as a case study, this article explored how the foundation can portray itself as an integral part of the community and the president's role in doing so.

Carnes, Lana Wilson. "Careers in Higher Education Fund Raising: Perceptions and Experiences of Middle- and Senior-Ranked Female Development Officers." EdD, University of Kentucky, 1996. 1.4, 6.5.

Based on interviews with 17 mid-level and senior female development officers, this thesis explored the opportunities and challenges that shaped their communities. Findings emerged in five areas: the emerging profession, women influencing the field, culture, support systems, and advice.

Carrier, S. M. "The Relationship of Selected Institutional Variables to Community College Foundation Revenue." PhD dissertation, University of Florida, 2002. 1.3, 8.2.

This thesis examined the factors influencing community college fundraising success using systems theory. College endowment, the role of foundation board members, and college size had significant, positive impacts on revenue; the regression model explained half of the variance in outcomes.

Carrier, S. M. "Key Variables Account for Greater Revenue among Community College Foundations." *International Journal of Educational Advancement* 5 no. 1 (2004). 1.3, 8.2.

This paper was based on the author's dissertation, "The Relationship of Selected Institutional Variables."

Carringer, Paul T. "The Community College President: Working with and through the Media to Advance the Institution." Colorado State University, 2013. 2.3, 6.1, 8.2.

The role of the community college president in using the media was explored in four case studies of award-winning marketing and public relations campaigns. Teamwork emerged as important in each case. Organizations presented stories to the media that were closely tied to their mission.

Carter, Linnie Smith. "The Philanthropic Motivations of Community College Donors: A Study of the Educational Foundation of a Mid-Sized, Multi-Campus Community College in Virginia." PhD, Old Dominion University, 2009. 1.2, 8.2.

Using one community college as a case study, this thesis studied donor motivation using a survey and interviews. Most donors were older white women with an income of at least $75,000 who had no direct ties to the institution. Communications from the institution played an important role in donor motivations no matter what motivated donors.

Carter, Linnie Smith. "A Donor-Focused Fundraising Model: An Essential Tool in Community College Foundations' Toolkit." *Community College Journal of Research and Practice* 35 (2011): 99–110. 1.3, 8.2.

The W. K. Kellogg Foundation Donor-Focused Fundraising Model was introduced for community colleges. The article described the inputs, activities, outputs, outcomes, and impacts that a college should have.

Carter, Linnie Smith, and Molly H. Duggan. "Philanthropic Motivations of Community College Donors." *Community College Journal of Research and Practice* 32 no. 1–2 (2010): 61–73. 1.2, 8.2.

This paper was based on Carter's thesis, described above.

Caruana, A., B. Ramaseshan, and M. T. Ewing. "The Marketing Orientation-Performance Link: Some Evidence from the Public Sector and Universities." *Journal of Nonprofit and Public Sector Marketing* 6 no. 1 (1998): 63–82. 3, 5.4.

This study examined whether a marketing orientation produced better results in universities in Australia and New Zealand using survey data. Performance was defined as high scores on service, cost effectiveness, and overall performance. Market orientation was found to have a significant effect, via responsiveness.

Cascione, Gregory Lawrence. *Philanthropists in Higher Education: Institutional, Biographical, and Religious Motivations for Giving.* New York: Routledge, 2013. 1.2.

This book is based on the author's dissertation, below.

Cascione, Gregory Lawrence. "Religion, Motivation, and Philanthropy to Higher Education." PhD, University of Michigan, 2000. 1.2.

Based on interviews with 25 major donors (million-dollars or more) to the University of Michigan, this dissertation explored the role of religion in motivating major donors to higher education. The role of religion varied among Jewish, Christian, and unaffiliated donors. Other factors examined included the role of education, impact on the community, institutional involvement, and demographics.

Cash, Samuel Gresham. "Private, Voluntary Support of Public Research Universities in the United States: 1785–1958." EdD, University of Georgia, 2000. 7.1.

In this historical account, the author divided the history of private support for public institutions into four eras: 1785–Morrill Act passage, the emergence of the land-grant institution, 1900–World War II, and the postwar era. Private support varied but was significant throughout each era.

Cash, Samuel G. "Private Voluntary Support to Public Universities in the United States: An Early History." *International Journal of Educational Advancement* 4 no. 1 (2003): 65–75. 7.1.

This article explored the era 1785–antebellum period. During this time public institutions followed the model of extant private American colleges and received funds from both public and private sources.

Castain, Cornelius Anthony. "Development and Implementation of the University of Northern Iowa's 'Students First' Capital Campaign: A Case Study." EdD, University of Northern Iowa, 2003. 1.6.

This case study looked at the forces, participants, and activities in a university's capital campaign based on 17 interviews of participants. Relevant activities included planning, research, and capacity building. Participants included development staff, a consultant, and the president.

Cates, Damon W. "Undergraduate Alumni Giving: A Study of Six Institutions and Their Efforts Related to Donor Participation." EdD, University of Pennsylvania, 2011. 4.3.

This study looked at the view of development officers at three selective private universities on undergraduate alumni participation in annual giving. Three themes emerged: presidential and vice presidential involvement, campus culture, and staffing and technology.

Caton, C. S. "Preference for Prestige: Commentary on the Behaviour of Universities and Their Benefactors." *Canadian Journal of Higher Education* 29 no. 2 (1999): 145–73. 1.7, 5.1.

This study of philanthropy in Canadian higher education was based on interviews with major donors to universities, hospitals, and art organizations in Toronto. Donors to higher education were less likely to be board members, more likely to view it as a civic responsibility, and were less sure their gift would make a difference. They felt the institutions were not good at building donor relationships.

Celly, Kirti Sawhney, and Brenda Knepper. "50th Anniversary Commemoration at a Major Public University: Benefits of an Integrated Branding and Communications Approach to Event Planning." *International Journal of Nonprofit and Voluntary Sector Marketing* 16 no. 251–74 (2011). 3.3.

This case study of the fiftieth anniversary commemoration at CSU-Dominguez Hills explored how the university's branding and integrated communications led to a significant increase in fundraising for the year. Campaign objectives included engaging internal and external audiences, positioning the university as a local asset, and developing partnerships, all within a limited budget.

Chance, Shannon. "Proposal for Using a Studio Format to Enhance Institutional Advancement." *International Journal of Educational Advancement* 8 no. 3/4 (2008): 111–25. 1.1.

The author proposed reorganizing advancement operations using a design studio metaphor in order to pool talent, promote collaboration, and align diverse interests. An alternative organizational chart was suggested as well as reorganization of responsibilities.

Chapleo, Christopher. "The Real Impact of Integrated Marketing Communications on Colleges and Universities." *CASE International Journal of Educational Advancement* 3 no. 3 (2004a): 240–51. 3.2, 5.2.

UK senior marketing personnel participated in a Delphi technique process regarding branding in higher education. All respondents had brands, although some limited the concept to visual identity and some had trouble communicating a unified brand. Brands were often based on an institution's history and communicated via publications, websites, and attitude. Structure of marketing programs varied widely.

Chapleo, Christopher. "Interpretation and Implementation of Reputation/Brand Management by UK University Leaders." *International Journal of Educational Advancement* 5 no. 1 (2004b). 3.3, 5.2.

Based on interviews with UK university leaders, the author explored their understanding of reputation and brand management. While they agreed their universities had reputations, leaders were less convinced their institutions had cohesive brands. Brands did not necessarily reflect reality. Also discussed was who was responsible for branding and what challenges universities faced.

Chapleo, Christopher. "Do Universities Have 'Successful' Brands?" *International Journal of Educational Advancement* 6 no. 1 (2005): 54–64. 3.3, 5.2.

Chapleo found that, based on interview with 40 opinion-makers, that few UK universities had successful brands. Participants did not agree on what inputs produced a successful brand, suggesting that marketing communication, reputation, location, and public relations were all important.

Chapleo, Christopher. "Is Communications a Strategic Activity in UK Education?" *International Journal of Educational Advancement* 6 no. 4 (2006): 306–14. 2.2, 5.2.

This paper queried 16 senior managers in UK higher education as to whether communications was a strategic activity or tactical tool. While it was seen as a strategy activity, there were obstacles to treating it as such in practice.

Chapleo, Christopher. "External Perceptions of Successful University Brands." *International Journal of Educational Advancement* 8 no. 3/4 (2008): 126–35. 3.3, 5.2.

Chapleo explored if and how UK universities brand themselves based on interviews with 12 external opinion-makers. Results suggested that UK universities were seen as distinct from each other but that few had well-developed brands.

Chapman, Brent S. "Best Practices in Grant Writing at Small Colleges." EdD, Ball State University, 2007. 1.1, 1.12.

Small private colleges were surveyed regarding grant writing and management. Over 80 percent of grants managers also had other duties and on average spent 33 percent of their time on grants. Over 75 percent helped faculty write grant proposals. About half felt their colleges were successful with grants.

Cheslock, John J., and Matt Gianneschi. "Replacing State Appropriations with Alternative Revenue Sources: The Case of Voluntary Support." *Journal of Higher Education* 79 no. 2 (2008): 208–29. 1.16.

The authors explored whether increasing fundraising to replace public funds increased financial disparities between public institutions using data from IPEDS and VSE. Private donations were shown to be more disparate than state appropriations with selective institutions benefiting the most. However, crowding-in rather than crowding-out occurred.

Chiang, Li-Chuan. "The Relationship between University Autonomy and Funding in England and Taiwan." *Higher Education* 48 no. 2 (2004): 189–212. 1.16, 5.2, 5.3.

The author compared university autonomy in two nations where universities are primarily state-funded. Funding alone was found not to be the sole influence on autonomy, and diversification of an institution's revenue base may therefore not necessarily increase autonomy.

Chiavacci, David. "Transition from University to Work under Transformation: The Changing Role of Institutional and Alumni Networks in Contemporary Japan." *Social Science Japan Journal* 8 no. 1 (2005): 19–41. 4.4.

In the 1980s and 1990s, university alumni networks in Japan were important to securing jobs for new graduates, but economic stagnation and labor market changes have eroded these networks. This paper documents these changes and how they occurred.

Chive, Joanne M. "Online Fundraising Trends among Selected Business Schools in the United States." EdD, University of Central Florida, 2007. 1.17, 8.7.

A survey of AACSB institutions found that 36 percent raised money online. Of those that did, 67 percent had an average gift size of $250 or less, and at most institutions online donations accounted for less than 10 percent of total annual donations.

Chung-Hoon, Tanise L. "Beyond Give and Take: A Donor/Organization Integration Model for Enduring Donor Relations in Public Higher Education Fund Raising." PhD, Brigham Young University, 2005. 1.7.

Based on a survey of 132 public institutions, this research sought to explain how personal relationships and formal organizational structure increase strategic integration via the Donor/Organization Integration Model. Institutions with more enduring donor relationships experienced greater fundraising success.

Chung-Hoon, Tanise L., Julie M. Hite, and Steven J. Hite. "Searching for Enduring Donor Relationships: Evidence for Factors and Strategies in a Donor/Organization Integration Model for Fund Raising." *International Journal of Educational Advancement* 6 no. 1 (2005): 34–53. 1.7.

This article presented the Donor/Organization Integration Model, based on interviews with fundraisers at three institutions. The research supported DOIM's constructs of relational embeddedness and structural interaction. In addition, a third construct, integration, arose.

Chung-Hoon, Tanise L., Julie M. Hite, and Steven J. Hite. "Organizational Integration Strategies for Promoting Enduring Donor Relations in Higher Education: The Value of Building Inner Circle Network Relationships." *International Journal of Educational Advancement* 7 no. 1 (2007): 2–19. 1.7.

This article was based on Chung-Hoon's dissertation, "Beyond Give and Take."

Church, Mary Barbara. "An Experimental Investigation of Donor Behavior and Commitment." PhD, Memphis State University, 1994. 1.2.

The Schwartz and Howard model of helping behavior was utilized to test factors in donor motivation. Appeals to 270 alumni in a university phonathon were varied on attention, motivation, and commitment to see their effect on pledge/donation proportions and amounts. Only the high/low commitment variable was found to influence giving.

Ciampa, Donna Lynn. "Community College Vice Presidents for Institutional Advancement: Role Expectations, Fundraising Responsibilities, Professional Relationships, and Commitment to the Institution." EdD, Dowling College, 2009. 6.3, 8.2.

This thesis tested whether vice presidents of advancement should follow the American College Public Relations Association model and answered affirmatively, based on interviews with vice presidents and archival data. Also, clear policies were needed, and advancement offices needed to build stronger relationships with alumni.

Clark, Sylvia D. "Perceptions and Positionings of Colleges in New York City: A Longitudinal Study of Brand Images." *International Journal of Educational Advancement* 5 no. 2 (2005). 3.3.

A study of high school seniors in New York City in 1979 of area college brands was replicated in 2002. A perceptual map showed two clusters in the earlier survey but a continuum in the later. Perceptions did not necessarily match *U.S. News* rankings.

Clarke, Rebecca Jean Grandstaff. "Giving Voice to Student and Alumnae Opposition during the Transition to Coeducation by a College for Women." PhD, Virginia Commonwealth University, 2011. 4.

This case study examined alumnae and student challenges to and experiences during the transition of a women's college to coeducation. Alumnae leaders funded a legal challenge to the change. They referred to the institution as "dead," and refused to donate or visit campus in the future.

Cleveland, Denise Cates Butler. "Perceptions of Career Path Barriers to Women in Educational Fundraising at the University of Alabama." EdD, University of Alabama, 2003. 1.4, 6.5.

This thesis examined barriers to senior-level positions in fundraising at the University of Alabama utilizing survey data. Most women believed there were gender-based barriers to their advancement—such as hiring and promotion that discriminated by gender—and that institutional policy changes were necessary.

Clotfelter, Charles T. "Who Are the Alumni Donors? Giving by Two Generations of Alumni from Selective Colleges." *Nonprofit Management and Leadership* 12 no. 2 (2001): 119–36. 4.3.

This study examined correlates of alumni giving at 14 private, selective institutions. While older alumni gave more, it was impossible to disentangle the effects of age, generation, income, and demographics. Larger gifts were given by men, the wealthy, extracurriculars leaders, those who could recall a college mentor, those who graduated from one's first institution, legacies, and those who were satisfied with their college experience. Political affiliation had no effect, and the effect of SAT scores were mixed.

Clotfelter, Charles T. "Alumni Giving to Elite Private Colleges and Universities." *Economics of Education Review* 22 no. 2 (2003): 109–20. 4.3.

This study examined the correlates of alumni giving at 14 private, selective institutions. Attending one's first choice college, having a college mentor, being satisfied with life, attending a public high school, graduating, having an MBA, and income all had a strong positive correlation with both higher levels of giving and with giving or not giving. Factors that influenced one cohort but not the other were extracurricular participation; having a graduate degree from the same institution; being white, single, and satisfied with nonteaching aspects of the institution; and earning honors.

Coates, Hamish. "Universities on the Catwalk: Models for Performance Ranking in Australia." *Higher Education Management and Policy* 19 no. 2 (2007): 69–85. 3.4, 5.4.

Three ways of evaluating/ranking universities in Australia were compared using survey data from recent graduates: ranking of aggregate performance, comparisons of change over time, and performance variation within fields. Aggregate methods were misleading, and the author concluded better methods were needed.

Cockrum, Lawrence Lee. "The Impact of Presidential Leadership Behavior on Success in Fund Raising." EdD, Peabody College for Teachers of Vanderbilt University, 2004. 6.1, 8.8.

Based on surveys and interviews with presidents at Council for Christian Colleges and Universities institutions, this thesis studied the relationship between presidential behavior and fundraising success. Effective presidents differed in seven ways from less-effective peers; they were more concerned with leadership than collegiality, had more experience, spent more time on, and had more control over fundraising.

Cohen, Chris, Warren Whisenant, and Patrick Walsh. "The Relationship between Sustained Success and Donations for an Athletic Department with a Premier Football Program." *Public Organization Review* 11 (2011): 255–63. 1.3, 8.4.

This study correlated the effects of the football team's winning percentage on donations to athletics at one university with a strong football team over 11 years. There was no correlation with the total amount of contributions, number of donors, or number of contributions; correlation with average contribution size was negative.

Cohen, Rodney T. "Black College Alumni Giving: A Study of the Perceptions, Attitudes, and Giving Behaviors of Alumni Donors at Selected Historically Black Colleges and Universities." EdD, Peabody College, Vanderbilt University, 2006. 4.3, 8.1.

HBCU alumni donors were surveyed regarding giving to their alma maters. Alumni were supportive and interested in giving, and felt their institutions were not in excellent financial health, but that their institutions could continue without their support. Alumni were four times more likely to support their churches than their college.

Cohen, Rodney T. "Black College Alumni Giving: A Study of the Perceptions, Attitudes, and Giving Behaviors of Alumni Donors at Selected Historically Black Colleges and Universities." *International Journal of Educational Advancement* 6 no. 3 (2006): 200–20. 4.3, 8.1.

This article is based on the author's dissertation, discussed above.

Cohu, Jeff G. "Factors Influencing Fundraising Success at Church-Related Colleges and Universities." EdD, Eastern Michigan University, 2012. 1.3, 8.8.

These five case studies examined fundraising strategies and leadership behavior at church-related institutions. Success was a product of a brand image, focused differentiation, donor segmentation, sticking to core competencies, an engaged board, skilled development staff, and a president who visibly embodied the institutional mission with boundary spanning, story-telling, and co-option.

Coles, Marlene. "A Quantitative Study of the Use of Newsmagazine Rankings in College Choice and the Effects of Social Capital." PhD, University of Michigan, 2007. 3.4.

This thesis explored how students used *U.S. News* rankings in the college choice process using CIRP data and how that usage varied by social capital. Low-income, minority, and first-generation students used rankings in a compensatory way; high-income, Asian American, and second-generation students used them to extend their advantage.

Collier, Alma Dacus. "A Survey of the Relative Effectiveness of Fund-Raising Activities in Private Colleges and Universities." EdD, George Washington University, 1996. 1.3.

The researcher collected qualitative and quantitative data on fundraising activities, policies, and practices. Important activities included having an active foundation, volunteers, gift clubs, phonathons/direct mail campaigns, athletic boosters, and solicitation of many individuals and organizations. Policies included planning, annual reports, involvement of senior leadership, and a board committee.

Collins, McLean. "Heeding the Rebel Yell: Identification and Communication in Managing Organizational Issues." *International Journal of Educational Advancement* 5 no. 4 (2005): 317–32. 2.5.

The transition from the Colonel Reb mascot to a new mascot at the University of Mississippi was analyzed using the issue development model. Most student and alumni criticism was directed at how the transition was handled rather than the decision itself. The university failed to examine multiple perspectives and communicate sufficiently.

Coloma, Jennifer. "Development and Validation of the University Website Evaluation Scale (UWES): A Tool for Assessing Website User Experience on a University Website." PhD, Alliant International University, 2012. 3.1.

The author developed, piloted, and tested the University Website Evaluation Scale using a university website and 198 testers. The UWES has four subscales (visual appeal, interactive links, university experience, and website as a resource) with strong internal validity.

Comegno, Marsha Hoffman. "Fundraising Effectiveness: Definition and Measurement at a Women's College." EdD, University of Pennsylvania, 2004. 1.3.

This interview-based case study attempted to measure fundraising effectiveness at Randolph-Macon Woman's College over two decades. Effectiveness was based on people, participation, proceeds, preparation, and pride.

Compton, Benjamin Hasty. "Essays in the Political Economy of Higher Education Funding." PhD, Clemson University, 2011. 1.16.

This three-essay dissertation explored the effects of politics on higher education funding in South Carolina. Using Andreoni's model of altruism, crowding out of private funding was demonstrated, but donors did not respond similarly to large private gifts.

Conley, A. "The Role of Student Organizations and Alumni Giving at Public Institutions." EdD, Indiana University, 1999. 4.3.

The impact of membership in the Indiana University Student Foundation was tested for impact on alumni giving. Membership had a positive affect, and steering committee membership had an additional impact.

Conley, Aaron, and Eugene Tempel. "The Student Foundation as a Community of Participation: A Study of Its Impact on Alumni Giving." *CASE International Journal of Educational Advancement* 1 no. 2 (2000): 120–33. 4.3.

This article was based on Conley's dissertation, "The Role of Student Organizations and Alumni Giving at Public Institutions."

Conner, Deborah Kay. "Factors That Affect Alumni Giving at a Southeastern Comprehensive University." PhD, Clemson University, 2005. 4.3.

The author created a structural equation model for whether alumni would give based on demographics, undergraduate and alumni involvement, educational gains, and value. Alumni involvement did not predict donations. Unusually, more recent graduates were more likely to be donors.

Cook, W. Bruce. "Courting Philanthropy: The Role of University Presidents and Chancellors in Fund Raising." PhD, University of Texas at Austin, 1994. 6.1.

Based on interviews with university presidents and fundraising documents, this thesis used role theory, prestige maximization, and social exchange to describe fundraising by university presidents. Conclusions include that the president is the center of a fundraising team; they should focus their energy on major gifts and administration, and context matters.

Cook, W. Bruce. "Fund Raising and the College Presidency in an Era of Uncertainty: From 1975 to the Present." *Journal of Higher Education* 68 no. 1 (1997): 53–86. 6.1.

This article provided an overview of presidential fundraising, 1975–1997. In this "era of uncertainty," many public institutions began fundraising and many private institutions expanded theirs. The first billion-dollar campaigns were held. Fundraising became a selection criterion for presidents and one of their main duties.

Cook, W. B., and W. F. Lasher. "Toward a Theory of Fund Raising in Higher Education." *Review of Higher Education* 20 no. 1 (1996): 33–51. 1.3.

This article is based on Cook's dissertation, "Courting Philanthropy."

Coupet, Jason, and Darold Barnum. "HBCU Efficiency and Endowments: An Exploratory Analysis." *International Journal of Educational Advancement* 10 no. 3 (2010): 186–97. 1.15, 8.1.

Efficiency (graduation rates compared to financial resources) was compared using Data Envelopment Analysis and HBCUs were found to be somewhat more efficient than PWIs. Endowment had a positive impact on efficiency; the authors suggested channeling funds raised into endowment rather than current operations.

Courtney, Barbara T. "Students and Graduates of the College of William and Mary 1756 to 1765: Plantation Owners, Planters, Merchants, and Politicians." EdD, George Washington University, 2011. 4.2, 7.2.

This thesis delved into what colonial graduates of William & Mary did postgraduation. Findings included class diversity in student origins, more curricular/cocurricular diversity than associated with the era, and the assistance to their careers that college attendance provided.

Cox, John L. "The Relationship between Private Giving and State Funding among Maryland's Four-Year Public Institutions." EdD, George Washington University, 2009. 1.16.

Using 10 years of data from 13 public institutions, this thesis examined the effect of fundraising on appropriations. While there was a correlation between giving and appropriations, changes in private giving produced a very small effect on state funding.

Cox, John L. "Private Giving and State Funding of Maryland's Public Institutions: New Perspectives on Support of Historically Black Institutions."

International Journal of Educational Advancement 10 no. 3 (2010): 166–85. 1.16, 8.1.

Based on data from his thesis, "The Relationship between Private Giving and State Funding," Cox compared the private and public support of HBCUs and traditionally white institutions. HBCUs received less private funding than TWIs but more public funds per FTE.

Cox, John L. "Private Giving versus State Funding: Perspectives on Funding of Maryland 4-Year Public Institutions." *International Journal of Educational Advancement* 10 no. 4 (2011): 181–210. 1.16.

This article is based on the author's dissertation, "The Relationship between Private Giving and State Funding."

Cristantello, David A. "Characteristics Describing Giving Behavior of Alumni of Three Historically Roman Catholic Colleges: Canisius College, D'Youville College and St. John Fisher College." PhD, State University of New York at Buffalo, 1992. 4.3, 8.8.

Alumni at three Catholic colleges were tested to see if demographic and attitudinal data could discriminate among nondonors, occasional donors, and regular donors. The data did not support this hypothesis: All three donor groups had positive feelings toward their institution.

Cross, Michael Edward. "The Run to Division I: Intercollegiate Athletics and the Broader Interests of Colleges and Universities." PhD, University of Michigan, 1999. 1.3, 8.4.

Case studies of four institutions that moved to Division I athletics examined their rationales. Institutions expected multiple benefits, including improved alumni support and development, community relations, and visibility. Institutions found that alumni donations increased but only for athletics. Community relations and visibility improved.

Croteau, Jon Derek, and Holly Gordon Wolk. "Defining Advancement Career Paths and Succession Plans: Critical Human Capital Retention Strategies for High-Performing Advancement Divisions." *International Journal of Educational Advancement* 10 no. 2 (2011): 59–70. 6.5.

The authors described the benefits of human capital investment strategies to retain high performers. This requires building viable career paths for employees to grow with.

Croteau, Jon Derek, and Zachary A. Smith. *Making the Case for Leadership: Profiles of Chief Advancement Officers in Higher Education.* Lanham, MD: Rowman & Littlefield, 2011. 6.3.

This book offered profiles of ten highly successful chief advancement officers and developed the Advancement Leadership Competency Model, which consists of 14 skills and characteristics.

Cunningham, B. M., and C. K. Cochi-Ficano. "The Determinants of Donative Revenue Flows from Alumni of Higher Education: An Empirical Inquiry." *The Journal of Human Resources* 37 no. 3 (2002): 540–69. 4.3.

Using a lagged model and VSE data, the authors regressed the effect of institutional characteristics, including student achievement, on alumni donations. Increases in student quality and faculty-student ratio resulted in higher donations. Negatively affecting giving were the percentage of students who attended business schools and being part of a system.

Curry, Janel, Scott Rodin, and Neil Carlson. "Fundraising in Difficult Economic Times: Best Practices." *Christian Higher Education* 11 no. 4 (2012): 241–52. 1.3, 8.8.

Based on surveys and interviews with leaders of Council for Christian Colleges and Universities, the authors found that macroeconomic conditions (such as a recession) and development staff size and budget do not influence fundraising performance, but that a transformational approach to development does.

Curtis, Mary Colleen. "A Model of Donor Behavior: A Comparison between Female and Male Donors to Men's and Women's Athletics Support Organizations at Division I NCAA-Affiliated Institutions within the Big Ten." PhD, University of Iowa, 2000. 1.2, 8.4.

Using Staurowsky's motivation theory, this thesis compared motivations for giving among donors to athletics. Donors were surveyed; factor analysis and regression were conducted. Lower-level donors were motivated by identity and belonging and a desire to increase institutional prestige (value-drive); higher level donors were motivated by personal benefits.

Curtiss, Jeffery Steven. "Case Study Regarding Perceptions of Donor Relations within a Private Liberal Arts College." PhD, University of South Florida, 1994. 1.1, 1.12.

This case study examined the process of soliciting donations, from identification of potential donors to recognition. Out of 41 fundraising elements that were used, fundraisers felt 16 influenced outcomes.

Daly, Siobhan. "Philanthropy, the New Professionals and Higher Education: The Advent of Directors of Development and Alumni Relations." *Journal of Higher Education Policy and Management* 35 no. 1 (2013): 21–33. 1.4, 5.2.

As British universities add development offices, the new professional identities of development officers are being constructed and affecting the institutions. Based on interviews with development officers and using Whitchurch's theory of professional identities, this study explored the roles and influence of development staff.

Daniels, Tatia Randilyn. "A Profile of Black Alumni Constituent Groups at Predominantly White Institutions." PhD, University of Virginia, 1999. 4.4.

This thesis explored the extent to which black alumni constituent groups are recognized at PWIs. A survey of research universities showed that 89 percent had constituent groups; 70 percent had BACGs. Nearly all groups were involved with socializing (97%); many also did recruiting (59%), mentoring (47%), and fundraising (55%).

Davis, Stephanie R. "Terry L. Fairfield: A Portraiture of Nonprofit Leadership in Educational Fundraising." PhD, University of Nebraska, 2013. 7.3.

This thesis used portraiture to examine the life of Fairfield, CEO of the University of Nebraska Foundation 1987–2005, primarily based on interviews.

Dean, Michael S. "Perceptions of Chief Development Officers about Factors That Influence Alumni Major Giving." PhD, Southern Illinois University at Carbondale, 2007. 1.8, 4.3.

This survey of doctoral university fundraisers examined their perceptions of factors influencing alumni giving. Demographic factors included marriage to another alumnus/a, income, studying business, time since degree, and multiple degrees. Student experience factors included overall satisfaction, satisfaction with faculty, and positive peer relations. Eleven alumni involvement factors were also important.

Dennis, E., and C. LaMay, eds. *Higher Education in the Information Age*. New Brunswick, NJ: Transaction Publishers, 1993. 2.3, 3.4.

This edited volume included essays on media rankings, athletics, and boosterism.

Dent, Nancy B. "The Philanthropic Motivations of Female Donors to Institutions of Higher Education: A Study of a Woman's Organization in Two Southwestern Cities." PhD, New Mexico State University, 2005. 1.2.

Members of two Junior Leagues were surveyed about their motivations to give to higher education. Desire to change, connect, and commit were found to be significant, whereas desire to create, collaborate and celebrate were not.

Dial, Daniel Dapat. "The Role Status and Qualifications of the Chief Advancement Officer in Selected Institutions of Higher Education." EdD, La Sierra University, 1993. 6.3.

> The author surveyed chief development officers at Seventh-Day Adventist-affiliated institutions, other religious institutions, and secular institutions. CDOs were found to be important to their institutions' fundraising programs and held similar views regarding successful fundraising.

Diamond, William D., and Rajiv K. Kashyap. "Extending Models of Prosocial Behavior to Explain University Alumni Contributions." *Journal of Applied Social Psychology* 27 no. 10 (1997): 915–28. 4.3.

> Survey data from business school alumni and institutional data were used in path analysis to find determinants of prosocial behavior. Obligation, perceived efficacy, and perceived need were found to influence intent to give. Intent to give and obligation influenced number of contributions. Obligation, individual attachment to the institution, and reciprocity influenced intent to attend reunions.

Diaz, Sandra L. "Raising the Cash: A Study of the Role of Leadership in a Capital Campaign." PhD, Capella University, 2013. 6.

> This case study of a capital campaign at New York University explored leadership dynamics. Both transactional and transformational leadership were needed. Both personal and professional relationships were necessary to reach campaign goals.

Dickerson, Frank C. "The Way We Write: A Profile of and Prescription for Fixing the Broken Discourse of Fundraising." *Journal of the DMA Nonprofit Federation* 12 no. 3 (2009a): 1–21. 1.9.

> This article is based on the author's following dissertation.

Dickerson, Frank C. "Writing the Voice of Philanthropy: How to Raise Money with Words." PhD, Claremont Graduate University, 2009b. 1.9.

> The author used linguistic and rhetorical analysis on a body of 2,412 fundraising texts from 880 nonprofits, surveyed writers of such texts, and measured the effect of hand personalization on fundraising appeals. Most of the texts sounded academic, was not interpersonal, and contained few narratives. Personalization increased response rates.

Diehl, Abigail Grosvenor. "The Relationship between Alumni Giving and Receipt of Institutional Scholarships among Undergraduate Students at a Public, Land-Grant Institution." PhD, Pennsylvania State University, 2007. 4.3.

> The effect of receiving institutional scholarship aid on subsequent alumni giving was examined with data from Penn State using Volkwein's

Conceptual Model of Gift-Giving Behavior. Scholarship receipt was found to influence whether or not alumni gave but not gift size; the number of scholarships received influenced both.

Dill, David D., and Maarja Soo. "Academic Quality, League Tables, and Public Policy: A Cross-National Analysis of University Ranking Systems." *Higher Education* 49 no. 4 (2005): 495–533. 3.4, 5.

University ranking systems from Australia, Canada, the United Kingdom, and the United States were compared. All relied in part on similar input measures (quality of incoming students and quality of faculty and research) but used more diverse process and output measures.

Dittman, Judith Lynn. "Intercollegiate Athletics at the University of Iowa: An Analysis of Donor Motives and Characteristics." PhD, University of Iowa, 1997. 1.2, 8.4.

Kotler's theory of exchange and Staurowsky's ACQUIRE-II Survey were used to examine motivation of donors to the University of Iowa's athletic programs. There were found to be significant differences between male and female donors and donors to men's and women's sports.

Dixon, Keith, and David Coy. "University Governance: Governing Bodies as Providers and Users of Annual Reports." *Higher Education* 54 no. 2 (2007): 267–91. 2.1, 5.4, 6.2.

Surveys of New Zealand universities examined how governing boards used annual reports. While governing boards are intended as external documents, about two-thirds of board members found them somewhat useful.

Dobson, Gretchen C. "Young Alumni Perceptions of English Universities in an Era of Tuition and Fees." EdD, University of Pennsylvania, 2013. 4.6, 5.2.

This thesis examined whether the introduction of student fees has affected alumni involvement in English universities via three case studies. In all three cases, the universities preemptively added alumni services; at two schools, alumni donations rose in response. Services include alumni volunteering and linkages to academic departments.

Dos Santos, Alves. "A Quantitative Analysis of Recessions and Financial Changes in Higher Education Institution Alumni Programs." EdD, University of Phoenix, 2013. 4.3.

The author examined if the 2000–2010 recession affected alumni giving for operational and capital expenses based on VSE data for 54 institutions. No difference in giving was found.

Doty, Donald G. "Institutional Strengths, Fundraising Messages, and Private Giving Outcomes in Tier One Research Extensive Universities: A Multiple Case Study." PhD, University of Nebraska—Lincoln, 2007. 1.9.

Using Shannon and Weaver's information processing model of communication, this six-university case study explored how communication of institutional strength was related to fundraising success. A review of publications, documents, and interviews found that they did communicate institutional strengths.

Dowd, Alicia C, and John L. Grant. "Equity Effects of Entrepreneurial Community College Revenues." *Community College Journal of Research and Practice* 31 no. 3 (2007): 231–44. 1.3, 8.2.

This paper tested whether community colleges in wealthy communities were more successful at raising private funds. Using Massachusetts colleges, the authors found that wealthier colleges were not more successful at raising money from either performance incentive programs or fundraising.

Drew-Branch, Vanessa L. "Student Engagement, Alumni Satisfaction, and Alumni Donations at a Public Four Year Institution: An Analysis of How the Undergraduate Experience Influences Alumni Donations." EdD, West Virginia University, 2011. 4.3.

Alumni at a comprehensive university were surveyed to see if there was a link between student satisfaction and giving. Student satisfaction was correlated with alumni satisfaction, and alumni satisfaction was correlated with giving time and money.

Drezner, Noah D. "Advancing Gallaudet: Alumni Support for the Nation's University for the Deaf and Hard-of-Hearing and Its Similarities to Black Colleges and Universities." *International Journal of Educational Advancement* 5 no. 4 (2005a): 301–16; doi: 10.1057/palgrave.ijea.2140222. 4.3, 7.2, 8.6.

Gallaudet University's alumni fundraising efforts were compared to those of HBCUs. Data used included historical documents and interviews. While federal funding provides a large part of Gallaudet's budget, and there have been a few alumni campaigns, concerted efforts did not begin until 1990, when campaign consultants were hired.

Drezner, Noah D. "Thurgood Marshall: A Study of Philanthropy through Racial Uplift." In *Uplifting a People: African American Philanthropy and Education*, edited by Marybeth Gasman and Katherine V. Sedgwick. New York: Peter Lang, 2005b. 7.3.

While Thurgood Marshall is best known for his accomplishments in jurisprudence, this article framed on his work as philanthropy. Marshall focused on achieving civil rights for all; many of his efforts, particularly in Maryland and for the NAACP, focused on access to higher education.

Drezner, Noah D. "Recessions and Tax-Cuts: Economic Cycles' Impact on Individual Giving, Philanthropy, and Higher Education." *International Journal of Educational Advancement* 6 no. 4 (2006): 289–305. 1.16.

Data from VSE, Giving USA, and other sources was used to study how recessions and tax cuts impact higher education fundraising. During recessions, giving went down. The impact of tax cuts was less clear-cut, but they seemed to lower giving by wealthy donors.

Drezner, Noah D. "Cultivating a Culture of Giving: An Exploration of Institutional Strategies to Enhance African American Young Alumni Giving." PhD, University of Pennsylvania, 2008a. 4.3.

This case study of the UNCF's National Pre-Alumni Council examined why young African Americans give to higher education. The author used prosocial behavior, organizational development, and relationship marketing theories, and found that NPAC used extrinsic and intrinsic motivation, created opportunities for involvement and uplift, and educated students about philanthropy.

Drezner, Noah D. "For Alma Mater and the Fund: The United Negro College Fund's National Pre-Alumni Council and the Creation of the Next Generation of Donors." *Triumphs and Troubles: Historical and Contemporary Essays on Black Colleges*. New York: Palgrave Macmillan, 2008b. 4.3, 7.2, 8.1.

This chapter is based on the author's dissertation, "Cultivating a Culture of Giving."

Drezner, Noah D. "Why Give? Exploring Social Exchange and Organization Identification Theories in the Promotion of Philanthropic Behaviors of African-American Millennials at Private-HBCUs." *International Journal of Educational Advancement* 9 no. 3 (2009): 147–65. 4.3, 8.1.

This article is based on the author's dissertation, "Cultivating a Culture of Giving."

Drezner, Noah D. "Philanthropy and Fundraising in American Higher Education." *ASHE Higher Education Report* 37 no. 2, edited by Kelly Ward and Lisa E. Wolf-Wendel. Hoboken, NJ: Wiley Periodicals, 2011. 1.0, 4.3.

This ASHE Report provided an outline of the major issues and current research findings in higher education fundraising. Drezner concluded that more research is needed on nontraditional donors, the effect of fundraising on mission, prosocial behaviors, senior leadership, and giving by different generations.

Drezner, Noah D., ed. *Expanding the Donor Base in Higher Education: Engaging Non-Traditional Donors*. New York: Routledge, 2013. 1.2, 4.3.

This edited volume focused on giving by nontraditional donors. See listings for individual chapters for more details.

Drezner, Noah D., and Anubha Gupta. "Busting the Myth: Understanding Endowment Management at Public Historically Black Colleges and Universities." *Journal of Negro Education* 81 no. 2 (2012): 107–20. 1.1, 8.1.

IPEDS panel data was used to compare financial management at HBCUs and PWIs to test whether HBCUs were more poorly financially managed. The authors found no evidence of a difference in endowment management for HBCUs, land-grant institutions, or institutions that were part of the Adams lawsuit (states with dual systems of higher education).

Drumm, Morris Don. "University Presidents' Leadership Frame and Giving." EdD, Tarleton State University, 2011. 1.3, 6.1.

This thesis examined whether the leadership frames used by university presidents affected fundraising. Presidents were surveyed using the Bolman and Deal leadership survey instrument. Those that used the human resources frame had a greater increase in giving over those that used symbolic, structural, or political frames.

Drummond, Jason S. "An Investigation of the Factors That Can Predict Philanthropic Support for Former Female Student-Athletes." EdD, University of Kansas, 2009. 4.3.

Based on a survey of female former student-athletes at the University of Virginia, this thesis examined their philanthropic motivations. The author found that age, attitude toward the athletic program, and willingness to give all impacted the decision to give; income affected how much alumnae gave.

Drummond, Mary Bea. "The Power of Money: Colleges and Universities Bank on the Boundary-Spanning Roles of Development Officers." EdD, Oklahoma State University, 1997. 1.4.

Based on interviews with development officers and the theory of boundary spanning, this thesis found that development officers play the roles of "gardener," "agent," and "matchmaker." These roles can be deployed at different times or may overlap, but result in different approaches to conflict management.

Dugan, K., C. Mullin, and J. Siegfried. "Undergraduate Financial Aid and Subsequent Giving Behavior." In Williams Project on the Economics of Higher Education Discussion Papers, 2000. 4.3.

Data on giving by Vanderbilt University alumni within eight years of graduation was used to explore the effect of undergraduate aid on giving. Adding scholarships to loans or eliminating loans from loan/grant financial aid packages increased the possibility of giving; larger aid packages or increasing the percentage of scholarships/grants had no effect.

Durand, Bonita R. "Demographic, Institutional and Leadership Characteristics Affecting Fund Raising Performance: A Study of Public Colleges in New York State." PhD, State University of New York at Buffalo, 2002. 1.3.

This study of fundraising by comprehensive SUNY-system colleges was described in this thesis. Institutions were ranked, potential success was predicted, and institutional leaders were surveyed. The author concluded that the most successful approach would be to solicit nonalumni.

Durango-Cohen, Elizabeth J., Ramon L. Torres, and Pablo L. Durango-Cohen. "Donor Segmentation: When Summary Statistics Don't Tell the Whole Story." *Journal of Interactive Marketing* 27 (2013): 172–84. 1.2, 1.3.

This article explored how alumni might be segmented, comparing models such as recency/frequency/monetary value (RFM) with Markov-chain based patterns of giving. The authors argue that RFM masks individual differences and that segmentation based on longitudinal segmentation is more accurate.

Durham, Margaret L. "Perceptions of the Development Process at a Large Public Research II University." EdD unpublished dissertation, Texas Tech University, 1999. 1.8.

This case study of a university's fundraising process used Curtiss' donor relations model. The institution used 46 of Curtiss' 57 elements; many had recently been added during a capital campaign. Five additional environmental factors emerged.

Durham, Margaret L., and Albert B. Smith. "Assessing the Fund-Raising Process at a Public Research II University and Refining the Process Framework." *CASE International Journal of Educational Advancement* 2 no. 1 (2001): 67–78. 1.1.

This article is based on the author's dissertation "Perceptions of the Development Process at a Large Public Research II University."

Durney, Lawrence John. "The Impact of Tax Reform and Related Donor Behavior on Fund-Raising at Small, Private Liberal Arts Colleges." EdD, Columbia University Teachers College, 1991. 1.16.

This thesis examined the impact of the Tax Reform Act of 1986 on giving at small liberal arts colleges, using VSE data. The author found it had a significant, negative impact in both the short and long terms. Total support dropped by 14 percent; alumni support by 33 percent; and property gifts by 39 percent.

Duronio, M., and E. Tempel. *Fund Raisers: Their Careers, Concerns, Stories, and Accomplishments.* San Francisco: Jossey-Bass, 1997. 1.4, 6.

Based on a study of over 1,700 fundraisers (not exclusively in higher education), this book discussed issues such as compensation, the status of women and minorities, ethics and regulations, turnover, and entry and promotion.

Dvorak, Tomas, and Shayna R. Toubman. "Are Women More Generous Than Men? Evidence from Alumni Donations." *Eastern Economic Journal* 39 no. 1 (2013): 121–31. 4.3.

Analyzing 31 years of alumni giving data from a liberal arts college, the authors found that women gave more often than men but in smaller amounts, when controlling for age, income, and participating in Greek life.

Dye, Ronald Keith. "The Relationship between Institutional Characteristics and Fund-Raising Outcomes at Selected Two-Year Colleges." PhD, Ohio University, 1992. 1.3, 8.2.

The effect of institutional characteristics on fundraising at community colleges was explored using VSE data. Age, control, education and general expenditures, endowment, expenditures per student, and tuition all affected the two-year average gift per student from foundations, corporations, alumni giving, nonalumni giving, and total support.

Ebersole, Tim. "Alumni Financial Donations, Life Cycle and Student Activities." EdD, Duquesne University, 2011. 4.3.

This longitudinal study examined giving by the class of 1973 at Shippensburg University over 36 years, considering the effect of student activities, gender, proximity to campus, and college. Based on ANOVA, proximity and activities mattered but gender did not. College mattered in later years only.

Ebiana, Bassey Iban Asuquo. "Deans as Fundraisers: An Analysis of Factors That Contributed to or Impeded Deans' Performance during a Capital Campaign." PhD, Michigan State University, 1993. 6.6.

The role of academic deans in MSU's first capital campaign was studied by interviewing deans and development officers. The author found that deans' leadership skills, planning, and organization mattered.

Edgington, Kyle Douglas. "Leadership in Higher Education Fundraising: Chief Fundraiser Leadership Style and Follower Self-efficacy." PhD, University of Texas at Dallas, 2013. 6.3.

Chief development officers of doctoral-granting universities were surveyed regarding leadership styles. CDOs had high levels of self-efficacy and were likely to use transactional leadership.

Edmiston-Strasser, Dawn M. "An Examination of Integrated Marketing Communication in U.S. Public Institutions of Higher Education." DMgt, University of Maryland University College, 2007. 3.2.

Eighty-two highly ranked public universities were surveyed about their use of IMC using the Four Stages of IMC framework; follow-up interviews were conducted at some institutions. Leadership, formal communications mechanisms, and an open system orientation influenced use of IMC. IMC resulted in increased selectivity and brand recognition. Universities did not linearly use the Four Stages model.

Edmiston-Strasser, Dawn M. "An Examination of Integrated Marketing Communication in US Public Institutions of Higher Education." *Journal of Marketing for Higher Education* 19 no. 2 (2009): 142–65. 3.2.

This article is based on the author's dissertation, discussed above.

Edwards, Chuck Cohnan. "Higher Education Development Officers' Use of Affinity-Seeking Strategies in Soliciting Contributions." EdD, Texas Tech University, 2003. 1.1.

University development officers were surveyed about their use of affinity-seeking strategies based on Bell and Daly's 25 strategies. A core of 10–12 strategies were consistently used; some strategies were considered mostly ineffective.

Ehrenberg, Ronald G. "Reaching for the Brass Ring: The US News & World Report Rankings and Competition." *Review of Higher Education* 26 no. 2 (2002): 145–62. 3.4.

Ehrenberg examined how institutions change their behavior to improve their *U.S. News* rankings. After discussing cases of institutional attempts to game their rankings, he discussed whether rankings inhibit collaboration. He concluded they do not.

Ehrenberg, R. G., and C. L. Smith. "The Sources and Uses of Annual Giving at Selective Private Research Universities and Liberal Arts Colleges." *Economics of Education Review* 22 no. 3 (2003): 223–35. 1.3, 1.15.

This paper used panel data from VSE to explore the varying philanthropic funding mixes and whether those funds are spent on current operations, endowments, or construction at private research universities. Factors influencing the funding mix were tax rates, median family income, alumni wealth, undergraduate major composition, undergraduate demographics and enrollment, and endowment per student.

Eisengrein, Mark Robert. "A Study of the Costs Associated with Athletic Fund-Raising at NCAA Division I Institutions." PhD, Ohio University, 1993. 8.4.

A survey of Division I institutes examined whether fundraising efficiency was linked to dollars raised per student. Higher expenditures led to more dollars raised per student; dollars per student was inversely related to efficiency. Overall, a 627 percent return on investment was found.

Elder, Stephen D. "Recruiting, Training, and Retaining High-Performance Development Teams." *New Directions for Higher Education* 149 (2010): 81–88. 6.

This article provided advice for leaders of development offices. The author advised leaders to have a compelling vision, be clear about priorities, provide training and tools, measure outcomes, coach team members, hiring the right staff, give employees territories, work together, eliminate silos, and build relationships.

Eldredge, Richard Grenville. "The Advancement President in Higher Education." EdD, Johnson & Wales University, 1999. 6.1.

Eight higher education presidents were interviewed regarding their role in advancement and the use of a fundraising foundation. Findings included that foundations have positives and negatives but are most beneficial for public institutions, and that transformational leadership is highly effective.

Eldridge-Karr, Claire. "An Investigative Study of Predictive Characteristics Associated with Alumni Planned Giving." EdD, University of Tennessee, 1991. 1.5, 4.3.

Using Delphi technique and analysis of data from the University of Tennessee, the author built a conceptual model for deferred giving based on demographic and attitudinal data. The model correctly predicted 81 percent of cases.

Eller, Dan Harold. "College Vice Presidents' Role in Fundraising Activities in the 2000s and Beyond: A Case in California." EdD, California Polytechnic State University, San Luis Obispo, 2010. 6.3.

This case study of a CSU institution was based on documents and interviews with four vice presidents regarding their roles in fundraising. Findings included that teamwork and collaboration and the elimination of silos were helpful for effective fundraising, although the vice presidents did not work closely together.

Elliott, D. *The Ethics of Asking: Dilemmas in Higher Education Fund Raising.* Baltimore, MD: Johns Hopkins University Press, 1995. 1.10.

This edited volume was divided into three parts: the social and moral foundations of higher education fundraising, discussions of ethical issues, and appendices of various codes of ethics.

Elliott, Deni. *The Kindness of Strangers: Philanthropy and Higher Education.* Lanham, MD: Rowman & Littlefield, 2006. 1.10.

This edited volume on ethics in higher education fundraising included chapters on mission, different donor segments, and fundraising as a business, as well as reprints of readings on foundations of fundraising ethics.

Enyard, Richard Keith. "A Study of the Effect of the Receipt of Financial Aid on the Rate of Giving by Alumni at a Public Mid-West University." PhD, University of Missouri—Columbia. 4.3, 1993. 4.3.

Institutional data was used to test the effects of financial aid on giving. Alumni who received both institutional scholarships and federal grants were more likely to give than alumni who received only institutional scholarships; the latter were more likely to give than recipients of only federal grants or no aid. Institutional scholarship recipients were more likely to be alumni association members.

Errett, Carole Diane. "The Giving Tree: Trends in Philanthropic Giving in Texas Community Colleges." PhD, University of Texas at Austin, 2004. 1.12, 4.3, 8.2.

Based on a survey of administrators at Texas community colleges and interviews, this thesis examined the motivations of alumni and corporate donors. Factors that influenced giving included reputation, allegiance, and corporate employee involvement.

Erwin, John Stuart. "Caterpillar Inc.'s Think Big Program at Illinois Central College: Sustaining Financial Support through Collaborative Partnerships." *New Directions for Community Colleges* 132 (2005): 59–65. doi: 10.1002/cc.214. 1.12.

The author examined one corporate/community college program that gave students an associate's degree and a position at the company and served as a prototype for similar programs elsewhere. Corporate funding paid for curricular design, marketing, facilities, equipment, and miscellaneous expenses.

Evans, Donald L., Jr. "Attitudes of Engineering Donors toward the Use of Electronic Communications for Fundraising in the College of Engineering at the University of Idaho." PhD, University of Idaho, 2005. 1.7, 8.7.

This qualitative case study examined the attitudes of donors toward the use of electronic communications for fundraising.

Eversden, Gregory Knight. "Characteristics of Selected Fundraising Programs: Case Studies of Two Carnegie I Research-Extensive Universities." PhD, Southern Illinois University at Carbondale, 2003. 1.3, 1.6.

> These case studies examined two universities with histories of successful fundraising. Findings included difficulty in defining fundraising success, the unique idiosyncrasies of each institution influencing fundraising success, efficiency as a function of planning, and the necessity of specific skills for leaders.

Farrell, Thomas J. "Comprehensive Fundraising Campaigns in the 21st Century: Non-Financial Elements and Factors Associated with Major Campaigns at Doctoral-Extensive Universities." EdD, University of Pennsylvania, 2005. 1.1, 1.6.

> This case study of Harvard's $2.6-billion campaign examined the campaign's nonfinancial objectives—what they were, whether they were produced, and how they could be more effectively achieved.

Ferrin, Scott Ellis. "Tasks and Strategies of In-House Lobbyists in American Colleges and Universities." *International Journal of Educational Advancement* 5 no. 2 (2005). 2.4.

> A survey of 105 in-house lobbyists was conducted using a survey used for other lobbying areas, and 20 in-house lobbyists were interviewed. All types of lobbyists felt personal presentations were most effective, but higher education lobbyists differed on their rankings of other tactics. Contact by constituents was second and organizing a public relations campaign was third.

Field, Kimberly Marie. "Engaging Institutional Environments and Alumni Donor Participation Rates: Is There a Linkage?" PhD, Florida State University, 2011. 4.3.

> Based on data from VSE and the National Study of Student Engagement, this thesis studied the relationship between engaging environments and alumni giving, measured in the same year. There was a relationship at baccalaureate colleges, but not at masters or doctoral universities.

Fife, E. Thomas. "Fund-Raising Effectiveness in Selected Community College Foundations." EdD, North Carolina State University, 2004. 1.3, 8.2.

> Community college foundation directors were surveyed using Bass and Avolio's Multifactor Leadership Questionnaire. Few variables, including the leadership ones, were found to be consistent across institutions; exceptions were enrollment and size of fundraising staff. Large colleges received more industry and foundation funds, and small colleges received more funds from individuals.

Filardo, Camille Elizabeth. "Alumni Student-Athletes' Attitudes towards Educational Philanthropy." EdD, University of Southern California, 2003. 4.3, 8.4.

This thesis examined which former student-athletes were most likely to donate. Good students and Division I athletes were most likely to give; income did not predict whether an alumnus gave.

Fincher, David Bradford. "Characteristics and Strategies of Bible College Fund-Raising Letters." PhD, University of Missouri—Columbia, 2003. 1.9, 6.1, 8.8.

Based on three years worth of fundraising letters from accredited Bible colleges, the author found that every strategy from the literature was used in at least some letters, but they did not always use every component. Personalization strategies were the most effective at raising funds.

Fisher, Brian. "Intercollegiate Athletics and College Rankings: An Analysis of the Relationship between Athletic Success and the U.S. News and World Report College Rankings." EdD, Florida International University, 2007. 3.4, 8.4.

This thesis discussed previous research on how athletic success affects applications and fundraising and explored whether success affected *U.S. News* rankings. There was little relationship, although institutions that regularly did well in Division I football tended to rank higher over time.

Fisher, Brian. "Athletics Success and Institutional Rankings." *New Directions for Higher Education* 148 (2009): 45–53. 3.4, 8.4.

This article is based on the author's dissertation, "Intercollegiate Athletics and College Rankings."

Flabiano, Heather Lynn. "Through the Lens of Maslow's Hierarchy: Understanding Endowment Accumulation at Private Colleges and Universities." PhD, University of Texas at Dallas, 2013. 1.15.

IPEDS, *U.S. News*, and National Center for Student Engagement data from 475 private institutions examined whether endowment levels affected financial and nonfinancial benefits. Larger endowments were found to improve the quality of enrolled students and donor loyalty; their effect on faculty quality was mixed.

Flores, Frank Cortez, Jr. "Academic Leadership in Advancement Activities: A Dimension of the Dean's Role in American Higher Education." PhD, Claremont Graduate University, 1993. 6.6, 8.3.

This thesis studied the organization of fundraising in American schools of dentistry via survey and interviews. Deans and development officers reported being involved in fundraising; 88 percent of deans used strategic

Fogerty, Glen. "College Rankings: Impact on MBA Admissions Policy and Practice." PhD, Arizona State University, 2008. 3.4.

planning for fundraising. The annual fund and alumni were the most important campaigns and donors, respectively.

Fogerty, Glen. "College Rankings: Impact on MBA Admissions Policy and Practice." PhD, Arizona State University, 2008. 3.4.

The use of *U.S. News* business school rankings by MBA admissions officers was explored at four schools of business. Admissions officers reported that rankings were important to potential students. Rankings were used to define institutional identity, market institutions, improve programs, and set admissions criteria.

Foley, Christopher R. "Differences in Motivation among High-Capacity Donors." *International Journal of Educational Advancement* 5 no. 3 (2005): 243–55. 1.2.

This study explored why wealthy donors gave at low levels, focusing on motivation variables, based on a survey of donors to the University of Virginia. Results were subject to varimax rotation and seven factors emerged, five of which influenced whether a donor gave high or low gifts: belief in institution, self-fulfillment, relational, and financial.

Foster, Donna Holland. "The Fiber of South Carolina Higher Education Philanthropy: A Historical Case Analysis of James C. Self and the Self Family Foundation." PhD, University of South Carolina, 2012. 1.12, 7.3.

This case study of one family foundation's giving to higher education used Prince and File's seven donor personalities. The Self Family Foundation has given over $14 million to higher education, including Lander College, Furman, The Citadel, and other private institutions in South Carolina.

Foxx, Laura R. "A Qualitative Study of Alumni Non-Donors of Historically Black Colleges and Universities." DM, University of Phoenix, 2013. 4.3.

This qualitative dissertation used snowball sampling to interview nondonors of HBCUs. Major findings included that college choice was determined by family tradition; social cohesion was important in college but participants lost touch after graduation; charitable giving is personal and trust-based; and colleges must communicate better with alumni to receive donations.

Franklin, Christopher. "Something for Everyone: The Marketing and Promotion of Alabama Community Colleges." EdD, University of Alabama Tuscaloosa, 2012. 3.3, 8.2.

Marketing and recruitment at three community colleges was the subject of this dissertation based on documents, focus groups, and interviews. The author found little planning and that institutions used traditional methods rather than innovative ones. This resulted in messages that were not cohesive.

Fraser, Gail E. "Institutionally-Related Foundation Boards: Processes and Perceptions of Performance." EdD, University of Pennsylvania, 2006. 1.3.

The author examined fundraising at the foundations of Kean and East Stroudsburg Universities. She found that factors that influence success on corporate and nonprofit boards also influence foundation boards: board composition, leadership, goal-setting, and opportunities to make meaningful contributions.

Freeman, Tyrone McKinley. "Beyond Hegemony: Reappraising the History of Philanthropy and African-American Higher Education in the Nineteenth Century." *International Journal of Educational Advancement* 10 no. 3 (2010): 148–65. 7.1, 8.1.

This paper used agency theory to reexamine historical fundraising by African Americans at Wilberforce University. While philanthropy for HBCUs has been portrayed as hegemonic and furthering the interests of the status quo, Wilberforce was founded under the auspices of the AME Church and actively fundraised among the African American community.

Frese, Dennis Wayne. "Analysis of Effective Athletic Fundraising Models in the State of California at the Division II, 4-Year College Level." EdD, University of San Francisco, 1995. 1.3, 8.4.

A survey of Division I and II athletic directors found that there was little difference between the attitudes of the two toward fundraising. Both felt it was important and led to athletic success. Other survey questions asked about skills, guidance, goals, donors, and institutional commitment to athletic fundraising.

Friedmann, Anita Story. "Building Communities of Participation through Student Advancement Programs: A First Step toward Relationship Fund Raising." PhD, College of William and Mary, 2003. 4.3.

Through a survey of alumni, interviews, and institutional data, this thesis examined how universities encouraged subsequent alumni donations and participation through student alumni associations and foundations. Using theories of prosocial behavior, communities of participation, and relationship marketing, it was found that students who participated in these activities did have different giving patterns.

Fygetakis, Elaine Christine. "A Study of the Relationship between Student Affairs Offices and University Development Offices in Fund-Raising for Student Extracurricular Activities." PhD, Florida State University, 1992. 1.8, 8.5.

A survey of administrators in development and student affairs at institutions with enrollments of 10,000 or more found that these professionals considered fundraising for student activities to be a joint endeavor. Offices worked either cooperatively or independently but not competitively; greater cooperation led to greater success.

Gaier, Scott E. "The Impact of Alumni Satisfaction with Their Undergraduate Academic Experience on Alumni Giving and Alumni Participation." PhD, Purdue University, 2003. 4.3, 4.5.

A survey of alumni at one institution asked about satisfaction, undergraduate involvement, current involvement, and demographics. Satisfaction with the undergraduate academic experience was correlated with current satisfaction and alumni involvement.

Gaier, Scott E. "Alumni Satisfaction with Their Undergraduate Academic Experience and the Impact on Alumni Giving and Participation." *International Journal of Educational Advancement* 5 no. 4 (2005): 279–88. 4.3, 4.5.

This article is based on the author's dissertation, discussed above.

Garcia, Esmeralda. "Texas Community College Fundraising: Strategies for Meeting Future Financial Needs." PhD, University of Texas at Austin, 2009. 8.2.

The author surveyed presidents and development officers at 50 Texas community colleges and conducted interviews. Smallest colleges had the highest wealth levels. Both coordination and centralization were limited. Effectiveness was correlated with enrollment, location, board/administrative leadership, and grant development.

Gardner, Brian. "The Role of Institutional Relations with Alumni Major Donors in Evangelical Higher Education." PhD, Loyola University Chicago, 2010. 4.3, 8.8.

Members of three Council for Christian Colleges and Universities examined the engagement, motivations, and perceptions of major alumni donors using two-way symmetrical communication and Jeavons and Basinger's theory of evangelical giving. Evidence of both theories was found; motivations and strategies aligned with previous literature.

Garvey, Jason C., and Noah D. Drezner. "Alumni Giving in LGBTQ Communities: Queering Philanthropy." In *Expanding the Donor Base in Higher Education: Engaging Non-Traditional Donors*, edited by Noah D. Drezner, 74–86. New York: Routledge, 2013. 4.3.

The authors argue that researchers and fundraisers need a better understanding of LGBTQ donors. Reasons for and barriers to giving were discussed, along with practitioner strategies.

Gasman, Marybeth. "Charles S. Johnson and Johnnetta Cole: Successful Role Models for Fund-Raising at Historically Black Colleges and Universities." *CASE International Journal of Educational Advancement* 1 no. 3 (2001): 237–51. 7.3, 8.1.

This paper examined the fundraising leadership strategies used by Johnson at Fisk and Cole at Spelman. Both presidents had above-average success at fundraising. Their experience with soliciting alumni donations, reaching white donors, and building fundraising programs were also discussed.

Gasman, Marybeth. "An Untapped Resource: Bringing African Americans into the College and University Giving Process." *CASE International Journal of Educational Advancement* 2 no. 3 (2002a): 280–91. 4.3, 4.5.

This paper discussed black giving patterns and made recommendations for higher education fundraising practitioners seeking to raise funds from black alumni. Black giving tends to focus on community giving, particularly to the church and to racial uplift, and trust is important.

Gasman, Marybeth. "W. E. B. Du Bois and Charles S. Johnson: Differing Views on the Role of Philanthropy in Higher Education." *History of Education Quarterly* 42 no. 4 (2002b): 493–516. 7.3.

In this article, DuBois's views of philanthropy were contrasted with those of Johnson, president of Fisk. DuBois was distrustful of philanthropy, while Johnson embraced it. The views of the two sociologists differed because of personal experience and ideological beliefs.

Gasman, Marybeth. "A Word for Every Occasion: Appeals by John D. Rockefeller, Jr. to White Donors on Behalf of the United Negro College Fund." *History of Higher Education Annual* 22 (2002c): 67–90. 7.3, 8.1.

This rhetorical analysis focused on Rockefeller's appeal letters to white UNCF donors. He positioned the UNCF as an "all-purpose" solution to the country's racial ills. His letters were tailored to the interests of specific donors, even when the beliefs of those donors were antiegalitarian.

Gasman, Marybeth. "Rhetoric vs. Reality: The Fundraising Messages of the United Negro College Fund in the Immediate Aftermath of the Brown Decision." *History of Education Quarterly* 44 no. 1 (2004): 70–94. 1.9, 8.1.

This article examined the response of the UNCF to the *Brown* decision, both supporting integration and HBCUs, as demonstrated in its fundraising appeals. The UNCF emphasized that economic barriers remained to equal education, the role of tradition in choosing to attend an HBCU, and the possibilities of whites attending HBCUs.

Gasman, Marybeth. "The Role of Faculty in Fund Raising at Black Colleges: What Is It and What Can It Become?" *International Journal of Educational Advancement* 5 no. 2 (2005). 6.8, 8.1.

> The role of faculty fundraising at HBCUs was explored. Historically, some faculty members were very involved. Today, they are involved in grant applications and speak to donors, and faculty with administrative roles become more involved.

Gasman, Marybeth. "Truth, Generalizations, and Stigmas: An Analysis of the Media's Coverage of Morris Brown College and Black Colleges Overall." *Review of Black Political Economy* Summer–Fall (2007a): 111–47. 2.3, 8.1.

> This article focused on media discussion of HBCUs, including a content analysis of coverage of Morris Brown College. Morris Brown's financial woes were portrayed within the frames of a general decline of HBCUs, desertion by students, failure, and religious devotion.

Gasman, Marybeth. *Envisioning Black Colleges: A History of the United Negro College Fund*. Baltimore, MD: Johns Hopkins University Press, 2007b. 7.2, 8.1.

> The story of the UNCF from its creation through the twenty-first century is told, based on interviews, oral histories, archival documents, and advertising. The organization's gradual growth from a cautious organization funded by white benefactors to its more empowering incarnation today is discussed.

Gasman, Marybeth. "Swept Under the Rug? A Historiography of Gender and Black Colleges." *American Educational Research Journal* 44 no. 4 (2007c): 760–805. 7.3, 8.1.

> Using an integrative framework that links gender and race, this article brought gender back into discussions of HBCU history. Gasman demonstrated that black women have often been positioned as invisible in previous historical work.

Gasman, Marybeth. "The Origins of the United Negro College Fund as the Cornerstone of Private Black Colleges." *Journal of Blacks in Higher Education* (2007d): 86–89. 7.2, 8.1.

> This article is based on the author's 2007 book, *Envisioning Black Colleges*.

Gasman, Marybeth, and Sibby Anderson-Thompkins, eds. *Fund Raising from Black-College Alumni: Successful Strategies for Supporting Alma Mater*. Washington, DC: Council for the Advancement and Support of Education, 2003. 4.3.

Based on survey research, this book offered advice for fundraisers at HBCUs and PBIs. It emphasized communication, working with a small staff, and understanding African American giving.

Gasman, Marybeth, and Nelson Bowman III. "Engaging and Soliciting African American Alumni." In *Expanding the Donor Base in Higher Education: Engaging Non-Traditional Donors*, edited by Noah D. Drezner, 15–25. New York: Routledge, 2013. 4.3.

The authors provided a literature-based overview of African American giving, including motivations and causes, mistakes institutions make, and how college experience influences the decision to give.

Gasman, Marybeth, and Noah D. Drezner. "White Corporate Philanthropy and Its Support of Private Black Colleges in the 1960s and 1970s." *International Journal of Educational Advancement* 8 no. 2 (2008): 79–92. 1.12, 7.1, 8.1.

This article focused on corporate giving to black colleges, based on papers from the Oram Group, the UNCF, the black oral history collection at Columbia University, and Giving USA. Corporate philanthropy grew in the 1960s, with many donations being given to colleges that companies hired from. Contributions were more likely to be from national corporations than at PWIs.

Gasman, Marybeth, and Noah D. Drezner. "A Maverick in the Field: The Oram Group and Fundraising in the Black College Community during the 1970s." *History of Education Quarterly* 49 no. 4 (2009): 465–500. 7.2, 8.1.

This case study of the Oram Group, a fundraising consultancy, focused on the group's work with HBCUs. Oram was unusual in its belief in the sector and in working with individual colleges rather than consortia or foundations. It is second only to the UNCF in funds raised for black colleges.

Gasman, Marybeth, and Noah D. Drezner. "Fundraising for Black Colleges during the 1960s and the 1970s: The Case of Hampton Institute." *Nonprofit and Voluntary Sector Quarterly* 39 no. 2 (2010): 321–42. 7.2, 8.1.

This article examines the case of Hampton Institute in dealing with the aftermath of the *Brown* decision. It launched its biggest campaigns, moved from foundation to corporate and individual giving, and withdrew from the UNCF. While risky in the short term, these strategies eventually paid off.

Gasman, Marybeth, and Edward Epstein. "Creating an Image for Black Higher Education: A Visual Examination of the United Negro College Fund's Publicity, 1944–1960." *Educational Foundations* 18 no. 2 (2004): 41–61. 1.9, 2.2, 7.2, 8.1.

UNCF publicity was examined in the postwar period focusing on why the organization used very mainstream techniques rather than specifically

African American ones. In part this was to appeal to white audiences as well as to situate HBCUs as players in the patriotic fight against communism.

Gasman, Marybeth, and Katherine V. Sedgwick, eds. *Uplifting a People: African American Philanthropy and Education.* New York: Peter Lang, 2005. 8.1.

This edited volume on African American philanthropy, including volunteering, fundraising, donors, and those who have dedicated their lives to helping others, focused on its historical roots.

Gatewood, A. C. "A Comparative Analysis and Evaluation of Community College Nonprofit Foundations in North Carolina." EdD, North Carolina State University, 1994. 1.1, 8.2.

Based on a survey of North Carolina community college foundations, this thesis described their characteristics, resulting in a list of 10 factors that can be used to evaluate such foundations' fundraising success. These include environmental factors, institutional characteristics, fundraiser characteristics, and institutional organization/effort.

Genovese, Suzanne Kim. "The Inside Story: Non-Alumni Women Philanthropists Connect to Institutions of Higher Education." PhD, Indiana State University, 2009. 1.2.

Based on 10 interviews with nonalumnae major donors to one university, the Revised Theory of Planned Behavior was used to explore how and why these women became donors. The author made recommendations for how institutions can solicit funds from nonalumnae women without immediate personal connections to the institution.

Gentile, Patricia A. "Ensuring the American Dream: Perceptions of New Jersey Community College Presidents on Fundraising as an Alternative Revenue Source to Preserve Access and Affordability." EdD, University of Nebraska—Lincoln, 2009. 1.15, 6.1, 8.2.

This case study of community college presidents used interviews, observation, and document analysis to explore their use of fundraising. While fundraising is a strategy they used, they did not view it as their primary alternative source of revenue. In addition to finding new sources of revenue, presidents also focused on cost-cutting.

German, Steven Dale. "Nonprofit Relationship Marketing: The Role of Identification." PhD, Texas Tech University, 1997. 4.3.

This thesis surveyed alumni of Texas Tech to find out their level of identification with and support of the university and the factors that influenced it. A LISREL model suggested that identification does not completely mediate the exchange model; it is a significant factor in it.

Gernhart, Kelly J. "Financing the Pursuit of Prestige: Finding Relationships between Prestige-Generating Expenses and Changes in USNWR Rank." EdD, University of Kansas, 2009. 3.4.

Using resource dependency and institutional theory, the author tested the effect of prestige-generating expenditures (from IPEDS) and *U.S. News* rankings. Resources devoted to administrative support and infrastructure activities at public institutions led to a change in ranking.

Gerstle, Katherine Marie. "Alumni Reactions to the Use of Prospect Research in Institutional Fund Raising." PhD, State University of New York at Buffalo, 1995. 1.10.

School of management alumni were surveyed regarding prospect research. The majority of respondents were not familiar with it and were worried about confidentiality, although they did not believe it necessarily constituted an invasion of property. They believed potentially damaging information should be kept out of a prospect's file.

Ghazarian, Peter Gregory. "Measuring Quality, Measuring Difference: International Rankings of Higher Education." EdD, Boston University, 2011. 3.4., 5.

In this thesis, the author tried to measure the impact of international rankings in policy-making decisions regarding higher education, with regional comparisons between Europe, east Asia, and Anglo-Saxon countries. One of the most significant impacts was pressure to increase research.

Gianneschi, Matthew Everett. "The Effect of Changes in State Appropriations on Voluntary Giving to State Supported Universities." PhD, University of Arizona, 2004. 1.16.

The effect of state appropriations on voluntary support was explored for 1993–2001. Donors were willing to support higher education when appropriations increased, but their donations did not replace lost funds when appropriations decreased. Donations were primarily restricted, and varied by institutional complexity and prestige.

Gibbons, LeRoy. "Philanthropy in Higher Education: Motivations of Major Donors to Two Utah Universities." EdD, Brigham Young University, 1992. 1.2.

This survey of 150 major donors to two universities asked about their philanthropic motivations. Motivations include institutional mission, respect for institution and its leaders, interest in particular programs, civic pride, tax incentives, and religion,

Gibbs, Annette. "The Role of Environmental Scanning in Effective Fundraising." *New Directions for Higher Education* 94 (1996): 57–67. 1.1.

The author explained why fundraisers should engage in environmental scanning and how it could help various components of a fundraising program.

Gibbs, Paul, and Patrick Murphy. "Ethical Marketing of Higher Education: What Might Be Done to Encourage Its Adoption?" *Higher Education Management and Policy* 21 no. 3 (2009): 75–90. 3.

The authors discussed how marketing can be used by higher education institutions without adopting a consumer orientation, based on Abela and Murphy's ethical tensions of marketing.

Gilmore, Charlotte Ann. "An Analysis of Fund-Raising Activities for the Solicitation of Private Donations at Selected Public Community Colleges." EdD, University of Memphis, 1996. 1.3, 8.2.

A survey of community colleges asked institutions to rank fundraising by category and expenditure. Sources, from largest to smallest, were individual donors, campaigns and events, large businesses, small businesses, and alumni. Spending, from most to least, was on campaigns and events, large businesses, individual donations, small businesses, and alumni.

Glass, J. C., Jr., and K. L. Jackson. "A New Role for Community College Presidents: Private Fund Raiser and Development Team Leader." *Community College Journal of Research and Practice* 24 no. 9 (1998a): 729–44. 6.1, 8.2.

This paper discussed the increasingly large role of the president in community college fundraising, as well as the role of the development team.

Glass, K. C., Jr., and K. L. Jackson. "Integrating Resource Development and Instructional Planning." *Community College Journal of Research and Practice* 22 no. 8 (1998b): 715–39. 7.1, 8.2.

This article compared the history of fundraising at community colleges with that of four-year institutions and explained how fundraising and planning might be integrated at community colleges. Several models of planning were discussed.

Glass, Sheryl Lee. "Women Donors: An Untapped Resource for Community Colleges." EdD, Morgan State University, 2002. 1.2, 8.2.

Based on a survey of female donors to one community college, this thesis presented a demographic and motivational profile of donors. Donors needed to have a connection to the college but were not necessarily alumnae. The typical donor was in her 50s, married, and a college graduate; most were present or past employees of the college.

Goddard, Corday. "Presidential Fundraising at Independent Colleges in the Midwest: A Case Study." PhD, University of Nebraska—Lincoln, 2009. 6.1

> Ten presidents were interviewed about their experiences with fundraising, and three themes emerged: preparation for fundraising came from a variety of experiences; fundraising was not regarded as a "necessary evil"; and presidents regarded fundraising as part of their legacies.

Goering, Elizabeth, Ulla M. Connor, Ed Nagelhout, and Richard Steinberg. "Persuasion in Fundraising Letters: An Interdisciplinary Study." *Nonprofit and Voluntary Sector Quarterly* 40 no. 2 (2009): 228–46. 1.8.

> This paper presented the results of an experiment that asked participants to allocate $100 between two fictional institutions based on fundraising letters. Letters varied by presence/absence of bulleted lists and readability/complexity. Letters with creditability appeals and a high level of readability garnered the highest donations.

Goldgehn, Leslie A. "Generation Who, What, Y? What You Need to Know About Generation Y." *International Journal of Educational Advancement* 5 no. 1 (2004). 1.2.

> The author presented advice on communicating with millennial prospective students, although the advice also applies to millennial alumni. Communication needs to be multichannel and two-way. Image is important, and online interaction is particularly crucial.

Golz, Carolyn. "The Impact of Student Engagement on Alumni Giving." PhD, Chicago School of Professional Psychology, 2013. 4.3.

> This thesis explored the relationship of alumni motivation, using NSSE data, to giving among three recent graduating classes at a SLAC. Enriching educational experiences, supportive campus environments, and being an international student positively influenced amount given and number of donations.

Gonzalez, Sandra Aida. "Latino Alumni Giving at a Major Southwestern University." PhD, University of Texas at Austin, 2003. 4.3.

> A survey of Latino alumni at a PWI and follow-up interviews found that they had the capacity and propensity to engage in alumni giving. While some had negative experiences, for most the positive outweighed the negative. Alumni were concerned about Latino underrepresentation.

Gottfried, Michael A. "College Crowd-in: How Private Donations Positively Affect Alumni Giving." *International Journal of Educational Advancement* 8 no. 2 (2008): 51–70. 4.3.

Using a fixed effects model at three universities over 12 years, the author sought evidence of crowding-in or crowding-out and found the former. Giving by parents, corporations, and foundations all positively influenced alumni giving.

Gottfried, Michael A. "School Urbanicity and Financial Generosity: Can Neighborhood Context Predict Donative Behavior in Spite of the Economy?" *International Journal of Educational Advancement* 9 no. 4 (2010): 220–33. 1.3.

This paper explored the effect urbanicity and other institutional neighborhood characteristics had on alumni, corporate, and foundation giving, using VSE and geospatial data. Only urbanicity was significant for alumni. Neighborhood vacancy rates, the percentage of black residents, and income affected corporate giving. Family size, urbanicity, and vacancy rates affected foundation giving.

Gottfried, Michael A, and Erica L Johnson. "Solicitation and Donation: An Econometric Evaluation of Alumni Generosity in Higher Education." *International Journal of Educational Advancement* 6 no. 4 (2006): 268–81. 4.3.

The authors explored the effect of percentage of alumni solicited on alumni giving using panel data from VSE, *U.S. News*, and the NCAA. The variable had a significant, positive relationship with alumni giving levels, as did endowment and enrollment; winning a bowl game had a significant, negative effect.

Graham, Mary Elizabeth Spring. "Board of Trustees for Public Two-Year Colleges: Perceptions of Fundraising from the Private Sector." PhD, University of Southern Mississippi, 1994. 1.8, 6.2, 8.2.

A survey of 154 board members collected demographic and perceptual data. Demographic (gender, education, years of service, participation in fundraising, and bequests) and institutional characteristics (board size, member selection method, college enrollment, and college budget) were related to perceptions of involvement in fundraising.

Grant, Angelique Sherita Celeste. "Major Gift Donor Stewardship in Higher Education." PhD, Washington State University, 2001. 1.7.

Using major donors at three institutions and the Quality Service Gap Model, the author found gaps in communication at each institution. These gaps reduced perception of stewardship quality.

Grant, Angelique S. C., and Mimi Wolverton. "Gaps in Stewardship Quality and Three Institutions." *International Journal of Educational Advancement* 4 no. 1 (2003): 45–63. 1.7.

This article is based on the author's thesis, "Major Gift Donor Stewardship in Higher Education."

Grant, John, Kathleen Schatzberg, and Wendy Northcross. "The Little College That Could...and Did! A Transformative Model for Small-College Fundraising." *Community College Journal of Research and Practice* 29 no. 8 (2005): 611–13. 1.6.

This case study of Cape Cod Community College's first capital construction campaign focused on the campaign's timing (starting just before September 11, 2001) and the factors that enabled its success: planning, positive public perception, and urgent space needs.

Grant, John L. "Productivity and Equity of Private Fundraising among Public Community Colleges: Does Local Financing Have a Social Capital Effect?" EdD, University of Massachusetts, Boston, 2009. 1.16, 8.2.

This thesis tested the effect of local funding on community college fundraising success using data from IPEDS and tax returns. Being in a wealthy locale with a larger, well-funded foundation with a large board led to fundraising success, but neither state nor local appropriations mattered.

Gray, Nancy. "Understanding Giving at a Successful Community College Foundation." PhD, Colorado State University, 2008. 1.6, 8.2.

Based on interviews, document review, and observations, this thesis explored how stakeholders at a community college saw giving. Communication, collaboration, and commitment mattered.

Greeley, Luke. "Creating an Engagement Model of Advancement for Young Alumni." In *Expanding the Donor Base in Higher Education: Engaging Non-Traditional Donors,* edited by Noah D. Drezner, 187–205. New York: Routledge, 2013. 4.3.

The author discussed the challenge of fundraising from young alumni and with some of the traditional frameworks to explain giving. College student development, he argued, is also alumni development, and should be actively practiced as such.

Green, Cami. "A Profile of Female Trustees at Independent Research I Universities with a Law School and Their Role in Fund-Raising." PhD, Barry University School of Education, 2000. 6.2, 8.2.

This survey of female trustees at 14 universities found that the trustees saw themselves as humanists. They had not been told about a financial commitment when they joined and saw their main role as making policy, including presidential selection and keeping their institutions fiscally sound. They wished to see more women on their boards.

Green, M. L. "Concerns Facing the Virginia Community College System in the Decade of the 1990s." PhD, North Carolina State University, 1994. 8.2.

Delphi technique with presidents, the state board, and state legislators compared their concerns for the two-year system. The three groups mostly agreed on issues, including fiscal, but only presidents were concerned about staff, central office, administration, enrollment, and adjunct faculty.

Griffith, Amanda, and Kevin Rask. "The Influence of the US News and World Report Collegiate Rankings on the Matriculation Decision of High-Ability Students: 1995–2004." *Economics of Education Review* 26 (2007): 244–55. 3.4.

Based on Colgate University Admitted Student Questionnaires, the authors examined the role of *U.S. News* rankings on matriculation decisions. Rank did matter, but it mattered more at higher levels of selectivity and for students receiving financial aid. Rank also mattered independent of other quality measures.

Grimes, P., and G. Chressanthis. "Alumni Contributions to Academics: The Role of Intercollegiate Sports and NCCA Sanctions." *American Journal of Economics and Sociology* 53 no. 1 (1994): 27–40. 4.3.

Thirty years of data from Mississippi State University were used to explore the effects of athletics on alumni giving to academics. Postseason play did not have an effect but television appearances had a positive effect; sanctions possibly had a negative effect.

Grunig, Stephen D. "A Model of Donor Behavior for Law School Alumni." PhD, University of Arizona, 1993. 4.3, 8.3.

This thesis tested factors that influenced alumni giving at 41 law schools using factor analysis. Factors included institutional quality, size, relative advancement effort, and age. Together, these account for 87 percent of variation in the total amount of alumni annual fund revenue.

Grunig, Stephen D. "The Impact of Development Office Structure on Fund-Raising Efficiency for Research and Doctoral Institutions." *Journal of Higher Education* 66 no. 6 (1995): 686–99. 1.1.

Grunig examined whether decentralized fundraising offices raised funds at a lower cost per dollar than centralized offices, based on a survey of universities. The results did not indicate this was the case. Offices with larger staffs and expenditures were more likely to be decentralized.

Gunsalus, Robert. "The Relationship of Institutional Characteristics and Giving Participation Rates of Alumni." *International Journal of Educational Advancement* 5 no. 2 (2005). 1.1, 4.3.

This study looked at institutional characteristics that influenced alumni donation at private masters institutions. Using *U.S. News* data, the best models explained 25 percent of the variation. Most influential were the first-year retention rate, graduation rate, percentage of students who live on campus, tuition, student-faculty ratio, and full-time enrollment.

Gustavsson, Janeric Arne. "Institutional Activities in International Higher Education: An Assessment of Advancement Strategies Used at Selected Small Church-Related Colleges and Universities." PhD, Andrews University, 2000. 1.1, 8.8.

Presidents and governing boards at Seventh-Day Adventist schools were surveyed regarding fundraising practices, compared to Willmer's model. The author found deficiencies in budget allocation and staff size for fundraising, a lack of involvement by presidents and trustees, and no evaluation, but sufficient authority and organization.

Gyllin, John. "Profiles and Giving Patterns of Donors to an Urban Southeastern Community College." EdD, University of Arkansas, 2013. 1.6, 8.2.

This case study of Seminole State College relied on institutional data. Most individual donors were current or former employees who gave small amounts. Most major donors were corporations.

Hagman-Shannon, Deborah A. "Endowed Faculty Positions: Institutional Considerations, Policies and Practices in the 1990s." PhD, Claremont Graduate University, 1993. 1.3, 1.15.

Based on a survey and five case studies, this thesis explored how institutions managed endowed faculty positions. The author found that the number of such positions is growing, and they improve institutions' ability to recruit nationally.

Haire, Constance M., and Laura S. Dodson-Pennington. "Taking the Road Less Traveled: A Journey in Collaborative Resource Development." *Community College Journal of Research & Practice* 26 no. 1 (2002): 61–75. 1.6, 8.2.

Southwestern Community College was used as a case study for how to build meaningful collaborations. SCC had raised over $15 million in grants over four years. The authors state that collaboration requires a supportive culture, long-term partnerships, resource development strategies, and creative projects.

Hall, Josefina S. "An Exploratory Study of Variables Associated with Trust Production during the Cultivation Process of Major Gifts in Higher Education." PhD, University of Iowa, 2003. 1.7.

This exploration of trust was based on interviews with development officers. Institutional trust was crucial in the early stages of donor/officer relationships, with interpersonal trust growing over time. Gifts were unlikely in its absence. Institutional and individual characteristics that engender trust were explored.

Hall, Margarete Rooney. *The Dean's Role in Fund Raising.* Baltimore, MD: Johns Hopkins University Press, 1993. 6.4.

This book examined the increasing role of academic deans in fundraising, discussing both why deans are involved and how to be more effective, and serving as a primer for deans new to fundraising. It also discussed how deans can work with development staff.

Hall, Margarete Rooney. "Building on Relationships: A Fundraising Approach for Community Colleges." *Community College Journal of Research and Practice* 26 no. 1 (2002a): 47–60. 1.7, 8.2.

Fundraising for two-year colleges was discussed in the context of relationship building. Exchange and communal relationships were broken down into components of trust, mutuality of control, satisfaction, and commitment. The author suggested ways colleges can leverage relationships to increase philanthropic support.

Hall, Margarete Rooney. "Fundraising and Public Relations: A Comparison of Programme Concepts and Characteristics." *International Journal of Nonprofit and Voluntary Sector Marketing* 7 no. 4 (2002b): 368–81. 1, 2.

Based on surveys and interviews, this article compared fundraising and public relations. Both were made successful by similar characteristics, including the support of their academic departments; demographics did not influence success. Universities provided appropriate support for public relations.

Hall, Margarete Rooney, and Gail F. Baker. "Public Relations from the Ivory Tower: Comparing Research Universities with Corporate/Business Models." *International Journal of Educational Advancement* 4 no. 2 (2003). 2.1.

Public relations programs at universities were compared with characteristics of excellent business public relations programs. Program leaders believed in those characteristics, although they were not reflected in priorities.

Hall, Zachary David Martin. "An Exploratory Investigation of the Influence of College President Perceptions on Organizational Commitment to Higher Education Marketing at High Performing California Community Colleges." EdD, University of California, Santa Barbara, 2007. 1.9, 6.1, 8.2.

California community colleges were ranked on the Marketing Index for Higher Education, presidential perceptions of marketing were measured with a Q-sort, and semi-structured interviews with chief marketing officers were conducted. Presidential perceptions of marketing contradicted the literature in several ways; marketing officers fell short of the ideal portrayed in the literature.

Hall, Zachary Martin. "Examining Marketing Officers' Demographic Factors' Influence on MIHE Scores at California Community Colleges." *Community College Journal of Research and Practice* 36 no. 2 (2012): 131–45. 3, 6.5.

This article is based on the author's dissertation, "An Exploratory Investigation."

Hammond, Russell E. "Exploring the Why of Volunteer and Philanthropic Commitment at One Community College: Case Study of a Capital Campaign." EdD, Fielding Graduate University, 2012. 1.6, 8.2.

This case study of major donors to a campaign relied on interviews and document review. Four mutually related themes emerged: Heritage philanthropic narratives, association, harmonics, and loyalty. These ideas were similar to Schervish's mobilizing factors for charitable giving theory.

Hancock, Ben E., Jr. "The Role of Philanthropy in the Development of British Universities during the Victorian Period (1851–1919)." PhD, University of Virginia, 2004. 5.2, 5.4, 7.1.

This thesis examined the role of philanthropy in the growth of British universities, particularly in the civic university movement, and the replication of this movement in New Zealand. Lessons for today's UK universities are drawn from this history.

Hanson, Sheila Kay. "Alumni Characteristics That Predict Promoting and Donating to Alma Mater: Implications for Alumni Relations." PhD, University of North Dakota, 2000. 4.3.

A regression model to predict donor/nondonor status was built for UND alumni; it correctly predicted 71 percent of cases. A model to predict giving amount found the following variables significant: income, perception of need, years since graduation, alumni activity attendance, and number of children.

Harasta, Joe. "Town-Gown Relations: University and Neighborhood Leaders' Perceptions of College and Community Relations." EdD, Wilmington University, 2008. 2.5.

This case study relied on interviews with university and community leaders to examine town-gown relations at one university. While both sides wished to improve relations, university and community perceptions about what the university was doing did not match. In addition to off-campus student housing issues, communication between both parties was the major problem.

Harbaugh, William T. "The Prestige Motive for Making Charitable Transfers." *American Economic Review* 88 no. 2 (1998): 277–82. 4.3, 8.3.

Using a framework of intrinsic and prestige benefits for donors, the author examined giving by a law school class over time. His model suggests that donors give in part because they enjoy prestige benefits.

Harris, Michael S. "Institutional Brand Personality and Advertisements during Televised Games." *New Directions for Higher Education* 148 (2009): 23–33. 3.3.

The author examined how institutions branded themselves during football bowl games advertisements using Aaker's five brand personality types. The ads were homogenous, emphasizing success, tradition, and appeal to prospective students, and did not differentiate institutions.

Harris-Vasser, Darlene G. "A Comparative Analysis of the Aspects of Alumni Giving at Public and Private Historically Black Colleges and Universities." EdD, Tennessee State University, 2003. 4.3, 8.1.

A survey of 75 HBCUs asked about alumni giving. Factors that influenced giving included studying business/education, gender, and race; institutional type and type of appeals did not affect giving. Suggestions for effective fundraising were included.

Harrison, William B. "College Relations and Fund-Raising Expenditures: Influencing the Probability of Alumni Giving to Higher Education." *Economics of Education Review* 14 no. 1 (1995): 73–84. 4.3.

Data from 17 institutions (cost of fundraising and college relations and institutional data) were used to build a factor analysis model to predict alumni giving rates. Three factors emerged: Fundraising effort, donor wealth, and institutional resources.

Harrison, W. B., S. K. Mitchell, and S. P. Peterson. "Alumni Donations and Colleges' Development Expenditures: Does Spending Matter?" *American Journal of Economics and Sociology* 54 no. 4 (1995): 397–412. 1.3, 4.3.

Using data from 18 institutions, the authors test the effects of development expenditures on alumni giving. Higher costs were found to increase giving. Other institutional factors that affected giving were the percentage of students in Greek organizations and percentage of part-time students.

Hartman, David E, and Sandra L. Schmidt. "Understanding Student/Alumni Satisfaction from a Consumer's Perspective: The Effects of Institutional

Performance and Program Outcomes." *Research in Higher Education* 36 no. 2 (1995): 197–217. 4.6.

Student and alumni satisfaction was examined within a customer satisfaction framework based on surveys from an undergraduate business school. Factor analysis revealed three factors that comprise satisfaction: communication, personal, and career skills.

Hasseltine, Donald. "Lessons for the Modern Campaign from the University of Virginia." *International Journal of Educational Advancement* 4 no. 1 (2003): 7–16. 1.6.

UVA's first capital campaign served as a case study. The author touched on goal-setting, economic trends, the importance of the quiet phase, and the role of leadership.

Hatfield, Sharon Lynn. "Exploring Entrepreneurialism in Community Colleges in the Appalachian Region." PhD, Old Dominion University, 2010. 1.15, 3, 8.2.

A survey of presidents and workforce development officers at 71 Appalachian community colleges explored entrepreneurial activities, including fundraising, at the colleges. Their rural location made fundraising more difficult.

Hauenstein, Daniel Ross. "Development of Strategic Fund-Raising Theory for Small, 2-Year Public Colleges." EdD, Nova Southeastern University, 2009. 1.3.

The author developed a fundraising effectiveness theory based on surveys and interviews at 31 community colleges. Recommendations included hiring full-time foundation leadership, accurate tracking of cost per dollar raised, the inclusion of fundraising funding in strategic planning, needs assessment, and cost-benefit analysis.

Hawkins, Fanny. "An Analytical Study of the Selection of Development Officers for Institutions of Higher Education." EdD, Texas Southern University, 1995. 6.5.

This thesis was based on a survey of presidents regarding search and selection procedures for development officers. Typical procedures included the use of committees and ads in *The Chronicle of Higher Education.* Common benefits were cars and tuition reimbursement. Honesty and good communication skills were important. Most development officers were predominantly male.

Hazelkorn, Ellen. "The Impact of League Tables and Ranking Systems on Higher Education Decision Making." *Higher Education Management and Policy* 19 no. 2 (2007): 87. 3.4, 5.

The impact of university rankings was explored based on a survey of higher education leaders. 57 percent felt rankings positively influenced their institution, although they did not accurately reflect the entire institution. They recognized that the audience for rankings included students and parents, industry, government, and the general public.

Head, John D. "A Study on the Influences of the 'U.S. News and World Reports': 'America's Best Colleges' Rankings on Policy and Decision-Making at Southern Comprehensive Colleges." EdD, University of Tennessee, 2005. 3.4.

A survey of baccalaureate college presidents asked about their use of *U.S. News* rankings. Tier 1 institutions were most likely to publicize their rank and to state that ranks were accurate. Presidents of institutions in other tiers felt that rankings were important to constituents and that a good ranking was important, but they were more critical of the rankings.

Hebing, Brad L. "Fundraising and Division I-A College Athletics: A Study of Alumnus Affiliation and Gender of Donors." EdD, University of Northern Colorado, 2004. 1.2, 4.3, 8.4.

This thesis explored the alumni status and demographics of donors to athletics at two universities using a survey adopted from the ACQUIRE-II instrument. Analysis of variation found that men were more motivated than women by influencing institutional decisions and loyalty; alumni were more motivated than nonalumni by loyalty.

Helmsley-Brown, Jane, and Izhar Oplatka. "Universities in a Competitive Global Marketplace: A Systematic Review of the Literature on Higher Education Marketing." *International Journal of Public Sector Management* 19 no. 4 (2006): 316–38. 3.

This literature review, now slightly dated, provided a good overview of international higher education marketing research. Extant research was found to be incoherent and atheoretical.

Hendrix-Kral, Constance L. "Capital Campaigns: Implications for Fund Raising for Student Affairs Divisions in Public Universities." EdD, University of Arkansas, 1995. 1.1, 8.5.

Surveys explored the roles of capital campaigns in student affairs fundraising. Campaigns were found to have little impact on student affairs fundraising capacity, in part because it was typically not a major campaign goal and in part because student affairs rarely had a full-time development officer.

Hennes, Dianne Tindall. "The Century II Capital Campaign of the University of St. Thomas: Catalyst for Change, 1983–1991." EdD, University of St. Thomas (Minnesota), 1993. 1.6.

This qualitative case study of a capital campaign explored the growth of the university under the president of 25 years and the role of the campaign in supporting that growth. While the campaign relieved some tensions caused by growth, it did not address them all.

Herbkersman, Neil, and Karla Hibbert-Jones. "Grants Development in Community Colleges." *New Directions for Community Colleges* 124 (2003): 63–73. doi: 10.1002/cc.135. 1.12, 8.2.

This article explored the role of grants and the grants office in community colleges, including a case study of Sinclair Community College. A successful grants office requires institutional commitment, a strategic structure, clear roles and procedures, and high-performing personnel.

Herley, Wade Thomas. "Public Higher Education Fundraising: Selected Florida University Leaders' Perceptions of Influences of Large Gifts." EdD, University of South Dakota, 2012. 1.8.

Based on five interviews with top leaders at four Florida universities, this thesis explored the role of major donors. Important issues were communication, leadership, and alignment.

Herrmann, Janet C. Lukomski. "An Examination of the Interaction between the Offices of Public Affairs and Fund Raising at Public Universities and Its Enhancement of the Fund Raising Efforts." PhD, The Union Institute, 1994. 1.1, 2.2.

Four universities served as the basis for this examination of the interaction between fundraising and public affairs offices. Two institutions had above-average interaction, one had below-average interaction, and one had none. Interaction was found to positively affect fundraising.

Heyes, Anthony G., and Catherine Liston-Heyes. "Brand Management in US Business Schools; Can Yale Learn from Harvard?" *International Journal of Educational Advancement* 5 no. 1 (2004). 3.3.

The authors used Data Envelopment Analysis to evaluate the efficiency of business schools in maximizing their reputation among recruiters and the academic community. Schools were ranked by the extent to which they perform well or underperform. Data was taken from *U.S. News*.

Heyns, Erla Petronette. "Fund Raising in Publicly Supported Academic Libraries of Institutions Belonging to the National Association of State Universities and Land-Grant Colleges." PhD, Indiana University, 1994. 1.3, 8.7.

This thesis compared fundraising success at academic libraries using the models of Pickett and Hunter and survey data. Based on the results, the theoretical model was revised.

Higgins, Leanne B. "Perceptions of Young Alumni toward Annual Giving at the University of Delaware." EdD, University of Delaware, 2000. 4.3.

> Twenty-seven donors and twenty nondonors who graduated in the past five years, as well as administrators, were interviewed regarding their perceptions, attitudes, and beliefs regarding UD and its annual campaign. Most were satisfied about the amount of communication the university engaged in, but they wished it was more personalized.

Hilbun, Ashlie Junot. "Liberal Arts Colleges during the Great Recession: Examining Organizational Adaptation and Institutional Change." EdD, University of Arkansas, 2013. 1.8.

> Case studies of three SLACs were built on interviews, documents, and observations to understand how they responded to the 2007 recession. While not focused on advancement exclusively, problems discussed in this thesis included poor endowment returns and solutions included fundraising.

Hiles, Thomas S. "Determining the Success of Fundraising Programs." *New Directions for Higher Education* 149 (2010): 51–56. 1.14.

> This article provided an overview of methods of evaluating fundraising, including the differences between new and established programs. Methods included traditional quantitative metrics, subjective judgments, and information sharing.

Hillman, Jan. "An Investigation of the Current Status of Fundraising Activities and Training within Student Affairs Divisions in Texas Colleges and Universities." EdD, University of North Texas, 2002. 1.1, 8.5.

> Based on a survey of development and student affairs professionals, 62 percent of chief student affairs officers were involved in fundraising. 18 percent had a dedicated fundraising officer and 30 percent had a shared fundraising officer. Most respondents viewed the two offices as cooperative rather than competitive.

Hixson, Nancy C. "Million Dollar Plus Donors within Intercollegiate Athletics: A Qualitative Analysis of Donor Motivations." PhD, University of Northern Colorado, 2012. 1.2, 8.4.

> Interviews with $100,000-plus donors to Division I athletics found that these donors had a history of philanthropy, donated for intrinsic reasons, were concerned about sustainable giving, and were focused on quality rather than simply on winning. The author noted that these motivations are similar to those of smaller donors.

Hodson, J. Bradford. "Leading the Way: The Role of Presidents and Academic Deans in Fundraising." *New Directions for Higher Education* 149 (2010): 39–49. 6.1, 6.6.

This article focused on the role of presidents and deans in soliciting major gifts. The president's responsibilities as "fundraiser in chief" were broken down. Deans' roles are similar, although their role in fundraising is more recent. The author suggested using advisor boards, making time to fundraise, and working with fundraisers.

Hodson, J. Bradford, and Bruce W. Speck. "Perspectives on Fund Raising." *New Directions for Higher Education* 98 no. 149 (2010). 1.

This volume of *New Directions* included nine articles on best practices in higher education fundraising. Each individual article is listed separately in this section.

Holland, Andrea Priscilla Wisenbaker. "Faculty Motivations for Giving to Their Employing Institutions." EdD, University of Alabama, 1997. 1.2, 6.8.

Full-time faculties at three public universities were surveyed regarding their motivations for donating to their employer. Five of the six motives (conviction, self-fulfillment, celebration, attachment, and mission) were found to vary in a significant manner between institutions. Respondents were more motivated by mailings than phone calls or visits.

Holloman, Darryl B., Marybeth Gasman, and Sibby Anderson-Thompkins. "Motivations for Philanthropic Giving in the African American Church: Implications for Black College Fundraising." *Journal of Research on Christian Education* 12 no. 2 (2003): 137–69. 1.2, 8.1.

Based on the historical and current role of the church in African American giving and interviews with HBCU alumni, the authors explored the similarities and differences between giving to one's church and one's alma mater. Participants noted their colleges did not discuss philanthropy with students. Given low alumni giving rates, the authors recommend HBCUs emulate church fundraising practices.

Holmes, Jessica. "Prestige, Charitable Deductions and Other Determinants of Alumni Giving: Evidence from a Highly Selective Liberal Arts College." *Economics of Education Review* 28 (2009): 18–28. 4.3.

The author used 15 years of alumni giving data from Middlebury College to explore factors influencing donations. States that allow charitable tax deductions, collegiate athletic success, being female, living in a wealth neighborhood near the college, and having alumni relatives positively influenced giving; increased academic prestige decreased giving. Alumni major and occupation also affected giving.

Holmes, Jessica A., James A. Meditz, and Paul M. Sommers. "Athletics and Alumni Giving: Evidence from a Highly Selective Liberal Arts College." *Journal of Sports Economics* 9 no. 5 (2008): 538–52. 4.3, 8.4.

Fifteen years of alumni giving data from Middlebury College were used to test the influence of athletics in giving. Athletes were more likely to give, particularly younger athletes in high-profile sports (football and men's hockey). Winning seasons led to greater and larger alumni giving.

Holmes, Robert J. "The Challenge of Funding Fundraising." *New Directions for Higher Education* 149 (2010): 27–37. 1.1.

This article discussed the pros and cons of various sources of funding for fundraising foundations, including institutional support, gifts, endowment and gift fees, temporary investment earnings, and real-estate revenue.

Holquist, Gary W. "Identifying Key Determinants That Influence Athletic Alumni Intent to Give Financially to Intercollegiate Athletic Department Fundraising Campaigns." EdD, University of Minnesota, 2011. 4.3, 8.4.

A survey of University of Minnesota Duluth former athlete alumni asked about demographics and philanthropic motivation for giving to athletics. Altruism, organizational identification, social identification, utility satisfaction, receiving services, and relationship marketing were the models explored; the first four each played a role.

Honeyman, D. S., J. L. Wattenbarger, Jr., and K. C. Westbrook, eds. *A Struggle to Survive: Funding Higher Education in the Next Century, Yearbook of the American Education Finance Association*. Thousand Oaks, CA: Corwin Press, 1996. 1.16.

This ten-chapter edited volume on higher education finance was not focused on advancement, but it included discussions of investment returns, patterns of community college support, and competition for resources.

Hopkins, Linda Rovtar. "An Analysis of the Relationships of Selected Variables and the Financial Support Provided to Comprehensive Coeducational Catholic Colleges and Universities by Their Alumnae." PhD, University of Pennsylvania, 1998. 4.3, 8.8.

A survey of Catholic comprehensive university alumnae used Burnett and Wood's Donation Decision Process to explore factors influencing giving. Five age cohorts had different preferences and campus experiences. 1930s/1940s alumnae preferred being solicited by women; 1950s alumnae preferred in-person solicitation and required spousal permission to give. Alumnae from the 1930s, 1940s, 1980s, and 1990s wished to see stronger female representation.

Horgan, Thomas R. "Higher Education Consortia: Raising Aspirations through Collaboration." *New Directions for Philanthropic Fundraising* 40 (2003): 65–77. 1.1.

Fundraising consortia were discussed, including their history, realism in mission, the importance of infrastructure, leadership, and staffing. The Claremont Colleges, founded in 1925, were one of the earliest consortia, but the number of consortia grew in the 1960s.

Horrigan, David Wayne. "Integrated Marketing Communications in Higher Education." PhD, University of Connecticut, 2007. 3.2.

This case study of one university examined its integrated marketing communications program and its attempts to reposition itself, including coordination, data collection, market segmentation, relationship building, branding, return on investment, performance measurement, budgets, and leadership.

Hossler, Don, and Erin M. Foley. "Reducing the noise in the college choice process: The use of college guidebooks and ratings." *New Directions for Institutional Research* 88 (1995): 21–30. doi: 10.1002/ir.37019958804. 3.4.

The author reviewed the research on the effect of rankings on the college choice process and found that guidebooks and ratings had very small effects on enrollment decisions.

Hou, Angela Yung-Chi, Robert Morse, and E. Shao Yueh-jen. "Is There a Gap Between Students' Preference and University Presidents' Concern Over College Ranking Indicators? A Case Study of 'College Navigator in Taiwan.'" *Higher Education* 64 no. 6 (2012): 767–87. 3.4.

This paper compared students' and presidents' uses of a ranking system that allowed students to personalize rankings based on focus groups with students and a survey of presidents. Students were more interested in learning inputs; presidents focused on research.

Hou, Angela Yung-Chi, Robert Morse, and Chung-Lin Chiang. "An Analysis of Mobility in Global Rankings: Making Institutional Strategic Plans and Positioning for Building World-Class Universities." *Higher Education Research & Development* 31 no. 6 (2012): 841–57. 3.4.

The authors examined four international university rankings to determine what factors most influenced institution mobility using K-means clustering. The factors that influenced moving into the top 100 varied. Of those that are relatively easy to influence, awards, size, peer and employer review, and citations mattered most.

Howard, G. Daniel. "Analysis of What Constitutes Productive Case Statements for Higher Education Capital Campaigns." PhD, Indiana University, 1993. 1.9.

Qualitative analysis of 20 campaign case statement and a supplemental survey found that these statement resembled Fortune 500 annual reports, with college-level language that was positive and optimistic. Length varied. All included specific monetary goals and clear spending priorities.

Hueston, F. R. "Predicting Alumni Giving: A Donor Analysis Test." *Fund Raising Management* 23 (1992): 18–23. 4.3.

The methodology and results of creating a model to discriminate between likely alumni donors and nondonors to New Mexico State University were presented. Factors that influenced higher probabilities included graduation from the college of engineering and being over 45 years of age; however, some commonly accepted factors were not stored in the university's database.

Hull, Mimi Stockover. "Corporate Fund-Raising Strategies in Public Community Colleges." EdD, University of Virginia, 2004. 1.12, 8.2.

A survey of 43 community college chief advancement officers sought to discover the extent to which they agreed upon factors influencing fundraising success and whether they used them. They agreed on what practices were effective, but they were unable to engage corporate and institutional leaders as much as they wished.

Humphreys, Brad R., and Michael Mondello. "Intercollegiate Athletic Success and Donations at NCAA Division I Institutions." *Journal of Sport Management* 21 no. 2 (2007). 1.3, 8.4.

This article explored the effect of football bowl game and Division I postseason tournament participation on fundraising success, using IPEDS and NCAA data. Both increased restricted (but not unrestricted) giving to public institutions the following year; only basketball success affected restricted giving at private institutions.

Hunter, Bruce. 1995. "College guidebooks: Background and development." *New Directions for Institutional Research* 88 (1995): 5–12. doi: 10.1002/ir.37019958802. 3.4.

The author provided an overview of the history of guidebooks, different types, their impact on colleges and students, and trends in them.

Hunter, Catrelia Steele. "A Study of the Relationships between Alumni Giving and Selected Characteristics of Alumni Donors of Livingstone College." EdD, Fayetteville State University, 1997. 4.3, 8.1.

Alumni of an HBCU were surveyed and major alumni donors at similar institution were interviewed to explore what factors influenced giving and how giving could be increased. Factors influencing giving included some demographic variables as well as beliefs in adequate career preparation, in mission, and that HBCUs are still needed.

Hunter, Catrelia S., Enid B. Jones, and Charlotte Boger. "A Study of the Relationship between Alumni Giving and Selected Characteristics of Alumni Donors of Livingstone College, NC." *Journal of Black Studies* 29 no. 4 (1999): 523–39. 4.3, 8.1.

This paper is based on Hunter's dissertation, discussed above.

Hurst, Frederick Matthew. "Philanthropic Giving Preference Differences: Nontraditional and Traditional Alumni at Northern Arizona University." PhD, Union Institute and University, 2008. 4.3.

A survey sought to compare traditional and nontraditional alumni giving at NAU. The two groups made similar numbers of donations of similar sizes and were involved with NAU at similar rates. Nontraditional alumni who took most courses off-campus were less interested in giving to scholarships for traditional students, students in their major, faculty funding, new buildings or renovations, and research.

Hurvitz, Lori A. "Building a Culture of Student Philanthropy: A Study of the Ivy-Plus Institutions' Philanthropy Education Initiatives." PhD, University of Pennsylvania, 2010. 4.3.

This qualitative study used student development theory to examine student philanthropy initiatives at Ivy Plus institutions. The author found that these initiatives should be part of a long-term strategy and congruent with campus culture. Early results show increased senior class giving rates.

Hurvitz, Lori A. "Building a Culture of Student Philanthropy." In *Expanding the Donor Base in Higher Education: Engaging Non-Traditional Donors*, edited by Noah D. Drezner, 138–51. New York: Routledge, 2013. 4.3.

This chapter is based on the author's dissertation, above.

Hyre, Jimenez. "A Study of the Attitudes of Faculty toward Marketing Programs at Northeastern Ohio Institutions of Higher Education and the Extent of Faculty Participation in Marketing Programs." EdD, University of Akron, 1991. 3.

Four-year colleges and universities were surveyed about their marketing practices and faculty attitudes toward them. Faculty members were positively disposed toward the marketing practices used (audits, marketing offices, consultants, consulting with marketing faculty, formal plans congruent with strategic plans, environmental analysis, and promotional tools), although faculty at private institutions were more involved.

Iarrobino, Jon D. "Turnover in the Advancement Profession." *International Journal of Educational Advancement* 6 no. 2 (2006): 141–69. 6.5.

Advancement office turnover was explored through a case study of a small college with a high turnover rate, which impacted fundraising. Topics discussed included the roles of positive and latent stakeholders, the costs of turnover, and advice to reduce turnover.

Ikenberry, John P. "Alumni Institutional Commitment: Connecting Student Involvement with Alumni Involvement and Institutional Commitment." PhD, Pennsylvania State University, 1999. 4.3.

Based on Tinto's model of student departure and data from Penn State, the author built a model to predict alumni association membership based on undergraduate experiences. Predictors of current membership included social involvement, past membership, and formal and informal alumni involvement. Time since graduation and location had negative effects on membership.

Ingram, Kathleen W., Linda L. Haynes, Gayle V. Davidson-Shivers, and Richard Irvin. "Building an Alumni Support Community: Tracking Alumni for Program Evaluation and Added Value." *College Student Journal* 39 no. 2 (2005). 4.5.

This paper documented efforts to build an alumni tracking system for an instructional design program, including a survey of alumni. Alumni indicated a desire to remain connected and preferred to be contacted via email.

Iqbal, Muhammad Jawad, Amran Bin Md. Rasli, and Ibne Hassan. "University Branding: A Myth or a Reality." *Pakistan Journal of Commerce & Social Sciences* 6 no. 1 (2012): 168–84. 3.3, 5.3.

Students from several countries were interviewed about their preferences in selecting a university to discover whether marketing constructs were being used in image development. Quality was the strongest construct, followed by prestige, financial incentives, and acceptance.

Ironfield, Elaine B. "Characteristics of Two-Year Public Colleges and Foundations with Successful Fund-Raising Programs." EdD, University of Massachusetts Amherst, 1991. 1.3, 8.2.

A survey of 72 community colleges asked about support for their foundations; highly successful institutions were interviewed. Sixty-one institutions had foundations. Both financial inputs and service area size positively influenced funds raised, as did presidential involvement and clerical/professional support.

Isaacson, Thomas E. "Evaluating the Crisis Response Strategies of a University Basketball Program: How Do Reactions Differ Based on Apologies, Crisis Severity, and Team Identification?" PhD, Michigan State University, 2012. 2.6.

Using Situational Crisis Communication Theory, students evaluated institutional responses to a crisis involving basketball team members. Corrective action, crisis severity, and team identification all influenced responses. Apologies were not always necessary, even when SCCT recommended them.

Iveson, Jon L. "Motivations behind Donations to Intercollegiate Athletics: A Case Study of a Mid-Western University." PhD, Ohio State University, 2000. 1.2, 8.4.

Factor analysis was conducted based on a survey of donors, utilizing Verner, Hecht, and Fansler's Motives of Athletic Donors and Mael and Ashforth's scale. Factors varied for donors based on their donation level (power/influence, benefits/reward) and gender (power/influence, benefits/rewards, and achievement). Organizational identification had little influence.

Jackowski, Mick Felix. "Toward a Quantitative Evaluation Model of Public Relations in Sport: Combining the Situational Theory of Publics and the Coorientation Model of Relationships to Identify Alumni Fundraising Publics and the Levels of Symmetry between These Publics and a Graduate Sport Management Program." EdD, University of Northern Colorado, 1998. 4.3, 8.7.

A survey of sport management program alumni (aware, latent, and active publics) and faculty/administrators in the program found that alumni felt less strongly than faculty and administrators that additional funding was needed. The majority of the alumni were aware (65%), and only members of the active public (13%) are likely to donate.

Jackson, K., and J. Glass. "Emerging Trends and Critical Issues Affecting Private Fund-Raising among Community Colleges." *Community College Journal of Research and Practice* 24 no. 9 (2000): 729–44. 8.2.

This paper is based on Jackson's thesis, discussed below.

Jackson, Karen Luke. "Emerging Trends and Critical Issues Impacting Private Fund Raising by North Carolina Community Colleges." EdD, North Carolina State University, 1997. 8.2.

This thesis used Delphi technique with 42 community college development officers to discover what current issues were impacting fundraising and what they anticipated would emerge in the next five years. Issues related to business and industry and image were most important.

Jaeger, Charlene Kay. "An Assessment of Factors Related to Successful Parent Fund-Raising Programs." EdD, University of Delaware, 1994. 1.3.

A survey of 44 colleges and universities and a document review explored approaches to parent fundraising. Institutions with high gifts per FTE sent personalized, focused letters; focused on mission; used special stationary; and sent four to six mailings per year. Factors affecting success included number of years of solicitation, varying by prospect level, using high-tech telemarketing equipment, and involving the president.

James, Russell N. "Charitable Estate Planning and Subsequent Wealth Accumulation: Why Percentage Gifts May Be Worth More Than We Thought." *International Journal of Educational Advancement* 10 no. 1 (2010): 24–32. 1.5.

The authors used data from the 1996–2005 Health and Retirement Study to compare wealth accumulation of those with and without charitable estate plans. Those with plans accumulated 50–100 percent more than those without, suggesting that traditional estimates of the value of percentage-based planned gifts are too low.

James, Russell N., and Pamala Wiepking. "A Comparative Analysis of Educational Donors in the Netherlands." *International Journal of Educational Advancement* 8 no. 2 (2008): 71–78. 5.6.

Using data from the Netherlands Panel Survey, the authors compared donors to education to donors to other causes and nondonors. Donors to education gave larger gifts than donors to religion or other causes, but gifts were smaller than in the United States. The authors speculated that, in the absence of well-developed fundraising programs, most Dutch gifts go to extracurricular activities.

Janney, Scott R. P. "The College President and Fund Raising Effectiveness." EdD, Temple University, 1994. 1.3, 6.1.

Based on a survey of 27 presidents at Christian College Coalition institutions and VSE data, the effect of presidential style were regressed on dollars raised per student. An open administrative style was significant but commitment to higher education was not.

Jenkins, L., and J. Glass. "Inception, Growth, and Development of a Community College Foundation: Lessons to Be Learned." *Community College Journal of Research and Practice* 23 no. 6 (1999): 595. 1.6, 8.2.

This article was based on Jenkins' thesis, discussed next.

Jenkins, Larry William. "Inception, Growth, and Development of a Community College Foundation: A Case Study." EdD, North Carolina State University, 1997. 1.6, 8.2.

This thesis looked at the founding of one community college foundation as a case study, using document review, observations, and interviews. The foundation was established to serve as a role model for other colleges, with the president and two trustees playing key roles. Another college's foundation and experience with the Association of Community College Trustees provided models.

Johnsen, Barbara Anne. "Creative Fund Raising Efforts in Three Virginia Community Colleges." EdD, College of William and Mary, 1995. 1.3, 8.2.

Based on a questionnaire of Virginia community colleges and case studies of three of them, the author compared fundraising practice to the models of Duronio and Loessin and of Kerns and Witter. The author found that the ten characteristics were present. In particular, a clear image, a professional fundraising office, and good communication led to fundraising success.

Johnsen, Lance Loren. "Understanding Deliberative Conflicts That Confront Academic Fund Raisers: A Grounded Theory Study." EdD, Arizona State University, 2005. 1.10.

Four academic fundraisers were interviewed to produce 22 deliberative conflicts, situations in which more than one resolution was attractive. Fundraisers attempted to resolve these conflicts by considering their responsibilities to the donor, their responsibilities to the institution, and conflicting responsibilities.

Johnson, Elizabeth Ann Miller. "Factors Associated with Non-Traditional and Traditional Undergraduate Alumni Giving to Alma Maters." PhD, Mercer University, 2013. 4.3.

Based on a survey of alumni from 101 institutions, giving by nontraditional and traditional alumni was compared. Traditional alumni gave more frequently. Factors that increased the chances of giving were being female, undergraduate participation in career or community service activities, identifying jobs for undergraduates, and attending athletic events.

Johnson, J. W., and P. D. Eckel. "Preparing Seniors for Roles as Active Alumni." In *The Senior Year Experience: Facilitating Integration, Reflection, Closure, and Transition*, edited by J. N. Gardner and G. VanDerVeer, 227–42. San Francisco: Jossey-Bass, 1997. 4.5.

This chapter from an edited volume focused on best practices for transitioning students to active, involved alumni.

Johnstone, D. Bruce. "A Political Culture of Giving and the Philanthropic Support of Public Higher Education in International Perspective." *International Journal of Educational Advancement* 5 no. 3 (2005): 256–63. 1.16, 5.

Successful advancement, the author argued, requires more than favorable tax laws; it also requires a political culture that accepts that parents and students should share in the cost of education. The failure of advancement to receive traction in many countries may be because of this.

Jones, Joree D. "Determining Factors Influencing the Propensity of Philanthropic Support of Alabama's Community Colleges." PhD, University of Alabama, 2007. 1.3, 8.2.

Based on interviews with potential donors and constituents of Alabama community colleges, this thesis explored attitudes toward those colleges and potential barriers to giving.

Jones, Para M. "Exploring Factors That Impact Success in Community College Fundraising." PhD, University of Nebraska—Lincoln, 2008. 1.3, 8.2.

Interviews with 12 community college chief development officers were the basis for collating strategies that lead to successful fundraising. CDOs believed that institutional commitment, presidential involvement, and cultivation of individual donors were necessary for success.

Jones, Thomas Oliver. "An Institutional Advancement Model for a Church-Related College or University." EdD, Pepperdine University, 1991. 1.1, 8.8.

This thesis put forth a model for successful fundraising based on a literature review, a survey of college presidents, and interviews. The advancement model focused on the organizational hierarchy, specific advancement programs, and evaluation. Out of 23 characteristics and components of the model, all but 4 were supported by the presidents.

Joyce, Mary L., David R. Lambert, and Harlan E. Spotts. "Reflections on Integrated Marketing Communication As Higher Education Marketing Practice Enters the Twentieth Century." *CASE International Journal of Educational Advancement* 1 no. 2 (2000). 3.2.

The authors argued that Integrated Marketing Communications is not new and adds little value to traditional marketing concepts. IMC is only one part of marketing, they stated, and institutions should not mistake it for the entire field.

Kaiser, Sara, and Amy Wells Dolan. "Women as a Donor Group to Higher Education." In *Expanding the Donor Base in Higher Education: Engaging Non-Traditional Donors*, edited by Noah D. Drezner, 61–73. New York: Routledge, 2013. 1.2.

Women have traditionally not been as involved with higher education philanthropy as men, although that is changing. The authors stressed the importance of relationships and bequests for female donors, and discussed issues of who makes philanthropic decisions in families.

Karns, William Vernon. "The Transitional Considerations of Traditional Potential Community College Presidents: Fundraising and Other Concerns." EdD, University of California, Davis, 2008. 6.1, 8.2.

Ten vice presidents who were considering college presidencies were interviewed about their attitudes toward fundraising and other transitional considerations. The interviewees considered fundraising to be a negative and did not think they would be good at it, but they did not consider it to be a major problem.

Karsevar, Kent J. "Fundraising Practices of the University of California, the California State University, and California Private Universities." EdD, California State University, Fresno, 2012. 1.1.

A survey of advancement personnel and interviews with university presidents compared successful fundraising across UC, CSU, and private institutions. Differences were found in grant writing, corporate sponsorship, direct mail, and campus campaigns. All presidents spent at least one-third of their time on fundraising.

Keene, Anne. "Then and Now: Oxford Women Principals 1879–1920 as Exemplars for the Twenty-First Century Advancement Profession." *CASE International Journal of Educational Advancement* 2 no. 2 (2001): 114–24. 5.2, 6.6, 7.2.

The heads of Oxford women's colleges in this era were involved in activities such as alumni relations and soliciting donations.

Keene, Anne. "An Academic Business: Meeting of Minds at the Interface of Education and Enterprise." *CASE International Journal of Educational Advancement* 3 no. 3 (2003): 268–77. 1.12, 5.2.

Partnerships between business and academia are still new in the United Kingdom. This paper explored partnerships in business schools and business influences in academia and their implications for advancement.

Keener, Barbara J., Sharon M. Carrier, and Sherry J. Meaders. "Resource Development in Community Colleges: A National Overview." *Community College Journal of Research and Practice* 26 no. 1 (2002): 7–23. 8.2.

A nationwide survey of community colleges collected descriptive data on institutional fundraising. The oldest foundation was established in the 1940s, with the majority born in the 1970s and 1980s. The typical grant office was established in the 1990s. Foundation offices had larger staffs than grants offices; budgets and staff sizes varied by size and urbanicity.

Keith, Bruce. "The Institutional Context of Departmental Prestige in American Higher Education." *American Educational Research Journal* 36 no. 3 (1999): 409–45. 3.4.

This study examined three rankings of individual doctoral programs and found that peer ratings reflected the prestige of the university rather than the individual program. Further, over time ratings were quite stable.

Kelleher, Lisa Ann. "Alumni Participation: An Investigation Using Relationship Marketing Principles." PhD, University of Nevada, Las Vegas, 2011. 4.5.

Via interviews with alumni relations officers and reviews of websites and documents at four institutions, the author explored the extent to which alumni relations officers used relationship marketing principles. Each officer approached alumni relations with a different mix of programs and principles, although each considered relationships.

Kelley, Margaret Northern. "Institutionally Related Foundations at Public Colleges and Universities." EdD, University of Tennessee, 1999. 1.1.

Foundations at four-year public institutions were surveyed regarding their structure and activities. Nearly all had an executive director that was not a voting board member; many also reported to the institutional president. Foundations received some funds from the state, but most also charged fees. Boards were responsible for investments and cooperated with institutional presidents in priority-setting.

Kellogg, Karen Ondercin. "An Analysis of the Collaborative Programming between Student Affairs and Alumni Relations Professionals at Select Postsecondary Institutions in Missouri." PhD, University of Missouri—Columbia, 1996. 1.1, 8.5.

Collaboration between student affairs and alumni relations professionals was investigated via interviews, surveys, and document analysis. Respondents indicated collaborative experiences were positive, allowing alumni to interact more with students and savings costs via resource-sharing.

Kelly, Kathleen S. *Fund Raising and Public Relations: A Critical Analysis*. Hillsdale, NJ: Lawrence Erlbaum Associates, 1991. 1.4, 2.

In this landmark book, Kelly argued that fundraising was a subset of public relations, and grounded it theoretically in communications. When regarded as separate from public relations, she argued, it begins to encroach on public relations' proper role.

Kelly, Kathleen S. "Fundraising Encroachment on Public Relations: A Clear and Present Danger to Effective Trustee Leadership." *Nonprofit Management and Leadership* 4 no. 1 (1993): 47–68. 1.1, 1, 6.2.

Kelly conducted a national survey to document fundraising encroachment on public relations. Twenty-three percent reported structural encroachment. Forty percent agreed that fundraisers had more policy influence than public relations officers did.

Kelly, Kathleen S. *Effective Fund-Raising Management.* Hillsdale, NJ: Erlbaum, 1998. 1.3.

Written as a textbook for current and future fundraisers and grounded in research, this book addressed fundraising generally rather than higher education fundraising specifically. It included a historical overview, definitions, best practices, discussions of major fundraising program components, and suggestions for future research.

Kemper, Ann L., Catherine W. Rosenkrans, and Kim Leeder. "There When They Need Us: Library as Fundraiser and Campus Community Builder." *Journal of Library Administration* 53 (2013): 380–89. 1.6, 8.7.

This case study of a community college library that got involved in fundraising discusses how it raised funds for an endowed memorial scholarship. Funds were raised through many small donations via events and contests.

Kenton, Carol Piper, Mary E. Huba, John H. Schuh, and Mack C. II Shelley. "Financing Community Colleges: A Longitudinal Study of 11 States." *Community College Journal of Research and Practice* 29 no. 2 (2005): 109–22. 1.16, 8.2.

IPEDS data was used to demonstrate that reliance on tuition and fees grew while state appropriates declined. Fundraising, grants, and endowments provided little alternative revenue.

Kessels, Joop M. M., and Hans Ruijgers. "Benchmarking on Organization of Communications: University versus Private Companies." *CASE International Journal of Educational Advancement* 3 no. 3 (2003): 200–10. 2.1, 5.6.

Two universities (Utrecht University and a peer) and four private companies were benchmarked on strategic planning and experience in communications. The universities ranked last.

Khashan, Hilal. "How Grantees Relate to Grantor: A Study on a Lebanese College Scholarship Foundation." *Research in Higher Education* 33 no. 2 (1992): 41–59. 1.6, 1.12, 5.6.

This case study of a foundation that provided support to American University of Beirut students and 400 grant recipients found that the foundation was subject to external pressures that influenced the selection of grantees. In addition, grant recipients indicated a lack of professionalism from the foundation and did not wish to express appreciation for their grant monies.

Kimball, Bruce A., and Benjamin Ashby Johnson. "The Beginning of 'Free Money' Ideology in American Universities: Charles W. Eliot at Harvard, 1869–1909." *History of Education Quarterly* 52 no. 2 (2012): 222–50. 7.3.

Kimball and Johnson explored how Harvard built its large endowment, even without the megagifts other institutions received. President Eliot's "free money" strategy emphasized the need for funds, ongoing relationships with donors, the importance of unrestricted gifts, and full financial disclosure.

King, David A. "A Qualitative Analysis of Major Donor Decisions in Higher Education." EdD, Temple University, 2005. 1.2.

Interviews with major donors from three institutions, as well as development officers, were conducted to understand how donors decide when, how much, and to what cause they gave.

King, Elizabeth H., Eric L. Sexton, and James J. Rhatigan. "Balancing Fundraising in Academic Programs and Intercollegiate Athletics." *New Directions for Higher Education* 149 (2010): 65–71. 1.1, 8.4.

This article explored the challenge of balancing donations to athletics and academics and described two common models for doing so: the centralized and decentralized models.

King, Gregory A. "Donor Behaviors, Motives, and Attitudes of Alumni Athletes at a Selected College in the Northeastern Region of the United States." EdD, United States Sports Academy. 2011. 4.3.

A survey of alumni athletes was based on the ACQUIRE-II and O'Neil and Schenke's donor survey, and factor analysis was performed on the resulting data. Models explained 28 to 45 percent of the variation between donors and nondonors, between total giving of donors, between total giving of major donors, and between other donor groups.

Kirsch, R. P., and M. W. Shell. "Achieving Leadership Gifts: The Investment Returns of Lasting Relationships." *New Directions for Philanthropic Fundraising* 21 (1998): 35–60. 1.7.

This article on developing relationships that result in lead gifts was not focused exclusively on higher education, although many of its examples were drawn from it. Culture, volunteers, ongoing relationship, the chief development officer, the act of asking, and stewardship were discussed.

Kisker, Carrie B., and Rozana Carducci. "UCLA Community College Review: Community College Partnerships with the Private Sector-Organizational Contexts and Models for Successful Collaboration." *Community College Review* 31 no. 3 (2003): 55–74. 1.12.

This article explored workforce training collaborations at community colleges, including strategies for success and several examples. In addition to brining in funds, the authors argue that these partnerships offer colleges other benefits.

Klostermann, B. K. "Development and Concurrent Validity of a 'Motivation to Give' Scale." PhD, Southern Illinois University at Carbondale, 1995. 1.2.

Data from donors and nondonors to SIUC were subjected to hierarchical discriminant function analyses to explore whether donors at different levels had different motivations to give. Comparisons were made based on donor/nondonor status, major donors and prospects, and low and high affluence.

Knight, William E. "Influences on Participation in a University Faculty and Staff Annual Giving Campaign." *International Journal of Educational Advancement* 4 no. 3 (2004). 1.2, 6.8.

Using human resources and development records and interviews with faculty from Bowling Green State University, logit was used to predict giving status and qualitative analysis expanded upon this. Faculty suggested appeals directly to departments and the ability to direct their donations.

Koch, James V. "The Relative Decline of a Musgrave 'Merit Good': The Case of Public Support of Flagship Public Universities." *Journal of Economic Finance* 32 (2008): 368–79. 1.13, 1.15.

The author argued that declining state support for higher education has led to a decline in the rankings of public universities. One of the alternative revenue sources discussed was fundraising, although private institutions have greater relative success at fundraising.

Koelkebeck, G. R. "The Evaluation of Public Community College Readiness for Private Sector Fund-Raising." PhD, Fielding Institute, 1994. 1.3, 8.2.

A survey of California community college presidents, interviews, and documents were used to create factors for fundraising success that were then regressed on outcomes. Significant factors included president/trustee/faculty positive relations, policy development, and readiness for change.

Kotler, Philip, and Karen Fox. *Strategic Marketing for Education Institutions.* Englewood Cliffs, NJ: Prentice-Hall, 1995. 3.

This second edition was intended as a handbook for marketing. Practices it recommended included emphasizing quality, research, strategic planning, methods of estimating demand, and direct mail.

Kozobarich, Jeri L. "Institutional Advancement." *New Directions for Higher Education* 111 (2000): 25–34. 6.5.

This article described career paths in institutional advancement. Skills, education, ethics, and equity were discussed. The author discussed her own career.

Kreuter, Barbara A. "A Classical Capital Campaign in an International Setting." *CASE International Journal of Educational Advancement* 3 no. 3 (2003): 254–67. 1.6, 5.2.

This case study of a capital campaign at an international school in London relied heavily on individual gifts including from parents. Challenges included mobility of families, dealing with multiple cultures and laws, and fluctuating currencies.

Kroll, Diane M. "Role Expansion in Student Affairs: Student Affairs Officers and Fundraising in Selected Midwestern Liberal Arts Colleges." PhD, Ohio State University, 1991. 1.1, 8.5.

Based on surveys of presidents, chief development officers, and chief student personnel officers, the expansion of student affairs into fundraising was explored. Participation in, and recent changes in, student affairs fundraising was discussed.

Krzyminski, Janet Restivo. "A Survey of Selected Demographic Factors and Their Influence on the Implementation of Development Strategies for Female Donors Who Have Given Major Gifts to a Public University." PhD, University of Toledo, 2001. 1.2.

Major female donors to the University of Toledo were surveyed to discover their perceptions on cultivation, solicitation, and stewardship. Better work was needed in stewardship. Age, employment, and geography impacted perception of fundraising strategies.

LaBeouf, Joanne P. "Community College Foundations: An Alternative Model for Institutional Funding." *International Journal of Educational Advancement* 5 no. 3 (2005): 232–42. 1.1, 8.2.

The author provided suggestions for community college foundations, recommending multiple sources of funds, collaboration, and more involvement with academics.

Lackie, Mary Bane. "Alumni Giving at Arkansas Tech University: College Experiences and Motivations to Give as Predictors of Giving Behavior." EdD, University of Arkansas, 2010. 4.3.

In this study, the alumni who left Arkansas Tech 1973–1995 were surveyed, and the characteristics of donors and nondonors were compared. Differences were found with postgraduation involvement with Tech, college experiences, and current attitudes toward the university.

Laguilles, Jerold S. "What Kind of Alumni Do Low-Income Students Become? An Investigation of the Relationship between Income-Status and Future Alumni Involvement." EdD, University of Massachusetts, 2013. 4.3, 4.5.

Institutional data from a liberal arts college was used to examine alumni volunteering, donating, and donation size among former low-income students. Low-income status did not affect volunteering or donating, but it affected donation size.

Lamb, Keith Whitaker. "The Role of Brand Equity in Reputational Rankings of Specialty Graduate Programs in Colleges of Education: Variables Considered by College of Education Deans and Associate Deans Ranking the Programs." PhD, University of North Texas, 2010. 3.4.

Deans and associate deans of graduate education were surveyed to discover what variables they considered when ranking peer institutions. Results were subject to principle component analysis. Faculty research was the most important consideration with marketing having little to no effect.

Lamboy, Joy Victoria. "Implications of Branding Initiatives in Higher Education among Trademarked Institutions in California." EdD, University of San Francisco, 2012. 3.3.

A survey of college marketing employees queried respondents about their perceptions of the importance and impact of branding in higher education. The results found that trademark licensing was considered to have positive impacts on four-year institutions.

Lamm, Jean Ann. "Educational Institutional Advancement as a Career Path." PhD, Colorado State University, 1991. 1.4, 6.5.

This thesis reviewed advancement position advertisements in *The Chronicle of Higher Education* and surveyed members of CASE about their careers. Advancement professionals came from a wide variety of backgrounds and had at least a bachelor's degree. Job tasks, functions, and titles varied widely, and professionals changed positions; over 90 percent had moved to take advantage of an opportunity.

Lang, Milton. "Fundraising for Diversity Initiatives: A Comparative Analysis of Four Public Research Universities." EdD, Washington State University, 2008. 8.7.

Fundraising staff at four universities were interviewed regarding fundraising for diversity initiatives. Institutions were categorized using Cheatham's Institutional Awareness and Cultural Diversity Scale.

Langseth, Mark N., and Cassie S. McVeety. "Engagement as a Core University Leadership Position and Advancement Strategy: Perspectives from an Engaged

Institution." *International Journal of Educational Advancement* 7 no. 2 (2007): 117–30. 1.6.

This article reviewed Portland State University's strategic planning process, which resulted in a focus on engagement. The changing role of engagement and its implications for advancement were discussed.

Lanning, Paul I., Jr. "Developing Expertise in Higher Education Fundraising: A Conceptual Framework." EdD, University of the Pacific, 2007. 6.5.

This study of fundraising professionals who had earned the CFRE credential was undertaken to provide guidance to novice professionals. Most CFREs had entered the field nondeliberatively and relied on conferences and informal networking for learning. In addition, most were female.

Larsen, Phyllis C. "Academic Reputation: How U.S. News & World Report Survey Respondents Form Perceptions." *International Journal of Educational Advancement* 4 no. 2 (2003). 3.4.

Interviews with 13 public university presidents and 2 provosts explored how they defined academic reputation for purposes of *U.S. News* rankings. Factors used included faculty quality, credible rankings, fiscal resources, research strength, student quality, visibility of leadership, historic reputation, and program quality.

Latour, Terry Stephen. "Study of Library Fund-Raising Activities at Colleges and Universities in the United States." PhD, Florida State University, 1995. 1.1, 8.7.

A survey of academic library directors found that 66 percent of libraries engaged in fundraising, with research universities most likely to do so. Factors encouraging participation were increasing technology costs and university encouragement. Factors influencing activities used and fundraising successes included size and institutional type.

Latta, Marcia Sloan. "Characteristics and Motivational Factors of Major Donors to Bowling Green State University." PhD, Bowling Green State University, 2010. 1.3.

This study examined motivations of $25,000-plus donors to a BGSU campaign via survey data and institutional data. Older, male donors gave the most. Factors that influenced gift size were being asked, serving on a board, serving on the foundation board, and income.

Lauer, Larry D. "The Status of Integrated Marketing in Colleges and Universities." *CASE International Journal of Educational Advancement* 1 no. 2 (2000): 101–12. 3.2.

This paper examined the embrace of Integrated Marketing Communications by higher education. General principles and benefits were explained.

Lawley, Cecelia D. "Factors That Affect Alumni Loyalty at a Public University." PhD, Purdue University, 2008. 4.3.

Purdue alumni were surveyed with a revised version of NCHEMS' Comprehensive Alumni Assessment Survey to analyze the effects of undergraduate extracurricular involvement, alumni activities, discipline studied, and graduation year on the probability of donation. The first three were significant; for graduation year, only graduation prior to 1955 was significant.

Lawrence, Robert Ray. "Development Officers' Perceptions of the Characteristics of an Effective Private Fund-Raising Program for Protestant Colleges." EdD, Oklahoma State University, 1991. 1.8, 8.8.

Chief development officers at Christian College Coalition institutions participated in Delphi technique surveys to determine the characteristics of effective fundraising programs. The following factors were found to matter: A clear mission statement; presidential leadership; the chief development officer, staff, and trustees; training; and close ties to their affiliated church's mission.

Le Blanc, Louis A., and Conway T. Rucks. "Data Mining of University Philanthropic Giving: Cluster-Discriminant Analysis and Pareto Effects." *International Journal of Educational Advancement* 9 no. 2 (2009): 64–82. 4.3.

Institutional data from one institution was subject to cluster analysis based on alumni giving and alumni association participation. Four of the six groups provided 88 percent of major gifts, while the last two provided 88 percent of annual fund gifts.

Leahy, Patrick F. "To the Next Level: How Drexel University Improved Its Fundraising Performance from 1997 to 2007." EdD, University of Pennsylvania, 2009. 1.6.

This case study examined Drexel, which per VSE had the greatest improvement in annual giving from 1997 to 2007. Interviews revealed that Drexel already had an efficient fundraising operation but engaged in deliberate, broad-based change.

Leak, Halima N., and Chera D. Reid. "'Making Something of Themselves': Black Self-Determination, the Church and Higher Education Philanthropy." *International Journal of Educational Advancement* 10 no. 3 (2010): 235–44. 7.1, 8.1.

This historical exploration of black church support of higher education examined the role of motivated donors and black leadership. The Atlanta University Studies and contemporaneous newspaper accounts demonstrated the development of that leadership.

Lee, Hsiu-Ling. "The Growth and Stratification of College Endowments in the United States." *International Journal of Educational Advancement* 8 no. 3 (2008): 136–51. 1.2.

IPEDS, VSE, and NSF data were combined to build a model for endowment size. Several significant factors were related to institutional prestige. Research expenditures and the percentage of alumni that gave also influenced endowment size.

Leonard, Edward F. III. "The Advancement Value Chain: An Exploratory Model." *International Journal of Educational Advancement* 5 no. 2 (2005). 1.1.

This paper adopted the value chain model from business to advancement. VSE data from comprehensive and baccalaureate colleges was used to build a structural equation model of total voluntary support, which can function as a value chain.

Lepke, Phyllis J. "Psychological Type and Preferred Learning Styles of Institutional Advancement Officers: An Initial Study Using the Myers-Briggs Type Indicator in Three Geographic Areas." PhD, Iowa State University, 1991. 6.5.

Attendees of a CASE district conference were administered the MBTI. The most frequent type was ENTJ (19%). Intuitives (N) were overrepresented compared to the general population. Fundraisers were more likely to be extraverts than faculty were.

Levine, Wendy. "Communications and Alumni Relations: What Is the Correlation between an Institution's Communications Vehicles and Alumni Annual Giving?" *International Journal of Educational Advancement* 8 no. 3 (2008): 176–97. 4.7.

A survey of private colleges inquired about communications pieces and alumni giving. The total number of pieces was not related to giving levels, although the frequency of alumni magazines and newsletters was positively related to giving. The effects of annual fund and campaign appeal letters were mixed.

Lewis, Muriel Monahan. "What Motivates Doctoral Level Alumni to Contribute? Response to a Segmented University Fundraising Appeal." EdD, Indiana University, 1996. 4.3, 8.3.

Former doctoral students of a faculty member who had been asked to donate to an endowment in his name were surveyed, and regression and qualitative analyses were conducted. Factors that typically motivated undergraduate alumni were not found to have an effect. Personal attachment to the professor was not significant in regression but appeared as a theme in the qualitative analysis.

Liao, Mei-Na, and Adrian Sargeant. "Operationalizing the Marketing Concept: Just What Can Be Achieved When You Get It Right?" *CASE International Journal of Educational Advancement* 1 no. 1 (2000): 24–39. 3.2, 5.2.

This paper reviewed the literature that links marketing to organizational performance. A case study of Camborne Schools of Mines illustrated how public relations, advertising, and personal selling were able to improve student recruitment.

Lin, Hsien Hong (Joe). "Why Taiwanese Companies and Foundations Donate to Public Colleges and Universities in Taiwan: An Investigation of Donation Incentives, Strategies, and Decision-Making Processes." PhD, Kent State University, 2009. 1.12, 5.3.

Surveys of Taiwanese universities, corporations, and foundations and interviews explored why corporations and foundations gave to universities. Companies gave when they believed the donation could benefit the corporation; foundations gave to universities that they perceived as supporting social justice.

Lindahl, Wesley E. "The Major Gift Donor Relationship: An Analysis of Donors and Contributions." *Nonprofit Management & Leadership* 5 no. 4 (1995): 411–32. 1.2.

The cultivation process for major gift donors to Northwestern University was explored using institutional data. Cultivation took years rather than months, and the process varied by donor type (alumni status) and category of gift (bequest or outright gifts).

Lindahl, Wesley E., and Aaron T. Conley. "Literature Review: Philanthropic Fundraising." *Nonprofit Management and Leadership* 13 no. 1 (2002): 91–112. 1.0.

This literature review covered the topics of the philanthropic environment, the work and careers of fundraisers, and fundraising management from 1986 to 2001. While not focused on higher education exclusively, institutional advancement was included, and the article serves as a good, if dated, starting point for a literature review.

Lindahl, Wesley E., and C. Winship. "Predictive Models for Annual Fundraising and Major Gift Fundraising." *Nonprofit Management and Leadership* 3 no. 1 (1992): 43–64. 1.1.

Based on data from Northwestern University, two models were created to predict giving, one for gifts of $100,000-plus and one for annual gifts of $1,000-plus. Total past giving was the strongest predictor in both models. Salary, planned giving mailers, and national resource ratings mattered for major gifts. More variables were significant for the annual fund model.

Lindahl, Wesley E., and Christopher Winship. "A Logit Model with Interactions for Predicting Major Gift Donors." *Research in Higher Education* 35 no. 6 (1994): 729–43. 1.1.

This article refined the major gifts model developed in Lindahl and Winship (1992), discussed above. Interacting past giving with other variables provided better predictive power.

Lineberger, Jonathan David. "The DBU Brand: A Case Study over the Process of Branding at Dallas Baptist University." EdD, University of Alabama, 2009. 3.3, 8.8.

This case study relied on interviews and document reviews to examine institutional rebranding in the late 1980s/early 1990s at DBU. Factors in the rebranding effort's success included good financial management, the mission statement, and consistently following that mission.

Lischwe, Sheila Turner. "An Evaluation of the Impact of University-Linked Retirement Communities on the Development/Fundraising Function at Affiliated Institutions of Higher Education." PhD, Saint Louis University, 2007. 1.3.

This study examined the opinions of chief fundraising officers at institutions with retirement communities about the philanthropic possibilities these communities presented. Most fundraisers were unaware of the communities and did not alter their fundraising practices to take advantage of them, and it was unclear if gifts from residents were new gifts.

List, John A., and David Lucking-Reiley. "The Effects of Seed Money and Refunds on Charitable Giving: Experimental Evidence from a University Capital Campaign." *Journal of Political Economy* 110 no. 1 (2002): 215–33. 1.3.

The effect of seed money was tested on a capital campaign for a new academic center at the University of Central Florida. Three levels of seed money were tested as well as refunds if goals were not reached. Higher seed money levels resulted in higher donations, as did refunds but at a smaller magnitude.

Liu, Sandra S. "Integrated Strategic Marketing on an Institutional Level." *Journal of Marketing for Higher Education* 8 no. 4 (1998): 17–28. 3.2.

This theoretical paper proposed that institutions should integrate marketing to potential students with strategic planning.

Liu, Ying. "Determinants of Private Giving to Public Colleges and Universities." *International Journal of Educational Advancement* 6 no. 2 (2006): 119–40. 1.3.

This paper was based on the following author's dissertation, "Institutional Characteristics and Environmental Factors."

Liu, Ying. "Institutional Characteristics and Environmental Factors That Influence Private Giving to Public Colleges and Universities: A Longitudinal Analysis." PhD, Vanderbilt University, 2007a. 1.3.

Data from IPEDS, VSE, the Bureau of Economic Analysis, Volkwein and Malik's classification of administrative flexibility, and the Graduate Medical Education Directory were combined to create a longitudinal dataset to explore what factors influenced donations in six different categories. Factors that mattered in multiple categories included *U.S. News* ranking, Carnegie classification, tuition rates, total revenues, and endowment growth.

Liu, Ying. "Revenue Diversification: A Comparison of Russian and Chinese Higher Education." *Higher Education in Review* 4 (2007b): 21–42. 1, 5.3, 5.6.

Based on cost-sharing theory and Johnstone's five primary vehicles of revenue supplementation, the rise of nongovernmental revenue sources (including grants and philanthropy) were explored in Russia and China. Accompanying revenue diversification in these countries was the devolution of decision-making from the state to the institution.

Loessin, Bruce A., and Margaret A. Duronio. "The Role of Planning in Successful Fund Raising in Ten Higher Education Institutions." *Planning for Higher Education* 18 no. 3 (1990): 45–56. 1.1.

Ten diverse institutions that were all successful in fundraising were described. Planning was broken down into systems, components, and qualitative elements.

Lofton, William Joel. "Commonalities among Experiences of Supportive Alumni of the University of Southern Mississippi." PhD, University of Southern Mississippi, 2005. 4.3.

Data on alumni giving to USM was scrutinized to find commonalities among donors. Identifiable clusters of donors were found among alumni association members. In particular, alumni who were involved in student organizations as undergraduates were more likely to give.

Lorenzen, Michael. "Perceptions of Academic Library Development Officers Regarding Their Work in Fund Raising." EdD, Central Michigan University, 2009. 1.9, 8.7.

Development officers at Association of Research Libraries member institutions with successful fundraising operations were interviewed regarding their roles, the development process, donor identification, cultivation, challenges, and the effect of reporting structures.

Loveday, Christine Hawk. "An Analysis of the Variables Associated with Alumni Giving and Employee Giving to a Mid-Sized Southeastern University." EdD, East Tennessee State University, 2013. 4.3, 6.8.

Alumni and employee data was used to explore giving at one university. Four percent of alumni and 18 percent of employees were donors. Men and alumni with more degrees were more likely to give; faculty members were more likely to give than staff.

Lovell, Jeanie. "Women's Philanthropy Programs at Coeducational Colleges and Universities." *New Directions for Philanthropic Fundraising* 50 (2005): 141–55. 1.1.

Alumnae giving initiative at coeducational institutions were compared to identify effective practices. Interviews from development officers at eight institutions revealed that the programs had multiple purposes, included educational seminars and a steering committee, and produced positive outcomes for institutional giving, despite some challenges.

Loyd, Marta M. "Donor Relations and Stewardship and Their Relationship to Private Philanthropy in Universities." EdD, University of Missouri-Columbia, 2011. 1.7.

VSE data regarding stewardship at 45 institutions were tested for effects on scholarship fundraising. No effect was found.

Lunardini, Ronald. "Undergraduate Participation in Extracurricular Activities as a Factor in Alumni Involvement with Their Institution." EdD, University of Pittsburgh, 1993. 4.3, 8.4.

The class of 1965 at Indiana University of Pennsylvania was surveyed to test the effect of undergraduate activity participation on alumni affiliation. Participation in athletics, special interest groups, and governance organizations were significant in regression analysis.

Luy, Dale R. "Athletic Fundraising at NCAA Division III Colleges and Universities." DSM, United States Sports Academy, 2007. 8.4.

Division III athletic and annual fund directors were surveyed about athletic fundraising at their institution. About three-quarters of institutions raised funds for athletics. A variety of reasons for not conducting athletic fundraising was listed, including institutional philosophy.

Machung, Anne. 1995. "Managing the information overload: The case for a standard survey response." *New Directions for Institutional Research* 88 (1995): 61–72. doi: 10.1002/ir.37019958807. 3.4.

Given the increase in the number of surveys and rankings and the amount of time colleges spend completing them, the author argued they should be standardized. A format used by the University of California at Berkeley was recommended.

Mackey, Shawn C. "An Investigation of African American Donor Behavior at a Predominantly White Institution." EdD, University of Memphis, 2008. 1.2.

African American alumni giving at Delta State University was explored with a survey of alumni. Attitude toward the institution influenced the decision to give, as did demographic variables.

Mael, F., and A. E. Ashforth. "Alumni and Their Alma Mater: A Partial Test of the Reformulated Model of Organizational Identification." *Journal of Organizational Behavior* 13 no. 2 (1992): 103–23. 4.5.

A model of organization identification was tested with survey data from a men's college. Identification was associated with organizational prestige and distinction, individual satisfaction, and alumni participation (donations, advising others to attend, and participating in college functions).

Mahoney, James. "Accountable to the Death: A Model for Evaluating Public Relations." *CASE International Journal of Educational Advancement* 1 no. 1 (2000): 40–51. 2.1, 5.4.

The author explored the growth of public relations and the subsequent push for accountability in public relations. A case study of Australian National University was included, where accountability was introduced to the university newspaper and the media coverage.

Mallette, Bruce I. "Money Magazine, U.S. News & World Report, and Steve Martin: What do they have in common?" *New Directions for Institutional Research* 88 (1995): 31–43. doi: 10.1002/ir.37019958805. 3.4.

Mallette discussed some methodological problems with college rankings, how these shortcomings affect consumers, and how they might be improved.

Maniaci, Vince, and Rob Poole. "The Vulnerability Framework Integrates Various Models of Generating Surplus Revenue." *International Journal of Educational Advancement* 5 no. 1 (2004). 1.13.

This paper was based on Maniaci's dissertation, "The Relationship of Annual Giving."

Maniaci, Vince, and Rob Poole. "Increasing Efficiency in Academia: The Use of a Weaning Model in Fundraising." *International Journal of Educational Advancement* 5 no. 2 (2005a). 1.1.

The authors argued for gradually reallocating operating funds to quasi-endowment to increase efficiency and stability. Their model was built on Zemsky and Massey's balanced budget model.

Maniaci, Vince, and Rob Poole. "A Taxonomy Based on Revenue Dependency for Private Master's Universities." *International Journal of Educational Advancement* 6 no. 1 (2005b): 20–33. 1.14.

This paper was based on Maniaci's dissertation, "The Relationship of Annual Giving."

Maniaci, Vincent Michael. "The Relationship of Annual Giving and Endowment Payout to Future Tuition Dependency at Private Master's Universities." EdD, University of Pennsylvania, 2003. 1.15.

VSE data was used to test a model of annual giving, endowment payout, and net tuition. Four percent was the typical endowment payout; institutions were categorized by high/low annual funds and high/low endowment payouts. Subjective perceptions by presidents played a role in spending decisions.

Maniaci, Vincent M., Rob Poole, and Thomas L. Wilson. "The Relationship of Annual Giving and Endowment Payout to Future Tuition Dependency at Private Master's Universities." *International Journal of Educational Advancement* 4 no. 2 (2003). 1.15.

Using VSE data from 1992 and 2001, the authors regressed the effects of fundraising variables on tuition dependency. Reliance on annual funds increased dependency; reliance on endorsement decreased it.

Mann, Timothy. "College Fund Raising Using Theoretical Perspectives to Understand Donor Motives." *International Journal of Educational Advancement* 7 no. 1 (2007): 35–45. 1.2.

This article provided an overview of theoretical perspectives used to explain donor motivation, including charitable giving, organizational identification, social identification, economic, services-philanthropic, and relationship marketing. The author explored how they might be useful to fundraisers.

March, Karen S. "A Descriptive Study of Faculty and Staff Giving Practices at Public Institutions of Higher Education within the United States." PhD, State University of New York at Buffalo, 2005. 1.2, 6.8.

Chief advancement officers were surveyed about faculty and staff giving at public institutions to see if giving varied by size, Carnegie classification, or geographical region. Both faculty and staff giving varied on each factor, except for staff giving, which was not affected by geography. Both were less likely to give when solicited by students and more likely to give restricted gifts.

Marlin, Dan, William J. Ritchie, and Scott W. Geiger. "Strategic Group Membership and Nonprofit Organization Performance." *Nonprofit Management & Leadership* 20 no. 1 (2009): 23–39. 1.3.

Data from IRS Form 990s was used to create groups of institutional foundations with distinct strategies. The group with the best financial results focused the most on fundraising; the second best results belonged to the group with the highest ratio of contributions to total revenues combined with the highest level of slack.

Marr, Kelly A., Charles H. Mullin, and John J. Siegfried. "Undergraduate Financial Aid and Subsequent Giving Behavior." *Quarterly Review of Economics and Finance* 45 (2005): 123–43. 4.3.

The effects of financial aid on young alumni giving behavior were tested with data from Vanderbilt University alumni. Aid type received influenced giving more than the total amount of aid; adding a small scholarship to an all-loan package or eliminating a small loan from a mixed package increased the likelihood of contributing.

Marshall, Charminn B. "Exploring the Functions of Alumni Associations at Selected Urban Universities." PhD, University of Cincinnati, 2009. 4.4.

This mixed-methods study examined the structure and planning of alumni associations at 30 universities. The quantitative component found no difference in programming based on size or institutional type. Thirty-one programmatic, activity, and service variables were factor analyzed to product 12 factors that described alumni associations.

Martin III, Quincy. "Nontraditional Pathways to the Presidency: A Student Affairs Approach." EdD, Northern Illinois University, 2010. 6.1.

This thesis explored student affairs professionals who became college presidents. As fundraising is an increasingly important presidential role, most presidents viewed preparation for it as essential to securing a presidential position.

Martin, Joseph Clifton, Jr. "Characteristics of Alumni Donors and Non-Donors at a Research I, Public University." PhD, University of Virginia, 1993. 4.3.

A survey of alumni of one university was used to create a model that would discriminate between donors and nondonors. Six factors (income, perceived need, reading alumni publications, graduate enrollment, special interest groups, and alumni involvement) influenced donor status, with 65 percent correctly classified, and seven factors influenced donation size, with 87 percent correctly classified.

Martinez, George Andrew. "Attitudes and Perceptions about Private Philanthropic Giving to Arizona Community Colleges and Universities: Implications for Practice." EdD, New Mexico State University, 2009. 8.2.

Three community college districts and three universities in Arizona served as case studies to identify similarities and differences in philanthropic support. Data was gathered from interviews and surveys. Donor motivation varied, with institutional mission mattering more to some donors than others; connectedness and a desire to effect positive change were typical.

Martinez, J. Michael, Jeffrey L. Stinson, Minsoo Kang, and Colby B. Jubenville. "Intercollegiate Athletics and Institutional Fundraising: A Meta-Analysis." *Sport Marketing Quarterly* 19 (2010): 36–47. 1, 8.4.

This meta-analysis brought together research regarding the effect of athletics on higher education philanthropy conducted during 1976–2008. Athletics had a significant, small, positive effect on giving, moderated by whether giving was for athletics or academics, donor alumni status, NCAA division, and participation in football.

Mastroieni, Anita. "Doctoral Alumni Giving: Motivations for Donating to the University of Pennsylvania." EdD, University of Pennsylvania, 2010. 1.2, 8.3.

This thesis explored why doctoral alumni give, using social exchange theory, interviews, and institutional data. Donors gave out of gratitude and indebtedness. Donors who used rational choice theory gave less, as they believed their donations would be too small to have an impact.

Mastroieni, Anita. "Fundraising from Doctoral Alumni: Going Beyond the Bachelor's." In *Expanding the Donor Base in Higher Education: Engaging Non-Traditional Donors*, edited by Noah D. Drezner, 87–101. New York: Routledge, 2013. 1.2, 8.3.

This article was based on the author's thesis, "Doctoral Alumni Giving."

Mathis, Hugh Raymond. "Leadership Strategies of Effective Presidents in Fund Raising Programs at Small, Private Colleges." PhD, Union Institute, 1998. 1.3, 6.1.

A survey of presidents at Council of Independent College member institutions found that effective presidents spent at least 15 but more often at least 20 hours per week and 10 percent of their budget on fundraising, whereas typical presidents spent 10–15 hours and 5 percent of their budget.

Matsoukas, George E. "Relationship of Community College Internal Organizational Structure to Effective Granstmanship." *Community College Journal of Research and Practice* 20 no. 3 (1996): 277–88. 1.1, 1.12.

This paper explored the structure of community college grants offices based on a survey of grant officers. 85 percent of institutions had grants offices, typically with one full-time staff member and a part-time assistant. Half were located in the development office, and most were supervised by either the development or president's office.

Maurasse, David J. "Higher Education-Community Partnerships: Assessing Progress in the Field." *Nonprofit and Voluntary Sector Quarterly* 31 no. 1 (2002): 131–39. 2.5.

This article on partnerships drew primarily on the author's experience as a practitioner to examine issues of measurement and assessment. While outcomes measurement is important, the author also argued that process measures are important.

McAdoo, Anthony Dean. "Factors Affecting the Institutional Perception of Alumni of the University of Arkansas." EdD, University of Arkansas, 2010. 4.

Based on data from the Alumni Attitude Survey, this thesis sought to discover the factors influencing alumni perception of the University of Arkansas. Geography only played a small role, but history and tradition, athletic success, campus aesthetics, and alumni accomplishments had larger impacts. Only history/tradition and athletic success had any impact on loyalty.

McAlexander, James H., and Harold F. Koenig. "Building Communities of Philanthropy in Higher Education: Contextual Influences." *International Journal of Nonprofit and Voluntary Sector Marketing* 17 (2012): 122–31. 3.3, 4.

The effect of institutional size on alumni brand community and willingness to donate to the institution was explored via survey. Both size and brand community were significant; alumni of smaller institutions had more positive feelings regarding their education and a stronger bond to their institution, but these feelings did not affect intent to donate.

McAlexander, James H., Harold F. Koenig, and John W. Schouten. "Building Relationships of Brand Community in Higher Education: A Strategic

Framework for University Advancement." *International Journal of Educational Advancement* 6 no. 2 (2006): 107–18. 3.3, 4.

The components of brand community were discussed and tested based on data from one university via factor analysis and SEM. Support for the model was found using both techniques.

McAllister, Sheila Marie. "Toward a Dialogic Theory of Fundraising." *Community College Journal of Research and Practice* 37 no. 4 (2013): 262–77. 3.1.

New Jersey community college websites were content analyzed under the lens of Kent and Taylor's dialogic theory of fundraising. Each was rated for usefulness of information, ease of interface, generating return visitors, and creating a dialogic feedback loop. Websites did not have interactive features and did not enable two-way communication with publics.

McAllister, Sheila M., and Maureen Taylor. "Organizational Influences and Constraints on Community College Web-Based Media Relations." *Community College Journal of Research and Practice* 36 no. 2 (2012): 93–110. 3.1.

This paper explored how internal organizational operations affected the web initiatives of New Jersey community colleges by surveying public relations directors. Two factors were found to matter most: the level of control by public relations professionals over web content, and the level of agreement among stakeholders as to the website's purpose.

McCarthy, Kirstin, Jeanne Contardo, and Leila Morsy Eckert. "Corporate Investments in Education during an Economic Downturn." *International Journal of Educational Advancement* 9 no. 4 (2010): 251–65. 1.12.

Four corporate philanthropies were examined as case studies to study the effect of an economic downturn on corporate giving. Interviews and document reviews showed that the organizations used best practices during the economic downturn, including providing more community development grants.

McCormick, Irene S. "Factors Related to the Endowment Fund-Raising Outcomes of Maryland Public Community Colleges." EdD, University of Maryland College Park, 1995. 1.3, 8.2.

Seventeen community colleges participated in a three-year endowment donation incentive program; institutional data was used to test whether capacity, history, or effort affected outcomes. Capacity had little effect, but history and in particular effort did. Personal visits, the involvement of trustees, volunteers, and funds spent on fundraising influenced endowment fundraising success.

McCown, Peter Lewis. "A Comparative Case Study of Institutional Advancement Program Effectiveness within Selected Institutions of the Coalition for Christian Colleges and Universities." PhD, State University of New York at Buffalo, 2000. 1.3, 8.8.

Fundraising offices of three high-performing and three low-performing Council for Christian Colleges and Universities served as case studies to study variations in performance. Observations, interviews, focus groups, and document review were utilized. Seventeen points of difference were found in the general areas of the president, governing board, vice president for advancement, institution, and advancement practices.

McDearmon, J. Travis. "What's In It for Me: A Qualitative Look into the Mindset of Young Alumni Non-Donors." *International Journal of Educational Advancement* 10 no. 1 (2010): 33–47. 4.3.

A survey of young nondonor alumni at a public university explored why they did not give. Open-ended responses were examined and three themes emerged. Alumni were frustrated with a lack of career assistance from the university; they wished to receive incentives for donations; and they wanted to direct where their dollars went.

McDearmon, J. Travis. "Hail to Thee, Our Alma Mater: Alumni Role Identity and the Relationship to Institutional Support Behaviors." *Research in Higher Education* 54 no. 3 (2013): 283–302. 4.3.

A survey of alumni at a public university explored how alumni saw their role in relation to the institution and the effect of this on support behaviors using Stryker's theory of symbolic interactionalism. Alumni with increased role identity were more likely to join the alumni association, attend university events, and make donations.

McDearmon, J. Travis, and Kathryn Shirley. "Characteristics and Institutional Factors Related to Young Alumni Donors and Non-Donors." *International Journal of Educational Advancement* 9 no. 2 (2009): 83–95. 4.3.

Based on a survey of young alumni at a public university, the differences between donors and nondonors were explored. Nondonors were more likely to have high levels of student loan debt and less likely to give to other charitable causes. Residential status (in-state or out) and aid awards also influenced donor status.

McDonough, Patricia M., Anthony L. Antonio, Marybeth Walpole, and Leonor X. Perez. "College Rankings; Democratized Knowledge for Whom?" *Research in Higher Education* 39 no. 5 (1998): 513–37. 3.4.

This paper analyzed which students used college rankings and how they used them in making college choices. Most students did not rely heavily on rankings, although high-ability, affluent students were most likely to.

McEvoy, Chad Dowrick. "An Investigation of Donor Characteristics and Contributions to an Intercollegiate Athletics Fund Raising Program." EdD, University of Northern Colorado, 2002. 1.2, 8.4.

Responses to a survey of athletic donors to one university were subject to ANOVA, factor analysis, and cluster analysis to discover factors related to donation size. Larger gifts were the product of living close by or following sports closely; there was not a significant difference in alumni gifts versus nonalumni gifts.

McGee, E. Ann. "The Role of the President in Supporting the College's Foundation." *New Directions for Community Colleges* 2003 (124): 41–46. doi: 10.1002/cc.132. 6.1.

The author explored the role of the president in foundation fundraising at community colleges based on her experience at two institutions. She reported that donors wished to have access to the president and to be able to trust him or her.

McGraw, Michael S. "The Campus Art Museum and Gallery: Uniting Patronage and Scholarship." EdD, Seton Hall University, School of Education, 1996. 1.15, 8.7.

The growth of institutional art museums and galleries over two decades and the role fundraising played in this growth were explored via survey research. Philanthropic giving was a key factor enabling this growth.

McGuire, Janine Pisani. "Integrating Fund Raising with Academic Planning and Budgeting: Toward an Understanding of Strategic Fund Raising." PhD, University of Pennsylvania, 2003. 1.1.

Case studies of seven universities, based on interviews and documents, outlined their attempts to integrate fundraising with academic planning and budgeting. The thesis explored why this occurred and what challenges arose.

McGuire, Michael D. "Validity issues for reputational studies." *New Directions for Institutional Research* 88 (1995): 45–59. doi: 10.1002/ir.37019958806. 3.4.

Based on two studies of *U.S. News* rankings, the rankings likely have issues with validity and reliability.

McIntosh, Clifford Joe. "An Analysis of the Use of Gift Annuity Agreements at Selected United States Colleges and Universities for the Period 1988–1993." EdD, University of North Texas, 1995. 1.5.

A survey of CASE member institutions inquired about their use of gift annuity agreements. The majority of institutions used them, although they were most prevalent at church-related institutions. Institutions preferred a minimum beneficiary age of 50–59 years of age and a $5,000–9,999 minimum gift size. Many institutions received 11 percent or more of gifts through such agreements.

McLaughlin, Linden D. "Graduate Professional Training in Christian Education at Dallas Theological Seminary and Alumni Perceptions of Program Quality." PhD, University of North Texas, 2002. 4.6.

A survey of DTS graduate alumni used Stufflebeam's CIPP model (Context, Input, Process, and Product) to assess program quality. Most agreed they would choose the program again, there was quality faculty-student interaction, sufficient attention was paid to spiritual growth, and that their advisors were helpful. The majority were satisfied with coursework and relationships. They were neutral about the seminary's role in job placement.

McNamara, Lynne A. "International Advancement: The Alumni Constituency." *CASE International Journal of Educational Advancement* 2 no. 1 (2001): 37–50. 4.6, 5.6.

This paper was based on the author's dissertation, "Communication Used in Institutional Advancement Efforts."

McNamara, Lynne Ann McCann. "Communication Used in Institutional Advancement Efforts with International Alumni from United States Institutions of Higher Education." PhD, Southern Illinois University at Carbondale, 1998. 4.1.

A survey of 177 institutions inquired about their communication with international alumni. Institutions differed as to whether US citizens living abroad were included, the number of such alumni, and the size of gifts received from them. Contact with alumni did not vary by institutional type; the most common form of communications was mass mailings.

McWherter, Lisa Carol. "The Development, Design, and Implementation of a Community College Institutional Advancement Program." EdD, Peabody College for Teachers of Vanderbilt University, 2005. 1.6, 8.2.

This qualitative case study focused on Walters State Community College, which had a successful advancement program. The pursuit of fundraising success and obstacles to achieving it were discussed. The author presented Walters State as a model for other community colleges.

Meadows, Rita Emily. "Fund Raising in Small Colleges with Membership in the Accrediting Association of Bible Colleges (AABC)." EdD, Peabody College for Teachers of Vanderbilt University, 1999. 1.3, 8.8.

College presidents at Accrediting Association of Bible Colleges institutions were surveyed regarding the effectiveness of their fundraising programs, using Willmer's Theoretical Model for Institutional Advancement. Overall, programs were deemed effective, with 71 percent of institutions showing an increase in total gift income.

Meer, Jonathan. "Brother, Can You Spare a Dime? Peer Pressure in Charitable Solicitation." *Journal of Public Economics* 95 (2011): 926–41. 4.3.

Using 15 years of data from one university, this paper explored the effects of being asked to give by someone with social ties to the donor. Whether the donor's freshman roommate participated as a solicitor served as a proxy for ties. Social ties increased the probability of making a gift.

Meer, Jonathan. "The Habit of Giving." *Economic Enquiry* 51 no. 4 (2013): 2002–17. 4.3.

Using 17 years of data from one university, the author attempted to disentangle whether repeated giving is simply a habit or reflects underlying factors such as affinity. An instrumental variables model that relies on shocks that may affect giving was employed. Some evidence of habit was found, although it did not affect amount given.

Meer, Jonathan, and Harvey S. Rosen. "Altruism and the Child-Cycle of Alumni Giving." *American Economic Journal: Economic Policy* 1 no. 1 (2009a): 258–86. 4.3.

This paper used 17 years of data from one selective university to explore whether alumni were given in part because they hoped to receive benefits (here, admission of a child). Birth of a child increased the likelihood of giving; giving increased among alumni whose children were admitted and fell among those whose children were not.

Meer, Jonathan, and Harvey S. Rosen. "The Impact of Athletic Performance on Alumni Giving: An Analysis of Microdata." *Economics of Education Review* 28 (2009b): 287–94. 4.3, 8.4.

The effect of athletic success on alumni giving was tested with 17 years of data from one university. Winning a conference championship increased the general and athletic giving of men who were on the team by 7 percent. Being a member of a successful team subsequently increased male giving. Won-loss records in basketball and football had no significant effect.

Meer, Jonathan, and Harvey S. Rosen. "Does Generosity Beget Generosity? Alumni Giving and Undergraduate Financial Aid." *Economics of Education Review* 31 (2012): 890–907. 4.3.

Institutional data from 1993–2005 graduates at one university was used to test the effects of financial aid on alumni giving. Loans and larger loan sizes lowered the likelihood of making a gift. Scholarships reduced gift size. Campus jobs did not affect giving.

Mehl, Carolyn L. "Demographic and Attitudinal Characteristics of Alumni and Nonalumni Planned Giving Contributions to the University of Akron." EdD, University of Akron, 1995. 1.5.

Giving by alumni and nonalumni at the University of Akron were compared, replicating and extending a study by Eldridge-Karr, "An Investigative Study of Predictive Characteristics," discussed earlier. Surveys asked about demographic and attitudinal variables. Planned giving donors were distinguished by several demographic and attitudinal variables regardless of alumni status.

Meisenbach, Rebecca J. "Framing Fund Raising: A Poststructuralist Analysis of Higher Education Fund Raisers' Work and Identities." PhD, Purdue University, 2004. 1.4.

This thesis used grounded theory and interviews with 18 development officers to explore how fundraisers framed fundraising. Six frames were found: financial, relational, educational, mission, coordination, and magical. These frames were used to negotiate tensions and manage power relations in their work.

Melching, Sandra Fox. "Resource Development at the University of Alabama: Practices and Perceptions of Executive Administrators and Development Professionals." EdD, University of Alabama, 2001. 1.9.

A survey of University of Alabama administrators and fundraisers and a follow-up focus group inquired as to the preferred course of fundraising. Respondents said external constituents should be educated about designated funds and grantwriting should be pursued. More strategic planning, with the involvement of more parties, was also suggested.

Melton, Douglas Owen. "A Study of Institutional Advancement in Selected Southern Baptist Colleges and Universities." PhD, University of North Texas, 1996. 1.1, 8.8.

Based on a survey of Southern Baptist institutions, actual advancement practices were compared with Willmer's model. Institutions had limited budgets, small staff, and little involvement by volunteers or trustees. Fundraising programs were centralized, used a variety of programs, and were overseen by competent leaders with appropriate authority levels.

Meredith, Marc. "Why Do Universities Compete in the Ratings Game? An Empirical Analysis of the Effects of the US News and World Report College Rankings." *Research in Higher Education* 45 no. 5 (2004): 443–61. 3.4.

The effects on institutions of *U.S. News* rankings were explored. Changes in rankings affected admissions outcomes, moderated by ranking level and public/private status. Racial and socio-economic demographics were also affected by changes in rank.

Merkel, Ryan E. "The Influence of Sorority and Fraternity Involvement on Future Giving." In *Expanding the Donor Base in Higher Education: Engaging Non-Traditional Donors*, edited by Noah D. Drezner, 152–70. New York: Routledge, 2013. 4.3.

Based on interviews with alumni as part of a larger case study, the author explored the role Greek affiliation played in giving. Fraternities and sororities helped bring alumni back to campus and impacted students' understandings of philanthropy.

Mesisca, James J. "Does Ivy League Athletic Success Increase Unrestricted Contributions from Alumni?" EdD, University of Pennsylvania, 2009. 4.3, 8.4.

The effects of won-loss records in men's football and basketball on alumni donations to Ivy League institutions was studied using seven years of data. Football success led to larger giving to athletics, but not to general giving, and basketball success did not have an effect.

Metcalf, Paul. "An Exploratory Analysis of the Dimensionality of the Mechanisms That Drive Private Giving Among Alumni Association Members and Non-Member Donors." PhD, Florida Atlantic University, 2013. 4.3.

Alumni giving at one university was explored using Bekkers and Wiepking's mechanisms of private giving and survey data. Six factors (efficacy, solicitation, reputation, values, altruism, and awareness) were found to have a meaningful effect. Alumni association membership did not have an effect.

Meuth, Elsbeth Friederike. "Corporate Philanthropy in American Higher Education: An Investigation of Attitudes towards Giving." EdD, University of Akron, 1992. 1.12.

Fortune 500 companies were surveyed regarding corporate giving and responses from those that gave to higher education were analyzed. Enlightened self-interest and business influenced were reasons for giving. Company demographics, not respondent's attitudes, predicted giving levels. Future giving to secondary education was projected to provide competition with giving to higher education.

Millard, James Edward. "Student Debt and Undergraduate Alumni Giving to One's Alma Mater." PhD, University of Missouri—Kansas City, 2002. 4.3.

This thesis tested the effect of total, personal loan, and credit card debt on alumni giving. Mean giving and giving consistency were significantly different for alumni with and without debt. The amount of debt had no effect on average annual gift or gift consistency.

Miller, Lawrence Gordon. "Patterns of Philanthropic Giving in American Community Colleges." PhD, University of Texas at Austin, 1994. 1.3, 8.2.

A survey of community colleges development offices and VSE data examined institutions with high levels of giving. Structure and fund sources varied; development officers attributed their success to institutional reputation and service, leadership, and economic impact. All institutions were less successful than four-year institutions.

Miller, Myra E. "Why Alumni Give: How Campus Environment and Sense of Belonging Shape Nontraditional Students' Intent to Give Financially to Their University." PhD, Saint Louis University, 2013. 4.3.

A survey of traditional and nontraditional students from four campuses at Drury University found two factors impacted intent to give: campus attended and sense of belonging. Traditional alumni were more likely to give, although they were the minority at Drury.

Miller, M. F. "An Analysis of Selected Public Community College Foundations in Michigan." PhD doctoral dissertation, Michigan State University, 1997. 1.3, 8.2.

College presidents, foundation directors, and trustee chairs were interviewed to determine the factors affecting high or low foundation performance. Successful institutions attributed their success to planning, "friend-raising," positive college image, articulation of mission to the public, visibility of personnel in community, active participation by the president and board members; having a full-time director, support by employees and volunteers, community partnerships, and communication.

Miller, Matthew W. 2013. "The Role of the Community College President in Fundraising Perceptions of Selected Michigan Community College Presidents." EdD, University of Nebraska. 1.2, 6.1, 8.2.

Four college presidents were interviewed based on resource dependence theory regarding their role in fundraising. Presidents suggested that strategic planning, vision, adequate resources, community involvement, "friend-raising," and having a full-time development officer influenced success.

Miller, Michael Thomas. "The Personal Motivation of Chief Academic Development Officers." EdD, University of Nebraska—Lincoln, 1991. 6.3.

A survey of development officers based on the Spectrum 1 Test of Adult Motivation and NACUBO data on endowment growth to see if successful and unsuccessful fundraisers had differences in motivation. No significant difference was found. All officers rated higher on accomplishment than on power, recognition, and affiliation.

Miller, Scott Douglas. "The Relationship of Selected Factors with Success in Private Sector Resource Acquisition at Appalachian Higher Education Institutions." PhD, The Union Institute, 1991. 1.3.

This survey of Appalachian College Program institutions, along with six site visits, explored the factors affecting the gift income. Institutions were divided into high- and low-performing groups based on their increase in total gift income. Benchmarks were created to compare the performance of individual colleges.

Milliron, Mark David, Gerardo E. de los Santos, and Boo Browning. "Feels Like the Third Wave: The Rise of Fundraising in the Community College." *New Directions for Community Colleges* 124 (2003): 81–93. doi: 10.1002/cc.137. 8.2.

Using Toffler's metaphor of a third wave (the transition from an industrial to an information society), the authors divide the history of community colleges into waves: the first being the massive growth of the system in the mid-1900s; the second being entrepreneurial expansion in the 1980s; and the third being the rise of institutional advancement.

Minter, Michele. "Women's Volunteerism and Philanthropy at Princeton University." *New Directions for Philanthropic Fundraising* 50 (2005): 125–39. 4.3, 4.5.

The case of the Women in Leadership Initiative at Princeton was explored. The Initiative emphasizes volunteering and giving and does not build an ongoing membership. The program was developed after focus groups with alumnae and is headed by alumnae.

Mitroff, Ian I., Michael A. Diamond, and Murat C. Alpaslan. "How Prepared are America's Colleges and Universities for Major Crises?" *Change: The Magazine of Higher Learning* 38 no. 1 (2006): 61–67. 2.6.

Provosts were surveyed regarding their institutions' crisis management teams, the types of crises they were prepared for, institutional support for these programs, and their effects. Institutions were only prepared for crises they had previously experienced. Teams were comprised of different members than similar corporate teams.

Mitzel, David Poe. "A Study of Factors Affecting the Level of Private Support for Ohio's Public Two-Year Colleges and Campuses." PhD, Ohio University, 1991. 1.3, 8.2.

Ohio public institutions were surveyed regarding fundraising. Separate campus foundations resulted in higher median gifts than did system-wide foundations. Larger staffs, the use of more techniques, and time spent by presidents or board members increased gifts, as did the years of experience of the president and chief development officer.

Mokopakgosi, Brian T. "Self-Reliance and the History of Higher Education: The Botswana University Campus Appeal (BUCA)." *Journal of Southern African Studies* 34 no. 2 (2008): 293–304. 1.6, 5.5.

Based on archival research and interviews, this paper explored how funds were raised after Botswana University was created from part of a previous institution in 1975. Donors were rewarded with publicity, and the campaign was framed as part of nation-building by political leaders.

Monks, James. "Patterns of Giving to One's Alma Mater among Young Graduates from Selective Institutions." *Economics of Education Review* 22 (2003): 121–30. 4.3.

Recent alumni of 28 private, selective colleges and universities were surveyed; the data was used to build a model for the likelihood of giving. Income, race, marital status, citizenship, satisfaction with the institution, advanced degrees (except PhDs), loan debt, and academic and extracurricular activities influenced gift size.

Mooney, Claudia. "The Communication Strategies and the Role Enactment of Selected College and University Fundraisers." PhD, Michigan State University, 1991. 1.1.

Ethnography was used to study roles of three fundraisers at different institutions. Cultivation of donors was found to be non-linear and continuous. Fundraisers used a variety of communication strategies, including networking and listening.

Morgan, Nancy B. "Characteristics Associated with the Effectiveness of Resource Development Programs at Florida Community Colleges." EdD, University of Central Florida, 2005. 1.13, 8.2.

Grant development programs at Florida community colleges were surveyed and the data was used to develop models to predict grant development success. No statistically significant relationships were found with the variables used.

Morris, Leah Michelle. "Integrated Marketing: The Process and Challenge of Implementing This Evolving Concept at Three Private Universities." EdD, Texas Tech University, 2003. 3.2.

This case study of IMC at three universities found that none of the institutions had integrated marketing, recruitment, and fundraising, although institutional messages were integrated. Two institutions used cross-functional teams. Marketing had little connection to academics.

Morton, Cathy Coleman. "The Importance of Fund-Raising Education to Public Relations Practitioners and Students: A Curriculum Issue in Higher Education." EdD, Texas Tech University, 1993. 2.2.

Public relations practitioners and students were surveyed to see if they had formal education in fundraising and eight public relations textbooks were content analyzed. Both surveys and the content analysis indicated that practitioners received little formal education in fundraising, despite its importance.

Mosser, John Wayne. "Predicting Alumni/ae Gift-Giving Behavior: A Structural Equation Model Approach." PhD, University of Michigan, 1993. 4.3.

University of Michigan alumni giving was modeled with SEM based on a survey of alumni. Capacity to give mediated motivation to give, but other factors mattered as well.

Mount, Joan, and Charles H. Bélanger. "Entrepreneurship and Image Management in Higher Education: Pillars of Massification." *Canadian Journal of Higher Education* 34 no. 2 (2004): 125–40. 3.3.

This paper explored two consequences of massification in higher education: entrepreneurialism and differentiation via branding.

Muller, Helen S. "The Contribution of Organizational Identification and Induced Reciprocity to Institutional Support and Philanthropy by Expatriate Alumni of an American University Abroad: An Exploratory Theoretical Model." PhD, New York University, 2004. 4.3, 5.6.

The author proposed a model of alumni supportive behavior that used institutional identification as a mediating variable and tested it on an American university abroad. Alumni were surveyed. Induced reciprocity, years since graduation, and income influenced giving. Identification, prestige, and induced reciprocity influenced alumni institutional promotion.

Mulnix, Michael William, Randall G. Bowden, and Esther Elena Lopez. "Institutional Advancement Activities at Select Hispanic-Serving Institutions: The Politics of Raising Funds." *International Journal of Educational Advancement* 5 no. 1 (2004). 1.1, 8.6.

Presidents of institutions that were HACU members were surveyed to find out more about advancement at HSIs. They agreed advancement and enrollment management were important. 70 percent believed sponsored programs were important and half had lobbyists in Washington, DC. Endowment growth was healthy.

Mulnix, Michael William, Randall G. Bowden, and Esther Elena López. "A Brief Examination of Institutional Advancement Activities at Hispanic Serving Institutions." *Journal of Hispanic Higher Education* 1 no. 2 (2002): 174–90. 1.1, 8.6.

Based on the same dataset as the authors' other article, "Institutional Advancement Activities," the findings here are similar.

Mulugetta, Yuko, Scott Nash, and Susan H. Murphy. "What Makes a Difference: Evaluating the Cornell Tradition Program." *New Directions for Institutional Research* 101 (1999): 61–80. 4.5.

The Cornell Tradition program, which encouraged alumni involvement with Cornell, was evaluated using a theory of college effects. Alumni from the classes of 1990 and 1992 were examined three years postgraduation; they were more likely than a matched sample to donate to Cornell and volunteer in their communities.

Murillo, Laura Gonzalez. "The Factors That Hispanic Alumni/ae Give for Making Gifts to a Public Institution of Higher Education." EdD, University of Houston, 2003. 4.3.

University of Houston Hispanic alumni donors (28 out of 350) were surveyed regarding attitudes and demographics to examine cultivation, solicitation, and stewardship.

Murphree, Vanessa, and Cathy Rogers. "'A Hell of a Shock' when a Jesuit University Faces a Presidential Sex Allegation." *Public Relations Quarterly* 49 no. 3 (2004): 34–40. 2.6, 6.1, 8.8.

This case study about a presidential sex scandal at Loyola University of New Orleans discussed the institution's crisis management. Loyola did not have a crisis management plan, did not conduct postcrisis research, and kept details about the allegations that unseated the president sealed.

Murray, Lynne Ellen. "The Managerial Practices of Chief Advancement Officers: Practices That Promote or Inhibit Fundraising in Higher Education." PhD, Gallaudet University, 2008. 1.3, 6.3.

Chief advancement officers at baccalaureate institutions were surveyed regarding their management practices; additional interviews were conducted. Three-quarters were male and most had served for four years or less in their current role. In addition to supervising development and alumni and public relations, they had administrative duties and worked with major donors.

Myers, John Anthony. "Influences on Major Donor Decisions." PhD, University of Calgary, 2011. 1.2, 5.1, 5.3.

Donors, high net worth individuals, and fundraisers from Canada and India were interviewed regarding donation decision-making. The author proposed a model for decision-making and refined it based on feedback from participants.

Nardone, Mary S. "Reputation in America's Graduate Schools of Education: A Study of the Perceptions and Influences of Graduate School of Education Deans and School Superintendents Regarding U.S. News & World Report's Ranking of Top Education Programs." PhD, Boston College, 2009. 3.4.

Education deans and school superintendents were surveyed regarding the reputation component of the *U.S. News* education school rankings. Superintendents are not rankings participants, although they may be in a position to judge the schools' production of professional graduates. Deans, who had vested interests in their institutions' ranks, participated but reluctantly.

Narum, Jeanne L. "Building Alliances for Institutional Support." *New Directions for Philanthropic Fundraising* 23 (1999): 51–67. 2.5.

Drawing from examples, the author described ways of building alliances with foundations, federal agencies, and universities. The author stated that alliances have many benefits and suggested scenarios for alliance-building.

Ncube, Peggie Mathaba. "A Rhetorical Analysis of Theodore Hesburgh's Fund-Raising Speeches for the University of Notre Dame." PhD, Andrews University, 2002. 1.9.

This thesis analyzed fundraising speeches to Notre Dame alumni by President Hesburgh using the Burkean dramatistic approach. His speeches stressed five points: alumni connection with the world, universal values, working hard for the university, focus on alumni rather than students, and what the university already has rather than needs.

Nehls, Kimberly. "Presidential Transitions during Capital Campaigns." *International Journal of Educational Advancement* 8 no. 3 (2008): 198–218. 1.1, 6.1.

This article is based on the author's dissertation, discussed below.

Nehls, Kimberly Kay. "Presidential Transitions during Capital Campaigns: Perspectives of Chief Development Officers." PhD, University of Nevada, Las Vegas, 2007. 1.1, 6.1.

Using Schlossberg's theory of transition, the work of nine chief development officers engaged in capital campaigns during presidential transitions was explored. Most transitions were negative. Strategies for dealing with transitions included providing input into presidential selection, communication, educating and involving the new president, and creating new funding priorities.

Nesbit, Becky, Patrick Rooney, Gary Bouse, and Eugene R. Tempel. "Presidential Satisfaction with Development Programs in Research and Doctoral Universities: A Comparison of Results from Surveys in 1990 and 2000." *International Journal of Educational Advancement* 6 no. 3 (2006): 182–99. 1.9, 6.1.

Two surveys of presidential satisfaction with fundraising were compared. Perceived expertise of the fundraising staff and satisfaction with funds raised in the past year predicted overall satisfaction. Presidents were more satisfied in 2000 than in 1990.

Neuman, Lisa Kay. "Recapturing Culture: American Indian Identities at Bacone College, 1927–1955." Duke University, 2002. 1.15, 8.6.

Bacone College, originally founded to educate, assimilate, and convert American Indians, began to emphasize Indian identity in an era when this emphasis provided a distinctive basis for fundraising. Thanks to the oil boom, some Indians became wealthy and were able to support the college, and Bacone adapted to donor wishes.

Neuman, Lisa K. "Selling Indian Education: Fundraising and American Indian Identities at Bacone College, 1880–1941." *American Indian Culture and Research Journal* 31 no. 4 (2007): 51–78. 1.15, 8.6.

This article was based on the author's dissertation, "Recapturing Culture."

Newman, Melissa Dawn. "Determinants of Alumni Membership in a Dues-Based Alumni Association." PhD, University of Louisville, 2009. 4.4.

Alumni association data from one university found that alumni were more likely to join the association if they were older, donors, aware of other members, and satisfied with the association. They were more likely to become life members if they had heavy extracurricular involvement, were donors, were frequently involved, and were satisfied with the association.

Newman, Melissa Dawn. "Does Membership Matter? Examining the Relationship between Alumni Association Membership and Alumni Giving." *International Journal of Educational Advancement* 10 no. 4 (2011): 163–79. 4.3, 4.4.

This article is based on the author's dissertation, "Determinants of Alumni Membership."

Newman, Melissa D., and Joseph M. Petrosko. "Predictors of Alumni Association Membership." *Research in Higher Education* 52 no. 7 (2011): 738–59. 4.4.

This article is based on Newman's dissertation, "Determinants of Alumni Membership," discussed earlier.

Newman, Raquel H. "Perception of Factors Relating to Gender Differences in Philanthropy." EdD, University of San Francisco, 1995. 1.2.

Alumni at two private institutions were surveyed to explore the effects of gender on giving. Of 11 subscales, women differed from men on three: priorities, conditions, and altruism. Income also affected giving, and women were likely to have lower incomes than men.

Nicholson, William. "Leading Where It Counts: An Investigation of the Leadership Styles and Behaviors That Define College and University Presidents As Successful Fund Raisers." University of South Carolina, 2006. 1.3, 6.1.

The fundraising behavior of four presidents served as case studies, using Bass and Avolio's framework of transactional and transformational leadership. Presidents used both approaches, but transformational approaches in particular enhanced fundraising.

Nicolanti, David R. "Characteristics, Experiences, Attitudes, and Other Factors Related to Alumni Who Provide Financial Support to Their Podiatry Colleges." PhD, Kent State University, 1991. 4.3, 8.3.

A survey of alumni of podiatry colleges compared donors and nondonors. While the two groups differed on 110 variables, 2 variables accurately predicted donor status for 82 percent of the sample: membership in the alumni association and a tally of the number of ways they were involved with the college.

Nicoson, Dan J. "Prospect Development Systems: Empowering Artful Fundraising." *New Directions for Higher Education* 149 (2010): 73–79. 1.1.

The author described methods of qualifying, cultivating, and assigning prospects.

Nielsen, Norm, Wayne Newton, and Cheryle W. Mitvalsky. "The Role of Community College Trustees in Supporting the Foundation." *New Directions for Community Colleges* 124 (2003): 33–39. doi: 10.1002/cc.131. 6.2, 8.2.

Based on a case study of Kirkwood Community College, the authors explored the role of college trustees in supporting the foundation. Trustees enhance college image, oversee and support the foundation, choose and support administration, and encourage innovation, according to the authors.

Nirschel, Roy Joseph. "Charitable Giving as Obligation or Option: An Analysis of Cuban Alumni and Jewish Alumni at a Private Research University." PhD, University of Miami, 1997. 4.3.

Jewish and Cuban alumni of the University of Miami were surveyed regarding charitable giving. Similar percentages of both populations donated, although Jewish alumni gave at higher levels. Alumni with strong religious beliefs viewed giving as an obligation, and giving was correlated with volunteerism in both groups. Jewish and Cuban alumni gave to somewhat different causes.

Niwagaba, Lillian Katono Butungi. "Shifting Paradigms, Changing Fortunes: Fundraising at Makerere University." PhD, University of North Texas, 2012. 1.1, 5.5.

This case study of Makerere University used Tierney's organizational culture framework and relied on interviews, document analysis, and observation. Problems included a governance structure that provided inadequate support, perceptions of corruption, and internal conflicts. Reforms to student and alumni experiences are producing some fundraising success.

O'Connell, Catherine. "Research Discourses Surrounding Global University Rankings: Exploring the Relationship with Policy and Practice Recommendations." *Higher Education* 65 no. 6 (2013): 709–23. 3.4.

This paper grouped research frameworks used in rankings research into four distinct discourses (dissensus, elite/a priori, consensus, or local/emergent). The discourse used in any given paper depends on the audience addressed and whether the proposal is structural or social justice oriented.

O'Connor, William J. "Factors That Motivate Hispanic Donors to Philanthropically Support Higher Education." PhD, State University of New York at Buffalo, 2007. 1.2, 1.3.

The author surveyed Hispanic alumni of the University of St. Thomas and Whittier College regarding philanthropic motivation. Giving to alma mater was rated as a high priority with motivations of loyalty and helping the next generation. Gender and age did not have significant effects.

Odom, Tara Leigh. "Predictors of Alumni Philanthropy in a Public University in South Mississippi." PhD, University of Southern Mississippi, 1995. 4.3.

Major donors at three levels to a university were surveyed to study factors that influenced donor level. Perceptual, undergraduate experience, and demographic variables were all related to donor category.

Oglesby, Rodney Allen. "Age, Student Involvement, and Other Characteristics of Alumni Donors and Alumni Non-Donors of Southwest Baptist University." PhD, University of Missouri—Columbia, 1991. 4.3.

Alumni of Southwest Baptist were surveyed to produce descriptive data regarding donors and nondonors. Age and student government participation predicted both donor status and level.

Okunade, A. A. "Logistic Regressions and Probability of Business School Alumni Donations: Micro-Data Evidence." *Education Economics* 1 no. 3 (1993): 243–58. 4.3, 8.3.

A survey of business school alumni to one university was used to create a logit model to predict donations. The probability of giving was influenced by major, time since graduation, having other graduates in the family, having children over 18, the number of other alumni known who gave, income, occupation, giving to other nonprofits, volunteering, access to matching gift programs, and perceptions of educational experiences.

Okunade, A. A. "Graduate School Alumni Donations to Academic Funds: Micro-Data Evidence." *American Journal of Economics and Sociology* 55 (1996): 213–29. 4.3, 8.3.

Giving information from University of Memphis graduate business school alumni was used to model predict the likelihood of giving a gift. Likely donors were male graduates with no other degrees from the institution; doctoral alumni gave more than masters alumni. Donations decreased over time.

Okunade, Albert A., and Robert L. Berl. "Determinants of Charitable Giving of Business School Alumni." *Research in Higher Education* 38 no. 2 (1997): 201–14. 4.3, 8.3.

Giving information and survey data from one university's graduate business school alumni was used to model predict the likelihood of giving a gift. Significant factors included time since graduation, academic major, willingness to recommend the university, household attributes, and family ties.

Okunade, A. A., P. V. Wunnava, and R. Walsh. "Charitable Giving of Alumni: Microdata from a Large Public University." *American Journal of Economics and Sociology* 53 (1994): 73–74. 4.3.

Institutional data on alumni donations to one university was used to build a life-cycle model that predicted the likelihood of giving based on age. The model predicted that donations would decline after age 52. Other significant factors included attending the business school, earning additional degrees at the university, and membership in non-Greek campus social organizations.

Oliver, Frank H. "Fellow Beggars: The History of Fund Raising Campaigning in United States Higher Education." EdD, Columbia University Teachers College, 1999. 7.1.

This history of fundraising campaigns traced the evolution of campaigns from 1641 to the 1997. Early campaigns relied heavily on volunteers. The early twentieth century saw some institutions adopting short, focused campaigns, while others raised funds more continuously, and institutions began to hire professional fundraisers. The field expanded greatly after World War II.

Oliver, Frank H. "The Roots of Academic Fund Raising." *CASE International Journal of Educational Advancement* 3 no. 2 (2002). 7.1.

This paper was based on the author's dissertation, "Fellow Beggars."

Oliver, Jenea Lynnette. "Individual Factors That Contribute to the Turnover of Fundraisers Employed at Institutions of Higher Education." PhD, University of Missouri—Kansas City, 2007. 6.5.

Fundraisers at eight higher education institutions were surveyed and interviewed to explore factors that influence turnover. Organizational commitment and job satisfaction were inversely related to intent to leave. The author identified six factors that influenced turnover.

Olsen, Deborah M. "Remaking the Image: Promotional Literature of Mount Holyoke, Smith, and Wellesley Colleges in the Mid-to-Late 1940s." *History of Education Quarterly* (2000): 418–59. 7.2.

The author examined changes in promotional literature at three women's colleges in an era when higher education for women had become established and antifeminist attitudes were ascendant. Materials were created to reach not only future career women but also future wives and mothers. Strategies included lighthearted tones, heterosexual images, linking students to marriage and family, and images and language related to motherhood.

O'Malley, Timothy Lawrence. "The Effects of Consortium Fund-Raising in Independent Higher Education." PhD, University of Oregon, 1991. 1.3.

Archival data and Delphi technique surveys from eight Oregon Independent College Foundation colleges were used to examine the effect of the consortium on fundraising. Communication practices, strategic prospect research, donor recognition, restricted giving, volunteers, and annual College-Business Weeks were found to be important.

O'Neil, Julie. "The Challenge of Promoting a Cohesive Institutional Identity: An Investigation of the Impact of External Audiences, Task Specialization, and the Overall Organization." *Journal of Nonprofit and Public Sector Marketing* 11 no. 2 (2003): 21–41. 3.3.

The University of Utah served as a case study to show the challenges of integrated marketing communications. Practitioners base decisions on departmental views, not student or public views. Multiple positioning efforts result in a multifaceted identity.

O'Neill, Patricia Purish. "The Impact of Undergraduate Greek Membership on Alumni Giving at the College of William and Mary." PhD, College of William and Mary, 2005. 4.3.

Using Astin's theory of undergraduate involvement and institutional data from William and Mary, the author tested the role of fraternity/sorority membership on alumni giving. Greek alumni were more likely to be donors, gave at higher levels, and gave more consistently over time. Age and Greek affiliation interacted to produce an additional giving increase.

Ostrower, F. *Why the Wealthy Give: The Culture of Elite Philanthropy*. Princeton, NJ: Princeton University Press, 1995. 4.3.

Ostrower interviewed close to 100 wealthy donors, focused in the New York City area. Philanthropic motivation and significance were explored. Philanthropy was found to serve as a marker of class status and was used to differentiate donors. Feelings of loyalty, responsibility, and altruism were not absent.

Owen, Sandy A. "Understanding Career Progression for Women in Higher Education Advancement: Gender Bias and Personal Choice." EdD, Johnson & Wales University, 2009. 6.5.

Based on surveys and focus group interviews with female development professionals, this thesis explored why women are overrepresented in the field yet underrepresented at top ranks.

Owston, James Martin. "Survival of the Fittest? The Rebranding of West Virginia Higher Education." EdD, Marshall University, 2007. 3.3.

In one decade, a startling number of West Virginia institutions rebranded, including college-to-university rebrandings. The author surveyed and interviewed administrators regarding the rationales, strategies, and implications in college-to-university rebrandings.

Page, Stewart. "Rankings of Canadian Universities: Pitfalls in Interpretation." *Canadian Journal of Higher Education* 25 no. 2 (1995): 17–28. 3.4, 5.1.

The author critically analyzed *MacLean*'s 1993 university rankings. Problems with rankings and correlations with some objective measures were discussed.

Palmer, Gladys Juanita Barwick. "The Nature and Status of Resource Development Activities in National League for Nursing Accredited Baccalaureate and Master's Degree Schools of Nursing." EdD, Florida State University, 1992. 1.1, 8.7.

Accredited nursing programs were surveyed regarding fundraising programs; follow-up interviews were conducted. While most institutions had an office for resource development, less than 25 percent had a dedicated officer for nursing. Dedicated officers were correlated with higher scholarship funds, endowed chairs, contingency funds, and total dollars raised.

Palmer, Stuart. "Characterisation of the Use of Twitter by Australian Universities." *Journal of Higher Education Policy and Management* 35 no. 4 (2013): 333–44. 3.1, 5.4.

Tweets and Twitter interactions from six Australian universities were analyzed by frequency and network analysis. The universities varied in their Twitter interactions, from regular and sustained to irregular and sparse. Gallaugher and Ransbotham's 3-M model of social media communications was used.

Parker, Steve Robert. "The Effect of Athletic Probation on Donor Contributions to the University's Development Office." EdD, University of Kentucky, 1995. 1.3, 8.4.

The effect of athletic probation on donations to universities was examined with data from 26 Division I institutions whose men's basketball or football teams were on probation in the 1980s and 26 institutions that were not. Probation showed no significant effect on total support, number of new donors, or corporate donations.

Parsons, Frank Ray, Jr. "Residential Life as a Correlate to Higher Education Fund-Raising." EdD, University of Alabama, 1998. 4.3.

Data from Samford University was used to test the effect of being a resident assistant during 1975–1990 on alumni giving. Resident assistants gave slightly more than non-RAs. They also participated more in alumni activities.

Parsons, Mark Hunter. "Negotiating the Planned Gift for Higher Education: A Learning Organization Paradigm." PhD, University of Minnesota, 1993. 1.5.

The author proposed a model of philanthropic giving and applied it to planned giving at Hamline University in a qualitative case study. The model is based on system dynamics methodology and defines philanthropy as a reciprocal social relationship.

Parsons, Pamela Hughey. "Women's Philanthropy: Motivations for Giving." PhD, University of Alabama, 2004. 1.2.

$250,000-plus female donors to the University of Alabama were surveyed based on Identification Theory. ANOVA found a significant difference between the donations of volunteers and nonvolunteers. Age and motivation were not significant. Qualitative analysis found that family and religion affected giving.

Pastorella, Mark J. "Keeping in Touch: Alumni Development in Community Colleges." *New Directions for Community Colleges* 124 (2003): 75–79. doi: 10.1002/cc.136. 4.7.

Monroe Community College served as the basis for this case study of alumni development in two-year institutions. Alumni were involved in multiple ways, including comprising 25 percent of the board and alumni events. The author recommended finding influential and affluent alumni, increasing alumni visibility, developing an annual fund, building relationships, having realistic expectations, and knowing your mission.

Patouillet, L. D. "Alumni Association Members: Attitudes toward University Life and Giving at a Public AAU Institution." PhD dissertation, University of Pittsburgh, 2000. 4.3, 4.7.

University of Pittsburgh alumni association members were surveyed, comparing donors to nondonors using several theories of fundraising. All respondents valued intangible benefits over tangible benefits. Significant differences were found in the rankings of factors that influenced satisfaction.

Patouillet, Leland D. "Alumni Association Members: Attitudes toward University Life and Giving at a Public AAU Institution." *CASE International Journal of Educational Advancement* 2 no. 1 (2001): 53–65. 4.3, 4.7.

This article is based on the author's dissertation, discussed above.

Pavlovich, Mark Gregory. "Environmental Conditions and Institutional Characteristics Which Enhance Fund-Raising Potential at Private Liberal Arts Colleges." PhD, University of Michigan, 1993. 1.3.

Information on 29 variables related to environmental conditions, donor motivations, and institutional characteristics at 305 liberal arts colleges was used to determine their impact on fundraising potential. At more selective colleges, average gift, number of alumni, and SAT scores accounted for most variability; at less selective colleges, endowment, average gift, SAT scores, budget, expenditures per student, and college age accounted for the variability.

Payne, A. Abigail. "Measuring the Effect of Federal Research Funding on Private Donations at Research Universities: Is Federal Research Funding More Than a Substitute for Private Donations?" *International Tax and Public Finance* 8 (2001): 731–51. 1.16.

The effect of an increase in federal grants on private giving was explored. The two funding sources were positively correlated for research institutions and negatively correlated for other institutions. Data sources included CASPAR, VSE, the NCAA, and several other sources.

Pearson, J. "Comprehensive Research on Alumni Relationships: Four Years of Market Research at Stanford University." *New Directions for Institutional Research* 16 no. 101 (1999): 5–21. 4.3.

Stanford University engaged in intensive market research among fundraising prospects, 1994–1999, and this paper reviewed some of these internal studies. Topics covered included undergraduate giving, the experiences of alumni of color, comparative data on undergraduates compared to peer institutions, graduate alumni giving, the online benefits alumni wanted, and the results of advertising.

Pearson, Jerold. "E-Mail Newsletters and Institutional Advancement." *CASE International Journal of Educational Advancement* 2 no. 2 (2001): 147–64. 4.7.

This article covers the same research as the author's article discussed above.

Pearson, William Edward. "A Study of Donor Predictability among Graduates of a School of Education within a Research I, Public University." PhD, University of Virginia, 1996. 4.3.

Based on a survey of alumni at one university, this thesis used discriminant analysis to distinguish between donors and nondonors. The model correctly classified 81 percent of donors based on demographic, participatory, attitudinal, and philanthropic behavior factors; donors were correctly classified as major or nonmajor at 86 percent.

Peeples, Yarbrah T. "Philanthropy and the Curriculum: The Role of Philanthropy in the Development of Curriculum at Spelman College." *International Journal of Educational Advancement* 10 no. 3 (2010): 245–60. 1.15, 8.1.

Spelman College's curriculum and the influence of philanthropy were examined with Spelman's history divided into presidential eras. Funds from philanthropists and foundations strengthened the institution and also influenced courses and majors.

Peet, Melissa R., Katherine Walsh, Robin Sober, and Christine S. Rawak. "Generative Knowledge Interviewing: A Method for Knowledge Transfer and

Talent Management at the University of Michigan." *International Journal of Educational Advancement* 10 no. 2 (2010): 71–85. 6.5.

Generative Knowledge Interviewing was tested as a method for passing down tacit knowledge, using fundraisers at the University of Michigan. This message could prevent the loss of knowledge in leadership transitions, according to the authors.

Peltier, James W., John A. Schibrowsky, and Don E. Schultz. "Leveraging Customer Information to Develop Sequential Communication Strategies: A Case Study of Charitable-Giving Behavior." *Journal of Advertising Research* July/August no. 23–41 (2002). 1.1.

The authors tested their model of sequential communication to build relationships by surveying alumni at one university. The structural equation model confirmed the importance of donor-organization relationships, donor-beneficiary relationships, relationship commitment, relationship motives, and category and relationship priorities.

Perez, Mario A. "Big Goals, Bigger Expectations: A Study of the Future Roles and Responsibilities for the Chief Development Officer in the Year 2015 and Beyond." EdD, University of La Verne, 2013. 6.3.

Delphi technique was used with a panel of 25 university presidents, chief development officers, and consultants regarding future roles and responsibilities of CDOs. Eight roles and 11 responsibilities achieved consensus. The top three future roles were advisor to president, campaign administrator, and communicator; the top three responsibilities were board development, creation of structures and systems, and gift procurement.

Perry, Pam. "Behind the Curtain of the Beauty Pageant: An Investigation of US News Undergraduate Business Program Rankings." PhD, University of Arizona, 2010. 3.4.

Ten each of deans and associate deans of top undergraduate business schools ranked in the top 50 by *U.S. News* were interviewed about how they rate peer institutions for the rankings. Deans valued quality from faculty and research; associate deans valued the undergraduate experience. Schools used IMC to influence peers.

Peterson, Lorna M. "Consortial Fundraising." *New Directions for Higher Education* 106 (1999): 59–65. 1.1.

Fundraising by higher education consortia was explored, drawing on the author's experience with Five Colleges, which has its own fundraiser. Policies were in place to avoid poaching, improve credibility, and handle grants administration; the author discussed these three policy issues.

Pettey, Janice Gow, and Lilya Wagner. "Introduction: Union Gives Strength—Diversity and Fundraising." *International Journal of Educational Advancement* 7 no. 3 (2007): 171–75. 6.5.

In this introduction to a special journal issue, the authors advocated for diversity in fundraisers and discussed some findings about non-US philanthropy.

Pettit, Joseph, and L. H. Litten, eds. "A New Era of Alumni Research: Improving Institutional Performance and Better Serving Alumni," no. 101, *New Directions for Institutional Research*. San Francisco: Jossey-Bass. 4.

This volume of *New Directions* focused on alumni research. Individual articles are discussed separately in this appendix.

Peyronel, Anthony C. "Higher Education Public Relations at the Year 2000: Assessing the Status of Public Relations at Colleges and Universities." *CASE International Journal of Educational Advancement* 1 no. 1 (2000). 2.

This article discussed the challenges of higher education's relationship with the media and what public relations professionals can do to improve it

Peyronel, Anthony C. "Media Scrutiny of Higher Education: An Ongoing Challenge and Long-Term Trend." *International Journal of Educational Advancement* 4 no. 3 (2004). 2.3.

While higher education and the media sometimes have an adversarial relationship, in this article the author argued for the importance of media relations.

Phelan, J. F., ed. *College and University Foundations: Serving America's Public Higher Education*. Washington, DC: AGB Publications, 1999. 1.1.

This edited volume provided advice for successful foundation fundraising. It also included survey results from a 1995 survey of foundations.

Phillips, Samuel Horace. "An Experimental Investigation of the Role of College and University Financial Statements in Alumni Support Decisions." PhD, University of Houston, 1991. 4.3.

In this experiment, alumni were presented with either an annual report or narrative, in either tabular or graphic format, and then asked questions about their willingness to provide support. Format mattered. In addition, general financial condition and efficiency were correlated with giving.

Piazza, Anthony F. "A Qualitative Study Examining the Role of Academic Deans and Fundraising." PhD, Capella University, 2008. 1.1, 6.6.

Academic deans were interviewed about their role in fundraising and their relationship with the relevant development officer. While deans understood the need to fundraise, most were not equipped to do so due to lack of experience. Newer deans were more enthusiastic about learning to do so.

Pichon, Doris Faye Jones. "A Study of Fundraising in Selected Urban and Suburban California Community Colleges: A Description of Programs and an Identification of Successful Strategies." PhD, University of Texas at Austin, 1999. 1.3, 8.2.

Eleven college presidents, one presidential assistant, and foundation directors were interviewed about why they were involved with fundraising, the means by which they fundraised, and the factors that contribute to fundraising success. Factors included institutional planning, staff quality and competency, level of quality, innovative strategies, and reciprocal giving.

Pike, Gary R. "Measuring Quality: A Comparison of US News Rankings and NSSE Benchmarks." *Research in Higher Education* 45 no. 2 (2004): 193–208. 3.4.

The *U.S. News* ranks and National Study of Student Engagement scores were compared for 14 public AAU-member universities using HLM. The two were not related, except that the *U.S. News* selectivity ranking was related to the NSSE Enriching Educational Experiences Score.

Pinchback, Garland Keith. "Fundraising and Community College Chief Executives: A Study of Development in the Southern Regional Education Board States." EdD, Arkansas State University, 2011. 1.1, 8.2.

A survey explored the president's role in fundraising. Most presidents had doctorates and came up through academic roles. A 65 percent had fundraised before becoming president; the majority had professional development in fundraising. Two-thirds said it was not one of the criteria for their hiring and over half were not evaluated on it. The majority spent less than 10 percent of their time on fundraising.

Piovane, Michael F. "An Analysis of Major Gift Programs and the Development of a Strategic Plan for Major Gift Cultivation at Kutztown University." EdD, Nova Southeastern University, 1996. 1.6.

Major gift programs at 77 public institutions were analyzed based on survey data and a strategic plan for major gifts was developed for Kutztown.

Plinske, Paul Michael. "Athletic Fund Raising: A Detailed Analysis of N.C.A.A. Division III Member Institutions." PhD, University of Minnesota, 1999. 1.3, 8.4.

Division III institutions were surveyed regarding athletic fundraising; 40 percent engaged in it. A 70 percent of programs aimed to provide budget relief for athletics. They relied on a variety of programs, averaging 380 donors and $143,000/year.

Poock, Michael C., and David J. Siegel. "Benchmarking Graduate School Development Practices." *International Journal of Educational Advancement* 6 no. 1 (2005): 11–19. 1.14, 8.3.

Based on a survey of Council of Graduate School members, the authors described development in graduate schools. About half engaged in development activities, with only 15 of 75 having a dedicated staff member. Most programs were begun between 2000 and 2004. Funds raised varied widely. 32 percent had no intent to begin fundraising.

Porter, Grace Aine. "Patterns of Giving to Urban Public Higher Education among Corporate Foundations in Virginia and Select Others Which Have a Significant Presence in Virginia." PhD, Old Dominion University, 1997. 1.12.

Corporate foundations with significant presences in Virginia were surveyed; tax returns were also analyzed. Analysis showed that four factors influenced giving to Virginia public higher education: altruism, profit maximization, mutual collective action, and geographical location.

Porter, Stephen R. "The Robustness of the Graduation Rate Performance Indicator Used in the U.S. News & World Report College Rankings." *CASE International Journal of Educational Advancement* 1 no. 2 (2000): 145–63. 3.4.

Differences in definition of "graduation rate" as used in *U.S. News* rankings, as well as sample size and missing data, can cause an institution's rate to fluctuate. The author modeled how these changes can occur and the changes that can result.

Powell, James R. "The Financial Management Practices of Small, Private, Non-Profit Colleges." PhD, University of Virginia, 2011. 1.8.

This qualitative study of seven tuition-dependent colleges examined their financial management practices. Most of the institutions felt they had to make fundraising a larger priority, cultivating donors that supported their missions, cultivating alumni, and supporting specific goals.

Pribbenow, Paul. "Pursuing Accountability: Organizing Integrity, the Advancement Profession, and Public Service." *CASE International Journal of Educational Advancement* 1 no. 3 (2001): 197–208. 1.10, 1.14.

The author argued that institutions have moral obligations to conduct assessment in order to purse accountability. The case of advancement was discussed, and a case of one assessment process was discussed.

Proper, Eve. "Bringing Educational Fundraising Back to Great Britain: A Comparison with the United States." *Journal of Higher Education Policy and Management* 31 no. 2 (2009): 149–59. 1, 5.2.

This article compared higher education fundraising in Great Britain and the United States. While it looks to the United States' higher education sector as a model, there are significant legal, historical, and cultural differences between the two nations that could limit the British higher education sector's capacity to increase voluntary support.

Proper, Eve. "The Outcomes of Board Involvement in Fundraising at Independent, Four-Year Colleges: An Organization Theory Perspective." PhD, Vanderbilt University, 2011. 1.3, 6.2.

This dissertation examined the effects of trustees on fundraising via a quantitative study, using Council of Independent Colleges data, and case studies of three colleges. Quantitative models explained little of the variation in funds raised. In the case studies, board members were not involved with fundraising beyond giving.

Proper, Eve, Timothy C. Caboni, Harold V. Hartley, and Wesley K. Willmer. "'More Bang for the Buck': Examining Influencers of Fundraising Efficiency and Total Dollars Raised." *International Journal of Educational Advancement* 9 no. 1 (2009): 35–41. 1.3.

Data from a Council of Independent Colleges survey were used to examine factors controlled by the advancement office that influenced fundraising efficiency and total dollars raised. Staff size was the only advancement variable that significantly influenced total dollars raised.

Proper, E., Wesley K. Willmer, Harold V. Hartley, III, and Timothy C. Caboni. "Stakeholder Perceptions of Governance: Factors Influencing Presidential Perceptions of Board Governance." *International Journal of Educational Advancement* 9 no. 3 (2009): 166–73. 1.8, 6.1.

Analysis of data from a Council of Independent Colleges survey found that presidents were most satisfied with their board's fundraising role when boards had received training, the board had a fundraising committee, the president was skilled at fundraising, the board had more female members, the institution had recently completed a capital campaign, and it was more difficult to recruit board members.

Puma, Michael. "Fostering Student Affairs and Institutional Advancement Partnerships." In *Expanding the Donor Base in Higher Education: Engaging Non-Traditional Donors*, edited by Noah D. Drezner, 171–86. New York: Routledge, 2013. 1.1, 8.5.

With partnerships between student affairs and development becoming more common, the author provided advice for institutions undertaking them.

Pumerantz, Richard Kenneth. "Alumni-in-Training: Institutional Factors Associated with Greater Alumni Giving at Public Comprehensive Colleges and Universities." PhD, Claremont Graduate University, 2004. 4.3.

Interviews at four top-performing California State University institutions and eight peer institutions explored the factors that led to higher levels of alumni giving. CSU campuses performed below average in all categories except total giving as a percentage of expenditures. CSU alumni played an unusually small role in institutional fundraising.

Pumerantz, Richard Kenneth. "Alumni-in-Training: A Public Roadmap for Success." *International Journal of Educational Advancement* 5 no. 4 (2005): 289–300. 4.3.

This article was based on the author's dissertation, "Alumni-in-Training."

Pumphrey, Kathryn Mitchell. "Characteristics That Motivate Alumnae Giving at a Research I, Public University." EdD, University of Virginia, 2004. 4.3.

Based on a survey of University of Virginia alumnae found that 11 of 23 motivations were positively correlated with gift frequency; two were correlated with gift size. Those who gave large gifts placed more importance on recognition and family influence but less on mailings and solicitations for women's programs.

Pung, Barnaby. "I Alumnus: Understanding Early Alumni Identity." PhD, Michigan State University, 2013. 4.6.

Based on interviews with university alumni who had graduated a decade earlier and the Identity Salience Model of Relationship Marketing Success, this thesis explored how graduates constructed their alumna/us identity. Alumni described their alumni experience as informal peer networks. Perceptions of academic and work preparation influenced their framing of postgraduate experience, as did the perceptions of others.

Pusser, Brian, and Simon Marginson. "University Rankings in Critical Perspective." *Journal of Higher Education* 84 no. 4 (2013). 3.4.

The authors examined rankings using critical power theory and by understandings of universities as political institutions. Rankings rely on intentionality, legitimacy, and ideology. Different ranking systems measure similar constructs: prestige and wealth.

Reilly, Thomas Joseph. "Motivations, Bilateral Relationships, and One Million Dollar Contributors: A Case Study of a Southwestern University." PhD, University of Arizona, 1992. 1.2.

Interviews with $1 million-plus donors (individuals, corporations, and foundations) to a university were conducted regarding factors that influenced their decision to give. Altruism was the biggest motivator, followed by profit maximization, reciprocity, and direct benefit.

Reimer, Jay Paul. "Motivating Factors for Philanthropy at a Ministry Preparation Graduate Institution." EdD, University of North Texas, 2013. 1.3, 1.9, 8.3.

This case study of the Graduate Institute of Applied Linguistics was based on four interviews. Respondents felt that organizational effectiveness was a motivating factor for major donors; watchdog agency evaluations were also thought to matter.

Rhoads, Thomas A., and Shelby Gerking. "Educational Contributions, Academic Quality, and Athletic Success." *Contemporary Economic Policy* 18 no. 2 (2000): 248–58. 1.2, 4.3, 8.4.

Fixed panel data from Division I football institutions were used to examine the impact of athletic success on fundraising. Alumni donors but not others responded to changes in athletic success. Athletic traditions also positively impacted giving, but less than student or faculty quality.

Rhodes, Frank Harold Trevor, ed. *Successful Fund Raising for Higher Education: The Advancement of Learning*. Lanham, MD: Oryx Press, 1997. 1.

This edited volume consisted of essays by presidents and chief development officers. They discussed teamwork, strategic planning, and key players.

Ridley, Dennis R., Nuria M. Cuevas, and Alexei G. Matveev. "Transitions between Tiers in U.S. News & World Report Rankings of Colleges and Universities." *International Journal of Educational Advancement* 4 no. 1 (2003): 30–43. 3.4.

This study examined how often changes in ranking occur in two categories of *U.S. News* rankings. The probability of change was calculated to be 0.14; the average change over four years for the Tier 1 institutions was 1.94 places. Institutions may not be able to significantly change their rankings.

Ridley, Dennis R., Alexei G. Matveev, and Nuria M. Cuevas. "Dynamics of Internet Visibility: Mutual Benefits for Distinguished Alumni and Alma Mater?" *International Journal of Educational Advancement* 5 no. 2 (2005). 3.1, 4.

This paper examined whether institutions are better able to leverage famous alumni such as US presidents via the web. Presidential names were Googled; dead presidents had a higher connection between eminence and visibility than living presidents. For dead presidents, there was some evidence that searches linked presidents with their alma maters.

Riggs, R., and O. Heleg. "Investment Policy for Community College Foundations: Are Commodity Futures Prudent?" *Community College Journal of Research and Practice* 20 no. 3 (1996): 219–31. 1.3, 8.2.

The article described risk-reward techniques that can be used to help foundations decide what to invest in. The authors suggested balancing risks with rewards.

Roberts, Danny Houston. "Targeting Potential Donors from the Ranks of Non-Traditional and Traditional Students at the Undergraduate and Graduate Levels: A Comparative Analysis for Institutional Development." PhD, University of Missouri—Columbia, 1999. 4.3.

Nontraditional and graduate students at one university were surveyed about demographics, institutional involvement, institutional solicitation, and institutional giving. Capability to give and employment status correlated with donor status.

Robinson, Denauvo M. "A Study of Selected Characteristics of Alumni Financial Support to Their Alma Mater." EdD, Grambling State University, 1994. 4.3.

Alumni of Grambling State, Louisiana Tech, and Northeast Louisiana were surveyed and donors compared to nondonors. Typical donors were white males who had participated in sports; lived either in a fraternity/sorority house or off-campus; majored in engineering, science, or business; visited campus 2–3 times per year; gave to other educational institutions; and also gave to athletics.

Robinson, Michael. "Efficacy of Fraternity Involvement on Leadership Development among Alumni Members of Alpha Phi Alpha Fraternity in the Workplace." PhD, Capella University, 2013. 4.6.

Alpha Phi Alpha alumni of one institution were interviewed regarding how their Greek leadership experience translated to the workplace.

Rodriguez, Charles G. "Alumni and the President: Presidential Leadership Behavior Effecting Alumni Giving at Small Private Liberal Arts Colleges." PhD, Union Institute, 1991. 4.3, 6.1.

Chief advancement officers were surveyed about presidential behavior and characteristics. Alumni donor participation rates were higher at colleges where presidents opened their houses to alumni, spoke to alumni about their institutions' historical value, did not sign direct mail appeals, and included seven to eight alumni on their donor prospect lists.

Rollwagen, Ingo. "Project Economy Approaches for Higher Education: Diversifying the Revenue Base of German Universities." *Higher Education Management and Policy* 22 no. 3 (2010): 1–21. 2.4, 2.5, 5.6.

This article described collaborative partnerships at German universities, including collaborations with industry partners, as a way of revenue diversification. The author believed these partnerships brought several benefits to the universities engaged in them.

Roney, Kay Finney. "Private Fund-Raising in Alabama Two-Year Colleges: Current Status, Perceptions of Presidential Involvement, and Perceptions of Success." EdD, University of Alabama, 1993. 1.9, 6.1, 8.2.

The author surveyed Alabama community college development officers regarding fundraising, presidential involvement, and perceptions of success. While 84 percent had foundations, 43 percent had assets under $25,000. Most had not hired consultants, had held fewer than four events, and published little. Respondents spoke positively about their president's involvement in fundraising.

Rooney, Patrick, Eleanor Brown, and Debra Mesch. "Who Decides in Giving to Education? A Study of Charitable Giving by Married Couples." *International Journal of Educational Advancement* 7 no. 3 (2007): 229–42. 1.2.

Using data from the Panel Study on Income Dynamics, the authors examined whether husbands or wives were more likely to decide where to donate and how much to donate. Women were the sole or more influential decision-maker more often then men, which led to more gifts to education, although this varied by income.

Rooney, Patrick Michael. "A Better Method of Analyzing the Costs and Benefits of Fundraising at Universities." *Nonprofit Management and Leadership* 10 no. 1 (1999): 39–56. 1.3, 1.14.

Rooney proposed an alternative to the CASE/NACUBO guidelines for analyzing the costs and benefits of fundraising. In particular, he recommended analyzing cost per dollar raised by type of fundraising rather than overall. Using one institution, Rooney compared methods and finds that this enables institutions to make better decisions.

Roper, Paula LaJean. "Black Alumni of the University of Missouri-Columbia: Financial Support as the Mirror of Attitudes." PhD, University of Missouri—Columbia, 2000. 4.3.

Black University of Missouri alumni were surveyed regarding perceptions of university leadership, image, correspondence, alumni association, student experience, and fundraising techniques. ANOVA did not find any statistically significant difference between donors and nondonors.

Rosenberg, Harris. "Nonstatutory Funding for Universities." *CASE International Journal of Educational Advancement* 1 no. 2 (2000): 135–43. 1.16, 5.2.

The author examined funding sources for European institutions, primarily UK universities, other than government. These sources include fundraising, operating some functions as a business, and selling degree courses.

Routley, Claire, Adrian Sargeant, and Wendy Scaife. "Bequests to Educational Institutions: Who Gives and Why?" *International Journal of Educational Advancement* 7 no. 3 (2007): 193–201. 1.5.

The authors reviewed the literature on charitable bequests. Topics covered included what prospects to solicit and motives for making bequests.

Rovig, Nicole G. "An Examination of the Relationship between Development Support Characteristics and the Amount of Funds Raised for Student Affairs Divisions." PhD, Saint Louis University, 2009. 1.3, 8.5.

This thesis tested the relationship between development support characteristics (development officer placement, involvement in fundraising of the chief student affairs officer, involvement in fundraising of other senior student affairs officers, support from the president of the institution, institutional type, and endowment size) and funds raised for student affairs. Having a development officer who reported to student affairs and involvement of certain other administrators affected funds raised.

Rowland, Terri Yvette. "Institutional Advancement Initiatives of Historically Black Colleges and Universities: A Multicase Study of African American Higher Education." EdD, North Carolina State University, 1997. 8.1.

This dissertation consisted of case studies of HBCUs based on interviews, content analysis, and observation. Factors important to advancement success were students, academics, athletic improvement, technology, community outreach, and cultivation.

Roy-Rasheed, Lupita D. "Alumni Giving: A Case Study of the Factors That Influence Philanthropic Behavior of Alumni Donors of Historically Black Colleges and Universities." PhD, Capella University, 2013. 4.3, 8.1.

The perceptions, triggers, and motivations of local alumni donors at two HBCUs were explored through interviews. Most had positive undergraduate experiences. Current perceptions were mixed. Donors were triggered to give by a sense of responsibility and by being asked.

Royce, Lee Gardner. "The Responsibilities and Effectiveness of Trustees at Church-Related Colleges and Universities." EdD, Peabody College for Teachers of Vanderbilt University, 1993. 6.2, 8.8.

Interviews with trustees, presidents, and church leaders inquired about trustee effectiveness. Fundraising was considered the second or third most important responsibility; current trustee selection procedures did not help trustees raise large gifts.

Rugano, Emilio Kariuki. "Motivations for Giving of Alumni Donors, Lapsed Donors and Non-Donors: Implications for Christian Higher Education." PhD, Biola University, 2011. 4.3, 8.8.

Alumni donors, lapsed donors, and nondonors of Biola were surveyed regarding demographics and motives for giving. Alumni motivations were primarily internal and included biblical motivations. Reasons for not giving were insufficient income, lack of emotional attachment to Biola, being unsure of what gifts would support, and believing their gifts would be too small.

Ruiz-Huston, Ines Marta. "What Can the Community Involvement Program Tell Us about Alumni Giving at the University of the Pacific." EdD, University of the Pacific, 2010. 4.3.

This thesis surveyed alumni CIP participants as to why they gave to the Community Involvement Program, which was designed to encourage donations from minority students and supported nontraditional, first-generation, and low-income students. Being African American and being asked to give by phone increased the chances of giving.

Ryan, Edward Francis. "Sources and Information: Development and Fundraising within Community Colleges." *New Directions for Community Colleges* 124 (2003): 95–104. doi: 10.1002/cc.138. 1, 8.2.

This article was an annotated bibliography of research on community college fundraising, including ERIC documents.

Ryan, G. Jeremiah, and James C. Palmer. "Leading the Fundraising Effort." *New Directions for Community Colleges* 132 (2005): 43–48. doi: 10.1002/cc.214. 1, 8.2.

This article provided an overview of community college fundraising.

Ryan, Lawrence J. "Behavioral Characteristics of Higher Education Fund-Raisers." *International Journal of Educational Advancement* 6 no. 4 (2006): 282–88. 1.4.

Development officers were surveyed regarding the importance they placed on four roles conceptualized by Worth and Asp: salesperson, catalyst, manager, and leader. Results indicated that all roles were regarded as equally important, perhaps due to the wide range of activities development officers must engage in.

Ryan, Ronald Raymond. "Impact of Donor Motivations and Characteristics on Giving to Higher Education." PhD, University of Oklahoma, 1997. 1.2.

Donors to Emporia State were surveyed regarding characteristics and motivations. Gift size was influenced by valuing higher education, satisfaction with the college experience, and belief that Emporia provided quality education. Older, wealthier, and higher net worth donors made larger donation; tax considerations and honoring loved ones also influenced gift size.

Salmi, Jamil, and Alenoush Saroyan. "League Tables as Policy Instruments: Uses and Misuses." *Higher Education Management and Policy* 19 no. 2 (2007): 31. 3.4, 5.

This article discussed university rankings, including a typology, controversies surrounding them, and implications for higher education policy. Controversies included a description of common criticisms, the worthiness of indicators used, and conditions that give institutions advantages or disadvantages.

Sanders, Denisha. "Factors Which Relate to Development Officer Turnover at Colleges and Universities in the Commonwealth of Virginia." PhD, University of Virginia, 1997. 6.5.

CASE members were surveyed regarding turnover. Discriminant analysis was used to distinguish between leavers and nonleavers. Leavers had less experience, less focus on retirement, and more interest in leaving. They were more interested in finding ideal positions, whereas nonleavers were more likely to leave for personal reasons.

Sanders, Karen M. "An Analysis of Florida Public Community College Foundations' Performance Measures from 2002–2004." EdD, University of Central Florida, 2008. 1.3, 8.2.

Information for each college was pulled from its IRS Form 990 and 27 financial ratios were calculated in 6 categories: fiscal performance, fundraising efficiency, public support, adequacy of resources for mission, use of resources to support mission, and investment performance. Benchmarks were set for future evaluations.

Sargeant, Adrian, Toni Hilton, and Walter W. Wymer. "Making the Bequest: An Empirical Study of the Attitudes of Pledgers and Supporters." *International Journal of Educational Advancement* 5 no. 3 (2005): 207–19. 1.5.

Based on a survey of bequest societies and legacy clubs, this paper explored motives for support and potential barriers to participating.

Sargeant, Adrian, and Stephen Lee. "Towards a Model of Donor Trust: Implications for HE Fund-Raising Practice in the United Kingdom." *CASE International Journal of Educational Advancement* 3 no. 3 (2003): 213–25. 1.2, 5.2.

The authors built a model of donor trust in which contextual and individual antecedents lead to trust, which leads to commitment and then to giving behavior. While based on the UK example, the model is likely applicable in other contexts.

Satterwhite, Christopher Robin. "The Function of University Presidents and CEO's in Fundraising: A Study of Public Universities with Capital Campaigns Less Than 100 Million." EdD, Texas Tech University, 2004. 1.1, 6.1.

Case studies of three public universities, based on interviews and archival data, focused on the role of the president in fundraising. Six presidential behaviors were found to be important: strategic planning, coordination of external stakeholders, team building, coordination of internal stakeholders, directing the fundraising process, and allocating resources.

Satterwhite, C. Robin, and Brent Cedja. "Higher Education Fund Raising: What Is the President to Do?" *International Journal of Educational Advancement* 5 no. 4 (2005): 333–42. 1.1, 6.1.

This article is based on Satterwhite's dissertation, "The Function of University Presidents and CEO's in Fundraising."

Saunders, Kenneth Kalso. "The Role of the President in Advancing Development at Community Colleges: A Case Study." EdD, University of Pennsylvania, 2009. 1.1, 6.1, 8.2.

The leadership of President Joseph Hankin at Westchester Community College was studied as a case of presidential involvement in advancement. Data included interviews, documents, and surveys of other SUNY community colleges.

Scarborough, Donald Alan. "The Impact of Older Adult Programs in Higher Education upon the Individual's Feelings of Loyalty toward the Sponsoring Institution." EdD, Peabody College for Teachers of Vanderbilt University, 1991. 4.6.

Participants in adult education programs at Brevard College were interviewed, observed, and analyzed to discover their relative loyalty to Brevard and their undergraduate alma mater. 68 percent were loyal to their alma mater; 100 percent were loyal to the adult education program. Most demonstrated loyalty through donations.

Schanz, Jeffrey M. "Differences in University Fundraising: The Role of University Practices and Organization." PhD, State University of New York at Albany, 2013. 1.3.

Data from IPEDS and VSE were used to develop an interview protocol for fundraising leaders at four institutions, two more successful and two less so. Successful organizations had mature fundraising organization, consistent leadership and vision, strong alumni engagement, and consistent marketing.

Schexnider, Alvin J. *Saving Black Colleges: Leading Change in a Complex Organization*. New York: Palgrave Macmillan, 2013. 1.6, 6.1, 8.1.

Schexnider described his experiences as chancellor of Winston-Salem State during a period of change and placed it in the context of issues facing HBCUs.

Schlichting, Kurt, and James Simon. "Using GIS to Identify Clusters of Potential Donors to Colleges and Universities." *CASE International Journal of Educational Advancement* 2 no. 1 (2001): 25–35. 1.1.

Geographic Information Systems can be used to find clusters of potential donors, leveraging Census and institutional data. An example of this using data on donors in Connecticut was included.

Schmidt, James Carroll. "Mining Philanthropic Data: Models for Predicting Alumni/us Giving at a Medium-Sized Public Master's University." EdD, University of Minnesota, 2001. 4.3.

This dissertation combined Winona State institutional data with proprietary data from Bernard C. Harris Publishing, the Composite Donor Index, to create two models that predicted alumni giving and one that predicted giving levels. The donor/nondonor models correctly predicted 70 percent and 61 percent of donors.

Schneider, John C. "Universities and Foundation Support: Working with Faculty and Administrators." *New Directions for Philanthropic Fundraising* 28 (2000): 97–110. 1.1, 6.8.

This article provided advice to development officers who work with faculty and staff regarding gifts, such as those from foundations.

Schoenecke, Marvin. "A Description of Successful Fundraising Programs in Student Affairs Divisions." PhD, University of Oklahoma, 2005. 1.3, 8.5.

Three case studies of student affairs programs at public universities and their involvement in fundraising were conducted, using interviews, observation, and documents, and organization theory. At each institution, the need for development originated with student affairs, not development, but the development office was crucial for functioning.

Schofield, Cathy, Debby Cotton, Karen Gresty, Pauline Kneale, and Jennie Winter. "Higher Education Provision in a Crowded Marketplace." *Journal of Higher Education Policy and Management* 35 no. 2 (2013): 193–205. 3.3, 5.2.

The websites of 19 institutions of higher education were examined and coded. Universities were focused on reputation, while further education colleges focused on graduate potential. They both communicated regarding student life and teaching and learning at similar rates.

Schubert, Philip J. "Assessing the Correlation between Longitudinal Changes in U.S. News World & Report Undergraduate College Rankings and the Broader Institutional Experience from 1999 to 2007." EdD, University of Pennsylvania, 2009. 3.4.

The rankings of over three hundred institutions were tracked over eight years. The author identified factors correlated with rankings changes and compared institutions that had improved their rankings with those that had not.

Schulze, C. J., Jr. "The Role of the Community College President in Successful Fund-Raising." EdD, Columbia University, 1991. 1.3, 6.1, 8.2.

This thesis explored the role of community college presidents in fundraising, quantitatively testing factors found in a literature review for their effect on institutional endowment. However, the analysis did not support these factors.

Sciple, Judith A. "Shaping Perceptions of Delaware Technical & Community College through a Comprehensive Brand Marketing Strategy." EdD, University of Delaware, 2010. 3.3, 8.2.

Based on focus groups with students, a survey of employees, and a survey of parents, counselors, and community leaders, this case study of Delaware Tech explored perceptions of the institution and ended with recommendations for the college.

Scott, LeKita Vaney. "A Description of Successful Fund-Raising Units at Public Historically Black Colleges and Universities." PhD, Florida State University, 2001. 1.3, 8.1.

Three case studies of HBCUs with successful fundraising programs were based on interviews, document analysis, and observations. The development office was the unit of analysis, and a framework of organization theory was used.

Scott, Michelle T. "Community College Trustees and Public Engagement: A Case Study of National Issues Forums Institute Network Community Colleges." EdD, Morgan State University, 2007. 2.5, 6.2, 8.2.

This thesis examined trustee engagement with the public at the five community colleges in the National Issues Forum Institute Network. Based on trustee interviews, the author concluded that trustees did not focus on public engagement and pursued their roles with minimum public engagement.

Selig, Camden Wood. "A Study of Donor Predictability among Alumni Athletes at the University of Virginia." EdD, University of Virginia, 1999. 4.3, 8.4.

A survey of alumni athletes at the University of Virginia was undertaken regarding demographics, attitudes, and behavior, and the data underwent discriminant analysis to tell donors from nondonors and high from low donors. Donors/nondonors were correctly categorized in 77 percent of cases; high/low donors were correctly categorized in 85 percent of cases.

Seligman, Joel Richard. "Institutional Strategy and Communications as Catalysts for Philanthropic Support of Private Research Universities in the United States." EdD, University of Pennsylvania, 2009. 1.3, 3.2.

This case study of five institutions was based on interviews with institutional leaders exploring the coupling of strategy, communications, and fundraising. Those that were more tightly coupled tended to be more successful.

Sevier, Robert A. "Image Is Everything: Strategies for Measuring, Changing, and Maintaining Your Institution's Image." *College and University* 69 no. 2 (1994). 3.3.

This article suggested engaging in image management via prioritizing audiences, market research, establishing clear goals, planning, and providing adequate resources to implement plans.

Sevier, Robert A. *Integrated Marketing for Colleges, Universities, and Schools: A Step-by-Step Planning Guide.* Washington, DC: CASE Books, 1998. 3.2.

Primarily a how-to guide for practitioners, this book addressed marketing, planning, and troubleshooting. It included a section with a guide to research sources and useful organizations.

Sevier, Robert A. "A Review of Perceptual-Mapping Techniques to Support a Comprehensive Institutional Image-Enhancement Strategy." *CASE International Journal of Educational Advancement* 1 no. 1 (2000): 74–87. 3.3.

This article reviewed one method of discovering what images an institution's constituents have of it. Data can be collected from focus groups, journaling, or survey questions (open-ended, Likert scale, and quadrant or sector analysis).

Shadinger, David. "Dialogistic Presence on Community College Websites in Nine Megastates." *Community College Journal of Research and Practice* 37 no. 12 (2013): 925–35. 3.1, 8.2.

This article was based on the following author's dissertation.

Shadinger, David Allen. "An Analysis of Dialogistic Presence on Community College Web Sites in Nine Mega-States." EdD, North Carolina State University, 2010. 3.1, 8.2.

A sample of 218 community colleges found that 215 of them used dialogic loops on their websites. These loops allow for two-way communication as described by Kent and Taylor. They were also likely to incorporate ease of navigation, encourage return visitors, and have updated information.

Shaker, Genevieve G. "Faculty and Staff as Prospects and Donors: Giving on Campus." In *Expanding the Donor Base in Higher Education: Engaging Non-Traditional Donors*, edited by Noah D. Drezner, 123–37. New York: Routledge, 2013a. 6.8.

The author provided an overview of research on faculty and staff giving to their employer and made recommendations for institutions interested in soliciting this population.

Shaker, Genevieve G. "The Generosity of the Professoriate: Faculty as Donors and Academic Citizens." *Metropolitan Universities* 23 no. 3 (2013b): 5–25. 6.8.

This study of ten faculty members who had given $25,000-plus to academics at one campus used interviews to explore why they gave. Most were older and all had served in an administrative capacity. The faculty felt obligated to be involved beyond the requirements of their job, regarded their entire life as integrated, and were interested in innovation.

Shapiro, Stephen L. "Donor Loyalty in College Athletics: An Analysis of Relationship Fundraising and Service Quality Effects on Donor Retention." PhD, University of Northern Colorado, 2008. 1.3, 8.4.

Current and lapsed donors to athletics at three institutions were surveyed to explore the role of service quality. Service quality constructs (responsiveness, effectiveness, and communication) explained 33 percent of the variation in donor satisfaction; only communication differentiated between donors and lapsed donors.

Shapiro, Stephen L. "Does Service Matter? An Examination of Donor Perceptions of Service Quality in College Athletics." *Sport Marketing Quarterly* 19 (2010): 154–65. 1.7, 8.4.

This article was based on the author's dissertation, "Donor Loyalty in College Athletics."

Shapiro, Stephen L, and Chrysostomos Giannoulakis. "An Exploratory Investigation of Donor Constraints for Former Student-Athletes." *International Journal of Sport Management* 10 no. 2 (2009): 1–19. 1.3, 8.4.

The authors interviewed 11 nondonor former student-athletes and used thematic content analysis to explore why they did not donate. Four themes emerged: importance (other causes ranked more highly), connection (which had deteriorated since graduation), communication/knowledge, and experience.

Shapiro, Stephen L., Chrysostomos Giannoulakis, Joris Drayer, and Chien-Hsin Wang. "An Examination of Athletic Alumni Giving Behavior: Development of the Former Student-Athlete Donor Constraint Scale." *Sport Management Review* 13 (2010): 283–95. 4.3, 8.4.

The authors developed the Former Student-Athlete Donor Constraint Scale based on work by Shapiro and Giannoulakis ("An Exploratory Investigation of Donor Constraints") and tested it on a sample from a Division I institution. Responses and the scale's five factors were tested and items revised to lack of importance, disconnect, communication issues, experience issues, and dissatisfaction.

Shaw, Karen Louise. "Financing Ontario Community Colleges: What Role Do Foundations Play in Augmenting Financial Support for Ontario Colleges?" PhD, Michigan State University, 1997. 1.12, 5.1, 8.2.

Twenty-one colleges that were part of the Association of Applied Arts and Technology of Ontario were surveyed and 18 individuals interviewed to discover the role of related foundations. Factors predicting success included presidential leadership, location, community linkages, the board (term length and size), staffing, and faculty involvement.

Shealy, Mary Ann Wertz. "Fund-Raising at Colleges of Education in Public Research Universities II." PhD, University of South Carolina, 1992. 1.1, 8.7.

Telephone surveys were conducted at 26 public universities to discover how centralized they were and whether development personnel were used in colleges of education. Most colleges had part-time development officers in central development offices. None had capital campaigns of $5 million-plus.

Sheridan, Brenda A. "Key Components of Successful Higher Education Online Fundraising Programs." EdD, University of Pittsburgh, 2004. 1.17.

Twenty-nine institutions were surveyed about fundraising online. Both highly successful and less successful programs had similar components, using website exposure, alumni email, a phone campaign, and direct mail to promote it. Both experienced technological difficulties as well as limited budgets and staffing. All experienced an increase in giving after September 11, 2001.

Shim, Jung-Min. "Relationship of Selected Alumnae Characteristics to Alumnae Financial Support at a Women's College." PhD, University of Florida, 2001. 4.3.

The author surveyed alumnae of one women's college to discover what variables affected gift size and frequency. Four variables affected gift size: participation in alumnae activities, number of postgraduation campus visits, perception of the college's financial need, and contact person from the college. Gift frequency was affected by participation in alumnae activities, number of postgraduation campus visits, and place of undergraduate residence.

Shoemaker, Craig. "The Current State of Marketing at Midwestern Private Higher Educational Institutions and the Role Played by the President." PhD, University of Iowa, 1997. 3, 6.1.

Surveys of presidents and case studies comprised of interviews at four institutions examined the president's role in marketing. Presidential involvement in planning, strategy development, initiating market research, and approving printed materials improved performance, as did the use of outside consultants. Marketing was not balanced or comprehensive, focusing primarily on student recruitment and donors.

Shuford, Monica Jean. "Factors Affecting the Success of North Carolina Community College Alumni Programs." EdD, Western Carolina University, 2007. 1.3, 8.2.

The author conducted five interview-based case studies of successful alumni programs at community colleges, exploring their establishment, operation, and future plans.

Simari, R. M. "Philanthropy and Higher Education: Women as Donors." EdD, Hofstra University, 1995. 4.3.

Hofstra alumnae were surveyed about philanthropy, and answers of donors and nondonors were compared. The two groups varied on 15 variables, including desire to help the next generation, institutional loyalty, feelings of rebuilding/repaying, communications from the university, and sense of obligation; they also differed on the purposes they preferred to support.

Simmel, L. L., and P. D. Berger. "The Art of the Ask: Maximizing Verbal Compliance in Telefundraising." *Journal of Interactive Marketing* 14 no. 3 (2000): 12–40. 1.9.

This experiment tested the effects various telemarketing techniques: a "how are you" inquiry (present/absent), asking about the prospect's initial refusal (present/absent), and the grammatical formulation of the ask. The first two had significant effects of pledge rates.

Simmel, Leslie L., Wendy Schneier Siegal, Paul D. Berger, and George Psathas. "A Conversation Analysis of Practices and Competencies in Telefundraising." *CASE International Journal of Educational Advancement* 3 no. 1 (2002): 22–39. 1.9.

Conversational analysis was applied to fundraising calls at one institution. Both participants adapt to each other; different conversational paths were discussed. Both sides used strategies to influence the conversation.

Simon, Jason Foster. "Does Campus Type Really Matter? National Patterns of Alumni Giving in the 2008 Voluntary Support of Education Study." PhD, University of North Texas, 2011. 4.3.

Using data from VSE, this study examined the impact of public/private status and baccalaureate/masters/doctoral classification on alumni giving, restricted giving, and unrestricted giving per FTE. Each of the three measures differed in a statistically significant way across the six institutional types.

Simon, Shirley R., and Maria Vidal De Haymes. "The Role of Alumni in Baccalaureate Social Work Education." *Journal of Social Work Education* 33 no. 3 (1997): 519–28. 4.6.

Directors of social work programs were surveyed about the role of alumni in their programs. Eighty-seven percent tracked graduates; 92 percent reported alumni involvement in some activities. Most common activities included field placement supervisors, speaking on campus, and serving on curriculum advisory boards. 20 percent had a formal organization for social work alumni.

Simone, Sean Anthony. "Examining the Influence of Selectivity on Alumni Giving at Public Universities: A Dynamic Panel Modeling Approach." PhD, University of Maryland, College Park, 2009. 4.3.

Using dynamic panel modeling and IPEDS data, this thesis modeled the effects of selectivity on alumni giving at public universities and compared the model to other typically used specifications such as OLS. Models differed in coefficients and errors; under the dynamic model, selectivity had no effect.

Simpson, Christopher, and Don Hossler. "Bringing in a Class: An Examination of the Effects of Linking Enrollment Management, Integrated Marketing, and Market Research at a Public University." *CASE International Journal of Educational Advancement* 1 no. 3 (2001): 253–65. 3.2.

This case study examined Indiana University's partnership between enrollment management and marketing. Both enrollment and alumni association membership increased, and a more precise public image of IU was developed.

Simpson, Douglas J., and William J. Hull. "Educational Philanthropy: An Instrument of Qualified Change." *Journal of Negro Education* (2007): 230–39. 1.12, 8.1.

The role of philanthropy in the education of African Americans, 1932–2007, was explored in this historical study. While philanthropists' motives were not always positive, African Americans were often able to leverage funds.

Sink, David W. Jr., and Karen Luke Jackson. "Successful Community College Campus-Based Partnerships." *Community College Journal of Research & Practice* 26 no. 1 (2002): 35–46.

The authors used Blue Ridge Community College as a case study for institutional partnerships. Twelve nonprofit and government agencies near campus reported on their partnerships with the college focusing on what made the partnerships successful.

Skari, Lisa Ann. "Who Gives? Characteristics of Community College Alumni Donors." EdD, Washington State University, 2011. 4.3, 8.2.

Based on social exchange theory, survey data from community college alumni at 18 institutions were used to build a model to predict whether they would give. Relevant factors were levels of satisfaction, involvement, relationships, age, giving to other organizations, time since attendance, income, and graduating with an associate's degree.

Slaughter, S., and L. L. Leslie. *Academic Capitalism: Politics, Policies and the Entrepreneurial University*. Baltimore, MD: Johns Hopkins University, 1997. 3.5.

The authors examined capitalism in public research universities in the Anglophone world. While this book was not focused on advancement, it touched on topics such as revenue diversification and marketing.

Smith, David Robert. "Effects of Perceived Goal Congruency upon Fund-Raising at Selected Church-Related Colleges." EdD, Peabody College for Teachers of Vanderbilt University, 1993. 1.3, 8.8.

The effect of goal agreement on fundraising at three church-related colleges was examined using Educational Testing Service and institutional data. ETS data included 787 employees, students, and constituents discussing goal attainment. Higher goals of goal congruence were linked to better fundraising productivity; the college with the least goal ambiguity was the most productive.

Smith, Lottie Jean. "Factors Which Promote or Limit Minority Alumni Support of a Predominantly White Private Church-Associated University." PhD, Marquette University, 1998. 4.3, 8.8.

This case study of one PWI examined minority, compensatory education program graduates. Participants were interviewed regarding their educational experience and philanthropic understandings. Different understandings of philanthropy, perceived racial discrimination, and feelings of not belonging to all were found to have potential impacts on the cultivation of these alumni as donors.

Smith, Mary Magnano. "An Understanding of Gift Giving in Chinese Universities: A Hermeneutic of Philanthropy." EdD, University of San Francisco, 1992. 1.2, 5.3.

The author explored philanthropic practices at Chinese universities seeking strategies that could be applied to Chinese alumni of American universities. Using critical hermeneutics, the author created a model for working with Chinese students to prepare them to be donors.

Smith, P. B. "Managing Successful Major Gift Programs." *New Directions for Philanthropic Fundraising: Developing Major Gifts* 16 (1997): 31–47. 1.3.

The author provided advice on overseeing major gift programs.

Smith, Stuart R. "Performance Benchmarking: Lessons on Using Performance Benchmarks to Maximize Fundraising Results." *New Directions for Philanthropic Fundraising* 49 (2005): 109–19. 1.14.

The author discussed benchmarking, arguing that rather than striving to meet a number, fundraisers should use it to improve fundraising performance.

Smith, Zachary A. "Assessing Educational Fundraisers for Competence and Fit Rather Than Experience: A Challenge to Conventional Hiring Practices." *International Journal of Educational Advancement* 10 no. 2 (2010): 87–97. 6.5.

The author argued that a traditional criterion for choosing fundraisers, experience, is less important than competence and fit. Employers should create a competency model, assessment tools, and evaluation tools for a position; commercial tools are available to assess workplace fit.

Snyder, Rachel A. "An Analysis of Charitable Giving Practices of Recent Optometry Alumni at Selected Institutions and Their Alumni Donor Support." PhD, Michigan State University, 1993. 4.3, 8.3.

Alumni of Ferris State's and Indiana State's schools of optometry were surveyed regarding their giving to higher education and other causes. No relationship was found with any of the 20 proposed factors and gifts. Qualitative questions indicated that those who did not give were affected by loans and income levels.

Somers, Marie-Andree. "The Effect of the Maclean's University Rankings on the Demand- and Supply-Side Outcomes of Canadian Universities." EdD, Harvard University, 2007. 3.4.

The first paper in this two-paper dissertation examined the effects of rankings on application decisions. The second examined the effects of rankings on institutional behavior, analyzing whether changes in behavior had the desired effects on subsequent rankings. These behaviors possibly were contrary to the social policy objectives of the institutions.

Song, Eun Jung. "The Relationship between Alumni Worldview and Motivation for Giving at Biola University." PhD, Biola University, 2011. 4.3, 8.8.

Biola alumni were surveyed to explore factors impacting donations to the university. Worldview factors were significant but small. Demographic factors influenced worldview and alumni motivations.

Sonn, Andrew C. "Institutions' Needs and Donors' Dreams: A Case Study of Successful Student Affairs Fundraising Collaboration at Three Private Research Universities." EdD, George Washington University, 2009. 1.2, 8.5.

Based on case studies of three universities, this thesis explored success factors for fundraising for student affairs, using interviews, document review, and observations. Experienced student affairs leadership and capital projects were important, as were organizational culture and department subcultures.

Spangler, Mary Schuhsler. "The Role of the College President in Facilitating Organizational Growth through Group Learning: A Qualitative Study of the Creation Phase in the Life-Cycle Process of a Community College Foundation." EdD, University of California, Los Angeles, 1994. 1.1, 6.1.

The Patron Association of Southern California Community College serves as a case study for how presidents encourage group learning in the development of a foundation. Group bonding, teacher scripting, and team building helped produce changes in outcomes, group behavior, and individuals' attitudes.

Spears, Lori D. "Fundraising Strategies in Higher Education: Black, White—Is There Any Gray In Between?" EdD, University of Pennsylvania, 2008. 4.3, 8.1.

Minority giving at Xavier (an HBCU) and St. Josephs (a PWI) Universities were studied using interviews, giving histories, documents, and observations. The strategies that worked with the majority population at each institution were not effective with their minority populations.

Speck, Bruce W. "The Growing Role of Private Giving in Financing the Modern University." *New Directions for Higher Education* 149 (2010): 7–16. 1.

Speck explored the benefits of fundraising for private institutions as well as its limits. Fundraising can provide facilities and scholarships, but the fruits of them, such as facilities that require maintenance, can add to an institution's costs.

Specter, Jennifer K. "Enhancing Alumni Engagement: Tradition-Building at the University of Delaware." EdD, University of Delaware, 2012. 4.5.

Delaware alumni were administered two surveys and administrators were interviewed regarding their perceptions of university traditions. The university has few events; those it has are undistinctive, such as commencement.

St. John, Edward P. "A Framework for Reexamining State Resource-Management Strategies in Higher Education." *The Journal of Higher Education* 62 no. 3 (1991): 263–87. 1.16.

The author provided a framework for states to reexamine finance policies, based on case studies of four public systems. While not centered on advancement, this article did discuss alternative revenue sources such as fundraising and endowments, as well as public attitudes.

Starace, Melissa D. "Transforming Nomads into Settlers: A Study of Community College Alumni Engagement Efforts in Pennsylvania." EdD, University of Pennsylvania, 2012. 4.5.

Based on interviews with presidents, advancement professions, and volunteers at five community colleges, this thesis explored how "nomadic" students can be transformed into alumni "settlers." Colleges should identify, engage, and educate former students about their alumni roles, which requires financial and human capital investments on the part of the college.

Staurowsky, Ellen J. "A Comparison of Motivations for Giving between Donors to Women's and Men's Athletic Support Groups." EdD, Temple University, 1994. 1.2, 8.4.

Donors to four athletic support groups (Division I men's, Division I women's, Division III men's, and Division III women's) were surveyed using the ACQUIRE-II instrument. Six factors that explained 70 percent of giving were found. Differences in motivation existed by athletic division, gender of donor, and gender of recipient.

Steeper, Daniel W. "The Effects of Selected Undergraduate Student Involvement and Alumni Characteristics on Alumni Gift-Giving Behavior at the University of Virginia." PhD, University of Virginia, 2009. 4.3.

Combining a survey of undergraduate alumni and institutional data, the author built models to predict giving, involvement, and attitude. Positive attitudes were predicted by extracurricular involvement, attending club meetings, and meeting with faculty. Involvement was predicted by participating in off-campus activities and meeting with faculty. Donations were predicted by undergraduate activities, maintaining faculty/staff contact, involvement in university events, perception of need, and income.

Stensaker, Bjørn. "The Relationship between Branding and Organisational Change." *Higher Education Management and Policy* 19 no. 1 (2007): 13. 3.3.

The author explored the benefits and problems associated with branding using the idea of organizational identity change. Branding can enhance development and facilitate organizational change.

Stephenson, Amber L. "The Effect of Brand Identification on Alumni Supportive Behaviors." PhD, Indiana University of Pennsylvania, 2013. 3.3, 4.3.

Based on a survey of alumni donors and nondonors and institutional data at a public university, this thesis explored the effects brand identification had on donations, promotional behavior, and competitive attitudes toward outgroups. Brand identity was found to influence donor behavior.

Stevens, Frederick Michael. "A Study of Capital Fund-Raising Campaigns at Peer Institutions of Northern Arizona University." EdD, Northern Arizona University, 1995. 1.1.

The author surveyed he fundraising practices at the 11 of 17 peer institutions of NAU that had conducted capital campaigns in the previous six years. Factors important for campaign success were reputation, presidential commitment, volunteer support, and strategic planning. In addition to funds raised, the campaigns had residual benefits for institutional fundraising.

Stevenson, Tommy J. "Fundraising Practices at Selected Midwestern Two-Year Colleges: Community, Junior, and Technical College Foundations in the Twenty-First Century." PhD, Bowling Green State University, 2001. 1.1, 8.2.

A survey of upper-level community college administrators asked about fundraising practices and their outcomes. Annual giving, visits, campus campaigns, and special events were somewhat successful, although institutions with larger staffs found events to be less successful. Benefits included more scholarships, increased enrollment, and improved technological infrastructure.

Stevick, Thomas R. "Integrating Development, Alumni Relations, and Marketing for Fundraising Success." *New Directions for Higher Education* 149 (2010): 57–64. 1, 3, 4.

The author argued that institutions should emulate corporations and integrate sales and marketing offices and discussed steps to successfully doing so.

Stewart, Kevin Dean. "The Community College President: Leader or Fundraiser?" EdD, Morgan State University, 2006. 6.1.

Based on a survey of community college presidents, this thesis found that 90 percent of presidents had no previous fundraising experience before becoming a president. Most spent 10–20 hours per week on fundraising. Age, professional and civic organization memberships, experience, and campus enrollment affected involvement levels.

Stewart, K. L. "Applying a Marketing Orientation to a Higher Education Setting." *Journal of Professional Services Marketing* 7 no. 2 (1991): 117–24. 3.

The author discussed the then-growing role of marketing in higher education as a response to enrollment declines.

Stewart, Mark E. "The Exploration of the 'Flutie Factor' and Philanthropic Contributions to NCAA Division II Football Championship Institutions from 1997–2010." EdD, University of Missouri–Columbia, 2012. 1.3, 8.4.

This thesis explored the effects that winning a football championship had on donations, using quantitative and qualitative data. Quantitative analysis indicated that winning positively affected total cash gifts and the number of alumni donors but had no consistent effect on other gifts. Survey data suggested that championships increased the pride of stakeholders.

Stinson, Jeffrey L. "The Effects of Intercollegiate Athletics Success on Private Giving to Athletic and Academic Programs at National Collegiate Athletic Association Institutions." PhD, University of Oregon, 2005. 1.3, 8.4.

Using VSE data, this thesis examined institutional characteristics that influenced donations to athletics. Athletic success influenced athletic but not academic giving. Institutions with better academic reputations were less affected by win-loss records and postseason appearances. Alumni gave more to both athletics and academics, but with similar influences as nonalumni.

Stinson, Jeffrey L., and Dennis R. Howard. "Scoreboards vs. Mortarboards: Major Donor Behavior and Intercollegiate Athletics." *Sport Marketing Quarterly* 13 no. 129–40 (2004). 1.2, 8.4.

Using data on annual gifts of $1,000-plus from the University of Oregon, the authors found that alumni gave larger portions of their gifts to academics. The percentage of alumni giving to athletics had increased over time, which the authors attribute to athletic success, while nonalumni giving to academics had decreased.

Stinson, Jeffrey L., and Dennis R. Howard. "Winning Does Matter: Patterns in Private Giving to Athletic and Academic Programs at NCAA Division I-AA and I-AAA Institutions." *Sport Management Review* 11 (2008): 1–20. 1.3, 8.4.

Using VSE data for Division I-AA and I-AAA institutions, the authors explored whether athletic giving crowds out academic giving. Successful men's basketball and football programs increased the number and size of gifts both to academics and athletics.

Stinson, Jeffrey L., and Dennis R. Howard. "Athletic Giving and Academic Giving: Exploring the Value of SPLIT Donors." *Journal of Sport Management* 24 (2010a): 744–68. 8.4.

Institutional data from three Division I universities were used to analyze the gifts of donors who gave to both athletics and academics. Compared to athletics-only donors, they gave higher average overall gifts but smaller gifts to athletics; compared to academics-only donors, they were retained at a higher rate.

Stinson, Jeffrey L., and Dennis R. Howard. "Intercollegiate Athletics as an Institutional Fundraising Tool: An Exploratory Donor-Based View." *Journal of Nonprofit & Public Sector Marketing* 22 (2010b): 312–35. 1.2, 8.4.

Sixty-five interviews were conducted with $1,000-plus donors to athletics and academic at two Division I-A universities. Four themes emerged: Athletics helped introduce and socialize donors to the institution; support for athletics was often driven by tangible rewards such as tickets; cultivation increased giving; and academic giving was increased by leveraging emotional connections to athletics.

Stoltz, Adam C. "An Analysis of the Perceptions of U.S. News and World Report College Ranking Systems by Enrollment Managers of American Jesuit Colleges and Universities." EdD, Saint Louis University, 2012. 3.4, 8.8.

Enrollment managers at Jesuit institutions were surveyed regarding their perceptions of *U.S. News* rankings. Overall, they agreed with rankings weights, except for peer ratings. They believed it affected enrollment management strategies, paying most attention to retention and graduation rates.

Stone, Melanie Lefferts. "National Media Coverage of Higher Education: A Case Study of Three Universities and the Role of Public Relations." PhD, University of Mississippi, 2005. 2.3.

National media coverage of the Universities of Mississippi and North Carolina and Louisiana State University for 2002 and 2003 were topically coded. The institutions were typically represented though faculty/staff/administration and students, although ten other topics emerged. Interviews with public relations officers explored their media relations techniques.

Stovall, William M. "A Case Study of Presidents' Approaches to Fundraising at Four Private and Public Historically Black Colleges and Universities." PhD, University of Missouri—Columbia, 2004. 6.1, 8.1.

Interviews, observations, and documents were collected from four HBCUs to explore presidential fundraising. The four presidents used three different approaches, but all believed presidential leadership was necessary and that a president ought to be able to articulate the institutional vision.

Strickland, Shelley. "Partners in Writing and Rewriting History: Philanthropy and Higher Education." *International Journal of Educational Advancement* 7 no. 2 (2007): 104–16. 7.1.

This paper compared today's higher education donors with those of the past, arguing that while donors of the past primarily created institutions, today's donors are more interested in transforming them. These gifts, despite their benefits, can be challenging for institutions to work with and may challenge institutional autonomy.

Strickland, Shelley. "The Kalamazoo Promise: A Study of Philanthropy's Increasing Role in the American Economy and Education." *International Journal of Educational Advancement* 9 no. 1 (2009): 16–34. 1.12.

The author examined the Kalamazoo Promise, a program that pays for the college education of every Kalamazoo, Michigan public school graduate and that was paid for by private donations. Current philanthropic models do not explain the gift and a new model is needed, she argued.

Strickland, Shelley Renae. "Internal or External: Community College Presidential Backgrounds and Management of the Presidency." PhD, University of Michigan, 2013. 6.1, 8.2.

This thesis examined whether community college presidents with fundraising career paths manage differently than those from academic career paths, based on interviews with 19 presidents. Findings included that the lines between the two career paths were somewhat fuzzy, and that fundraisers had advantages early in their presidencies in board relations.

Strmiska, Kenneth Dale. "Development Officers' Occupational Knowledge Acquisition Processes: A Qualitative Study of Six Fund Raisers." EdD, North Carolina State University, 1998. 6.5.

Six development officers were examined to discover how occupational knowledge was transmitted. They preferred to ask colleagues for information, preferred models over theories, and relied upon preenculturating theories. Both formal (i.e., conferences) and informal knowledge transfers were used.

Strode, James P. "Donor Motives to Giving to Intercollegiate Athletics." PhD, Ohio State University, 2006. 1.2, 8.4.

Athletic donors to one institution were surveyed based on McClelland's theory of needs and helping behavior. Achievement, followed by affiliation, was the most common motivation for giving. Level of fan identification was correlated with achievement motives. However, the motives explained only 1 percent of the variance in giving.

Stuart, Debra L. "Reputational rankings: Background and Development." *New Directions for Institutional Research* 88 (1995): 13–20. doi: 10.1002/ir.37019958803. 3.4.

The author described the history of college rankings.

Sturgis, Rhonda L. "Team Relationships within Institutional Advancement: Board of Trustees, President, and Vice President of Institutional Advancement." EdD, George Washington University, 2005. 6.1, 6.2, 6.3.

Presidents, vice presidents, and trustees at baccalaureate institutions completed Reichmann's Team Performance Questionnaire. Low response rates made analysis difficult. One finding was that president and vice presidents differed on competency and leadership attributes.

Sturgis, Rhonda L. "Presidential Leadership in Institutional Advancement: From the Perspective of the President and Vice President of Institutional Advancement." *International Journal of Educational Advancement* 6 no. 3 (2006): 221–31. 6.1, 6.3.

This paper was based on the author's dissertation, "Team Relationships within Institutional Advancement."

Sulaiman, Maliah, Mohd Akhyar Adnan, and Putri Nor Suad Megat Mohd Nor. "Trust Me! A Case Study of the International Islamic University Malaysia's Waqf Fund." *Review of Islamic Economics* 13 no. 1 (2009): 69–88. 1.6, 5.3.

The development and accounting practices of IIUM's Waqf Fund were examined. Begun in 1999, the fund was not legally registered as a waqf. It has several purposes including supporting needy students; funds come from the government, university staff, and donors. Fundraising agents are paid commission. The authors concluded the fund's structure, government, and management were sound.

Sun, Xiaogeng. "A Multivariate Causal Model of Alumni Giving at a Midwest, Public University." PhD, University of Nebraska—Lincoln, 2005. 4.3.

The author used data from an alumni survey conducted at one university to test factors influencing alumni giving. Significant factors included graduation year, gender, alumni motivation, alumni experience, student experience-relationships, and student experience-extracurricular activities.

Sung, Minjung, and Sung-Un Yang. "Student-University Relationships and Reputation: A Study of the Links between Key Factors Fostering Students' Supportive Behavioral Intentions towards Their University." *Higher Education* 57 no. 6 (2009): 787–811. 4.3, 5.3.

A survey of undergraduates at a private Korean university asked about supportive behavioral intentions. A structural equation model was built with seven hypotheses and was found valid. Students' active communication behaviors, perceived educational quality, perceived relationship with the university, and perceived university reputation all influenced intent to give.

Swanson, Lee. "College-Community Engagement in Response to Community Perceptions of Social and Economic Value Generated by a College." EdD, University of Calgary, 2008. 2.5, 8.2.

Using a social capital model, this thesis studied how community members perceived a Canadian college. Community members believed the institution created value, although their estimates were lower than that of researchers. Beliefs that the college increased community economic and social well-being increased engagement with it.

Sweitzer, Kyle, and J. Fredericks Volkwein. "Prestige among Graduate and Professional Schools: Comparing the US News' Graduate School Reputation Ratings between Disciplines." *Research in Higher Education* 50 no. 8 (2009): 812–36. 3.4, 8.3.

The factors influencing peer ratings in *U.S. News* graduate and professional rankings in business, education, engineering, law, and medicine were modeled. Full-time enrollment was the only factor to appear in all five models; average admissions test score, faculty productivity, and tuition appeared in four models. Models explained 47–88 percent of variance.

Sweitzer, Kyle V. "The Correlates of Changes in Prestige among American Colleges and Universities." PhD, Pennsylvania State University, 2008. 3.4.

Variables describing institutions that experienced the greatest change in peer rankings in *U.S. News* were subject to factor analysis. Student selectivity, six-year graduation rate, and faculty productivity influenced peer rankings most.

Tang, Yao. "Empirical Analysis on Revenues and Expenses of Taiwanese Higher Education." *International Journal of China Studies* 1 no. 3 (2010): 685–704. 1, 5.3.

Financial reports from 162 Taiwanese institutions of higher education were compared in regards to fundraising. The private institutions in the study received 87–90 percent of their funds from fundraising.

Taylor, A. L., and J. C. Martin. "Characteristics of Alumni Donors and Non-Donors at a Research I Public University." *Research in Higher Education* 36 no. 3 (1995): 283–302. 4.3.

Alumni donors and nondonors from one university were surveyed. Discriminant analysis was used to predict donor/nondonor (65% correct) and high/low donor (87%) statuses. Predictive factors included perceived need for support, family involvement, subsequent graduate enrollment, reading alumni publications, special interest groups, and alumni involvement.

Teague, Bradley Berris. "The Satisfaction, Influence, and Attitude among Donors to the Athletics Foundation of the University of Mississippi." PhD, University of Mississippi, 2000. 1.7, 8.4.

Active, inactive, and reactivated major athletics donors to the University of Mississippi were surveyed regarding their satisfaction, attitude, and influence. ANOVA found differences between all three groups on each indices.

Teich, Ira. "A Marketing Perspective of Donation Attitudes and Intentions: An Analysis of Selected Factors Which May Impact Alumni Contributions." PhD, New York University, 2001. 4.3.

The alumni of two private institutions were surveyed with questions based on Fishbein and Azjen's Theory of Reasoned Action. Analysis showed the theory was able to discern some factors that influenced alumni donation attitude. From the results, three donor profiles were created.

Terkla, Dawn Geronimo, and Marian F. Pagano. "Understanding Institutional Image." *Research in Higher Education* 34 no. 1 (1993): 11–22. 3.3.

Using Tufts University as a case, the authors explored the use of the semantic differential research tool (which requires survey data) to measure institutional image. The tool compares current and desired image as well as images among different constituencies. One finding was that incoming freshmen had different perceptions than other constituents.

Terry, LeRodrick. "Alumni Attitudes Study a Secondary Analysis of Auburn University Alumni Attitudes." EdD, Auburn University, 2010. 4.6.

Auburn Alumni were surveyed to discover the effects of their attitudes toward Auburn and its alumni association. Loyalty, demographic, and student, alumni, and overall experience variables influenced propensity to give.

Thelin, John R. "Institutional History in Our Own Time: Higher Education's Shift from Managerial Revolution to Enterprising Evolution." *CASE International Journal of Educational Advancement* 1 no. 1 (2000): 9–22. 1.16, 7.1.

The author argued that in the last quarter of the twentieth century, colleges and universities began to make much greater use of data. This enabled them to better respond to constituents including federal and state governments and donors. Key events and influences in this change were discussed.

Thomas, Christy. "Retaining Educational Fundraisers: Reducing Turnover by Investing in Human Capital Management." *International Journal of Educational Advancement* 10 no. 2 (2010): 99–107. 6.5.

The author discussed the use of Human Capital Management to reduce turnover of major gifts officers, which she argued is particularly necessary during capital campaigns.

Thomas, Rosemary M. "The Emotional Intelligence of Chief Development Officers in Public Higher Education Institutions of the Mid Atlantic Region and Organizational Climate Perceptions of Their Development Teams." EdD, West Virginia University, 2007. 6.5.

Chief development officers were administered surveys of emotional quotient and organizational climate. Analysis found a significant, positive relationship between EQ scores and perception of climate. Demographic data did not affect perceptions of climate. In addition, CDOs had higher than average EQs.

Thompson, Justin B. "Leader Succession and the Evolving Presidency at Public Doctorate-Granting Universities." PhD, University of Virginia, 2012. 6.1.

This thesis compared the time spent on fundraising by presidents with their preparation for it. High-level academic administrators were surveyed about their preparedness for and the appeal of presidential duties. They estimated that presidents spent 41 percent of their time on fundraising, but generally rated tasks outside of academic administration as unappealing.

Thompson, James D, Stephanie Katz, and Peter Briechle. "A High Level Annual Fund without the Annual Ask." *International Journal of Educational Advancement* 9 no. 4 (2010): 273–79. 1.3.

The authors proposed an annual fund model that may be less effort-intensive based on an initiative at the University of Rochester. The institution created the George Eastman Circle, in which donors pledged to give $1,500–5,000 per year for five years.

Thompson, Lori Ann. "Data Mining for Higher Education Advancement: A Study of Eight North American Colleges and Universities." PhD, North Dakota State University, 2011. 1.1.

Alumni advancement data from eight institutions was used to test the predictive power of the variables institutions provided. Individual variables had power; each institution's model had significant predictive power.

Thompson, Tomas Micheal. "Who Gives? A Study of Variables at Graduation and Their Predictive Value for Alumni Fund Raisers." PhD, University of Missouri—Kansas City, 1994. 4.3.

Delta State University seniors and alumni were surveyed to be determined if potential donors could be identified as seniors. Four variables predicted senior likelihood to give and one variable predicted alumni giving, but no relationship between the two groups was found.

Till, Jean Marie. "Correlates of Fund-Raising Effectiveness in Public Four-Year Institutions of Higher Education." EdD, University of Minnesota, 1999. 1.3.

Data from publicly available sources, including VSE, for the University of Minnesota at Duluth and 26 peer institutions, was used to test Hornbaker's findings on factors that influence total funds raised. Endowment market value and education/general expenses explained 65 percent of the variation.

Till, Jean M. "Correlates of Fund-Raising Effectiveness in Public Four-Year Institutions of Higher Education." *CASE International Journal of Educational Advancement* 2 no. 3 (2002): 209–19. 1.3.

This article was based on the author's dissertation, discussed above.

Tindall, Natalie T. J. "Fund-Raising Models at Public Historically Black Colleges and Universities." *Public Relations Review* 33 (2007): 201–5. 2.2, 8.1.

Based on Kelly's fundraising models, the author explored what fundraising models and communication strategies HBCUs employed. Thirty public HBCUs responded to a survey. The most common model was the press agentry model, followed by two-way symmetrical communication.

Tindall, Natalie T. J. "Working on the Short Grass: A Qualitative Analysis of Fundraiser Roles and Experiences at Public Historically Black Colleges and Universities." *International Journal of Educational Advancement* 9 no. 1 (2009): 3–15. 6.4, 8.1.

Twenty-seven advancement officers at HBCUs were interviewed regarding their roles. They believed they were part of their institutions' leadership coalitions but were constrained by financial and staffing factors. They served as prescribers, problem-solving facilitators, and technicians, as described by Kelly.

Tindall, Natalie T. J., and Richard D. Waters. "The Relationship between Fundraising Practice and Job Satisfaction at Historically Black Colleges and Universities." *International Journal of Educational Advancement* 10 no. 3 (2010): 198–215. 1.1, 2.2.

Communication strategies of HBCU fundraisers were examined in a survey of 87 fundraisers. Most used one-way rather than interactive communications strategies, whether the office was centralized and job satisfaction influenced communication styles.

Tisdale, James Terrell. "Critical Components of Mississippi Community College Foundations." PhD, University of Southern Mississippi, 2003. 1.3, 8.2.

Based on surveys and interviews with foundation directors, information on college characteristics, presidential participation, identity marketing, alumni/friend roles, and donor identification and cultivation were gathered. While the foundations were relatively new, they had experienced some fundraising success.

Titus-Becker, Katherine Corley. "Make That Gift: Exploring the Stoical Navigation of Gender among Women Fundraisers in Higher Education." PhD, Ohio State University, 2007. 6.5.

The author used narrative inquiry to explore how female development officers navigated gender. Eleven female development officers from one institution were interviewed. They reappropriated gendered skills to achieve success. They faced harassment and marginalization from coworkers and donors, which they mostly responded to with silence.

Tobolowsky, Barbara F., and John Wesley Lowery. "Commercializing College: An Analysis of College Representations during Bowl Games." *International Journal of Educational Advancement* 6 no. 3 (2006): 232–42. 3.3.

The authors analyzed bowl game advertisements for two years to see how institutions portrayed themselves. Ads were consistent across institutions emphasizing the innocence of college life, traditions and history, and an embrace of the future. Only a few ads took unique approaches.

Tofallis, Chris. "A Different Approach to University Rankings." *Higher Education* 63 no. 1 (2012): 1–18. 3.4.

The author explored technical difficulties with university rankings, particularly those regarding how data is normalized, weighted, and aggregated. Different approaches can lead to very different rankings. The author recommended the multiplicative approach.

Tolbert, Dawn. "An Exploration of the Use of Branding to Shape Institutional Image in the Marketing Activities of Faith-Based Higher Education Institutions." EdD, Union University, 2013. 3.3, 8.8.

This thesis examined printed recruitment materials, websites, and admission portals for the 112 members of the Council for Christian Colleges and Universities to measure how these institutions portrayed their faith and to test whether that measure was predictive of external perception. Scores on faith portrayal did not influence alumni giving rate, peer assessment score, and *U.S. News* rankings.

Toma, J. Douglas. "The Collegiate Ideal and the Tools of External Relations: The Uses of High-Profile Intercollegiate Athletics." *New Directions for Higher Education* 105 (1999): 81–90. 2, 8.4.

The author argued that high-profile sports are an important part of American higher education helping to share customs and traditions, and helping institutions to reach a broader constituency.

Toma, J. Douglas, Greg Dubrow, and Matthew Hartley. *Special Issue: The Uses of Institutional Culture: Strengthening Identification and Building Brand Equity in Higher Education.* 31 no. 2, ASHE Higher Education Report. Hoboken, NJ: Wiley, 2005. 3.3.

This monograph discusses how institutional culture (norms, values, and beliefs) can be used to build brand equity, which in turn reinforces culture. Strong culture and brand equity help institutions reach external constituents.

Townsend, R. Larry. "An Assessment of Professional Consultants' Perceptions about Institutional Advancement Organizations within Higher Education." PhD, Southern Illinois University at Carbondale, 1999. 1.3.

Advancement consultants were surveyed regarding organizational strengths, barriers, and trends. Consultants felt that presidents and advancement vice presidents had weak management skills regarding complex initiatives; advancement initiatives were more likely to succeed when aligned with institutional goals; and there were often barriers to forming relationships with potential donors.

Trainer, James F., and Mary Sapp. "Identifying Measures of Quality in American Higher Education." *CASE International Journal of Educational Advancement* 1 no. 2 (2000): 165–79. 3.4.

The authors sought to see how members of the Higher Education Data Sharing Consortium defined "quality" via a formal brainstorming technique. Final determinants of quality were quality of instruction, institutional profile, alumni outcomes, and financial information.

Trakas, Peter A., II. "Online Giving and University Development." EdD, University of Central Florida, 2003. 1.17.

Potential donors to one liberal arts college were surveyed regarding their propensity to give online. While some gave to other causes online, most were uncertain about it. Class year was not a factor. Potential donors were concerned about security and privacy. They also preferred to receive traditional mail to email from the college.

Trollinger, Richard W. "Philanthropy and Transformation in American Higher Education." PhD, University of Kentucky, 2009. 1.6.

Via three case studies (University of Richmond, Emory, and the University of North Carolina), the author examined the effect of transformational gifts. Each institution changed dramatically, but not in similar ways.

Tsiotsou, Rodoula. "The Giving to Athletics Model (GAM): An Investigation of the Factors That Explain Donations to Intercollegiate Athletics." PhD, Florida State University, 1996. 1.2, 8.4.

The author developed the GAM and tested it with survey data from Florida State University. The data was tested with structural equation modeling and the model revised. Involvement with athletics and emotional motivation were the most significant factors predicting athletic giving, but experiences with sports also had an effect. Athletic attendance affected emotional motivation.

Tsiotsou, Rodoula. "Investigating Differences between Female and Male Athletic Donors: A Comparative Study." *International Journal of Nonprofit and Voluntary Sector Marketing* 11 (2006): 209–23. 1.2, 8.4.

This article is based on the author's dissertation, "The Giving to Athletics Model (GAM)."

Tsunoda, Kozue. "Asian American Giving to US Higher Education." *International Journal of Educational Advancement* 10 no. 1 (2010): 2–23. 1.2.

Three case studies of Asian American giving (Stanford, Columbia, and the University of Maryland) were explored based on interviews with development officers. Fundraisers said they used the same strategies they would with white donors, emphasizing that personalized relationships are important for all major gift fundraising. Barriers and motivations were also discussed.

Tsunoda, Kozue. "Unraveling the Myths of Chinese American Giving: Exploring Donor Motivations and Effective Fundraising Strategies for US Higher Education." PhD, University of Maryland, College Park, 2011. 1.2.

Interviews with 14 Chinese America donors to higher education contrasted "traditional" (family obligations, community and institutional reciprocity, and appreciation for education) and "nontraditional" motivations. The ways in which donors gave were often nontraditional (large, institutionalized, and public).

Tsunoda, Kozue. "Chinese American Philanthropy: Cultural Contexts behind Major Gifts in Higher Education." In *Expanding the Donor Base in Higher Education: Engaging Non-Traditional Donors*, edited by Noah D. Drezner, 40–58. New York: Routledge, 2013. 1.2.

This book chapter was based on the author's dissertation, "Unraveling the Myths of Chinese American Giving."

Tucker, Irvin B. "The Influence of Big-Time Athletic Success on Contributions to the University." *Journal of Business and Economic Perspectives* 21 no. 2 (1995): 1–9. 1.3, 8.4.

The author used data on university contributions and AP rankings for football and men's basketball at 55 universities to see if AP rankings influenced contributions. He found they did.

Tucker, Irvin B. "A Reexamination of the Effect of Big-Time Football and Basketball Success on Graduation Rates and Alumni Giving Rates." *Economics of Education Review* 23 no. 6 (2004): 655–61. 4.3, 8.4.

A sample of big-time athletics universities was examined to see if athletic success (winning percentages, bowl/postseason participation, and AP poll appearances) affected six-year graduation rates and alumni giving rates. Football success positively influenced both, but basketball successful did not.

Tucker, Shauna K. "The Early Years of the United Negro College Fund, 1943–1960." *Journal of African American History* 87 (2002): 416–32. 7.2, 8.1.

This article explained the founding of the UNCF, its first campaign, the role of John D. Rockefeller, Jr., its growth and formalization, the *Brown* decision, and the setting of standards for membership.

Turner, Sarah E., Lauren A. Meserve, and William G. Bowen. "Winning and Giving: Football Results and Alumni Giving at Selective Private Colleges and Universities." *Social Science Quarterly* 82 no. 4 (2001): 812–26. 4.3, 8.4.

The effect of football success was explored at 15 selective, private institutions in Divisions I and III using College Board data. Winning percentages did not affect giving at Division I or Ivy League schools, although they had a moderate effect at other Division III schools, especially for former student-athletes.

Turpin, Andrea L. "The Ideological Origins of the Women's College: Religion, Class, and Curriculum in the Educational Visions of Catharine Beecher and Mary Lyon." *History of Education Quarterly* 50 no. 2 (2010): 133–58. 7.2.

The ideologies of Lyon, founder of Mount Holyoke, and Beecher, founder of Hartford Female Seminary, were contrasted. Beecher favored providing wealthier women with a more vocational education, whereas Lyon favored providing a liberal arts education to middle-class women. These differences arose from their backgrounds and theologies and affected the education their colleges offered.

Upton, Thomas A., and Marcela Orvananos de Rovzar. "Case Study of the American British Cowdray School of Nursing (ABCSN)." *CASE International Journal of Educational Advancement* 3 no. 2 (2002). 7.2, 5.6.

This case study of a nursing school in Mexico examines its structure and fundraising practices. The formal philanthropic sector in Mexico is less developed than its US counterpart, informing its operations. Marketing materials were examined to see how the institution presented itself.

van Fleet, Justin W. "Corporate Giving to Education during Economic Downturns: General Trends and the Difficulty of Prediction." *International Journal of Educational Advancement* 9 no. 4 (2010): 234–50. 1.12.

The author examined trends in corporate giving during economic downturns over the past 40 years using data from several public sources, findings that downturns do affect giving. Information technology, the largest sector donor to higher education, maintained giving rather than increasing in following the recession of 2007.

van Fleet, Justin W. "A Half Billion Dollars Adding Up To Small Change: The Promises and Pitfalls of Corporate Philanthropy to Support Global Education." PhD, University of Maryland, College Park, 2011. 1.12, 5.5.

This thesis explored the role of US corporate philanthropy to support education, including higher education, in developing countries. Companies give over half a billion dollars annually, targeting emerging economies. Many gifts are small, short-term, and uncoordinated with other funding sources.

Van Horn, Drew Layne. "Satisfaction with the Undergraduate Experience as Motivation for Smaller Dollar Alumni Donations." PhD, University of South Carolina, 2002. 4.3.

Alumni of two private colleges were surveyed to explore the effect of satisfaction with the undergraduate experience on alumni donations. While the relationship between satisfaction and donations was strong, it was not predictive. Only motivation to give was significant.

van Nostrand, Innes. "A Quantitative Model for Evaluating Advancement Effectiveness." *International Journal of Educational Advancement* 4 no. 2 (2003). 1.14.

Based on data from previous surveys, the author created five indices measuring the donor-institution relationship: the Student Experience, Reputational, Connectivity, Participation, and Donor Indices. These indices were used at Upper Canada College for information and goal-setting.

Vanderbout, Jenne L. "Impact the Undergraduate Experience Has on the Development of Alumni Loyalty." EdD, University of Missouri–Columbia, 2010. 4.6.

Through structured interviews with thirty alumni donors and nondonors from one university and two focus groups, this thesis explored the role of the student experience in developing alumni loyalty. Donors had stronger long-term relationships, believed they had changed during college, and thought their education had given them a foundation for life. They often had multiple degrees from the university and had fewer loans.

VanderKelen, Barry Lee. "Institutional Conditions Fostering Corporate Development Officers' Advocacy of Corporate Interests." PhD, University of California, Los Angeles, 1997. 1.12.

Twenty-five corporate development officers at 10 institutions were interviewed to test if overall program focus and accountability affected the CDO's level of advocacy. The hypothesis was not supported. Half the CDOs were not held accountable for reaching fundraising goals.

Violand, Laura T. "An Analysis of Donors of $10,000 or More to the $75 Million Campaign at the George Washington University." EdD, George Washington University, 1998. 1.2.

This thesis explored the characteristics of major donors to GWU's medical center campaign using institutional data. Donors and prospects differed on 26 of 49 variables. The most likely prospects had a desire to designate their gifts; formal relationships with GWU; were male and graduated pre-1950 or were female, older, and single; had alumni relatives; and had served on institutional boards or received honorary degrees.

Vogel, Stephanie Huefile. "Development of a University Alumnae Mentoring Program." *International Journal of Educational Advancement* 4 no. 3 (2004). 4.7.

This case study of one university's alumnae mentoring program describes its creation, membership, structure, challenges, result, and value. The program was developed in response to focus group research. Both students and mentors said they received value from the program.

Voigts, Michael C. "Understanding the Relationship between Asbury Theological Seminary and Its Alumni 'Metacommunity.'" DMin, Asbury Theological Seminary, 2004. 4, 8.3.

Based on a survey of Asbury alumni, the author made recommendations for how the seminary could improve its alumni relations. While alumni had positive perceptions of Asbury, the institution primarily engaged with them for fundraising and admissions.

Waddell, John Kenneth. "A Study of Fund-Raising at the National Association for Equal Opportunity in Higher Education (NAFEO) Affiliated Public Black Colleges and Universities." EdD, Florida State University, 1992. 8.1.

Statistical data on fundraising was collected for public NAFEO members; state colleges and land-grant institutions were compared. Land-grants had larger budgets and received more donations. Also, urban institutions received larger gifts than rural institutions.

Wæraas, Arild, and Marianne N. Solbakk. "Defining the Essence of a University: Lessons from Higher Education Branding." *Higher Education* 57 no. 4 (2009): 449–62. 3.3, 5.6

This case study of branding a university in Norway discussed the challenges faced. Faculty challenged the branding strategy, which positioned the university as regional, preferring a national brand, and saw the proposed core values as meaningless platitudes. The author concludes the university did not have a coherent identity but identities, and that the proposed identity better represented the university's past than its future.

Wagoner, Richard L., and Rudolph J. Besikof. "Community College Fundraising: The Voluntary Support of Education Survey as a Sampling Tool for Research." *Community College Journal of Research and Practice* 35 no. 1–2 (2010): 74–87. 1.14, 8.2.

This article discussed the VSE and what it can be used for, stressing that it contains more relevant data than alternatives. They related one use of it to study community college fundraising.

Walker, Sharianne. "The Athletic Department and the Institutional Development Office: A Systems Approach to Athletic Fund-Raising." PhD, University of Massachusetts Amherst, 1994. 1.1, 8.4.

This thesis built a model for athletic fundraising, which was then compared with fundraising at Division I institutions. Data was gathered by interviews with athletic fundraisers. They reported that relationships between athletics and development were poor.

Walker, Stephanie J. "Development of a University Alumnae Mentoring Program: A Case Study." EdD, University of Nebraska—Lincoln, 2002. 4.7.

Using qualitative data from participants, this case study described the developing of an alumnae mentoring program at one university. While the program had some formal mentoring characteristics, it had an unstructured approach and no formal outcomes. The program's development was aided by the support of the alumni association, the program's executive coordinator, and its executive committee.

Walter, Michele Corcoran. "Effective Presidential Leadership in Fund-Raising: A Case Study of a Community College Foundation." PhD, Saint Louis University, 1993. 1.3, 6.1, 8.2.

This case study of a multicampus community college explored presidential leadership's role in starting a new fundraising program, using archival data and interviews. The program did not reach its dollar goal but did achieve passage of a fee referendum. Effective presidential leadership was not present in all areas.

Walton, Andrea. "Rethinking Boundaries: The History of Women, Philanthropy, and Higher Education." *History of Higher Education Annual* 20 (2000): 29–57. 7.1.

This chapter profiled Grace Hoadley Dodge, a trustee and treasurer of Teacher's College, and Elsie Clews Parsons, a patron and scholar at Columbia. Philanthropy has the possibility to blur the lines of who is inside/outside of an institution, and it enables women to participate in a meaningful way.

Walton, Andrea. "To Bind the University to Nothing: The Giving of Clementine Miller Tangeman as a Case Study in Donor Motivation." *CASE International Journal of Educational Advancement* 2 no. 2 (2001): 126–45. 7.3.

This historical paper examined the giving of Tangeman to Smith, Butler, Christian Theological Seminary, and Yale and explores the factors that made her a dedicated philanthropist. Family and church played an important role in her philanthropic development.

Walton, Andrea, ed. *Women and Philanthropy in Education, Philanthropic and Nonprofit Studies*. Bloomington, IN: Indiana University Press, 2005. 7.1.

While women have not historically been major donors, they have played an important role in philanthropy. This edited volume profiled some of these women who were involved in higher education philanthropy in the 1800s and 1900s.

Walton, Andrea, and Marybeth Gasman, eds. *Philanthropy, Volunteerism & Fundraising in Higher Education*, ASHE Reader. New York: Pearson Learning Solutions, 2012. 1.0, 7.1.

Like other ASHE Readers, this volume compiled classic readings on the subject. Readings emphasize the role of private giving in shaping US higher education, the role of voluntary action on education policy, the role of donors in shaping research and campus culture, and the role of philanthropy in access.

Wampler, Fredrick Hoopes. "Bridges to a Lifelong Connection: A Study of Ivy Plus Young Alumni Programs Designed to Transition Recent Graduates into Engaged Alumni." EdD, University of Pennsylvania, 2013. 4.7.

Ivy Plus institutions were surveyed and Cornell and Penn's young alumni programs served as case studies in this thesis. While not all 10 members had young alumni programs, all prioritized the involvement of recent graduates. The cases showed the importance of institutional culture, the importance of beginning alumni identification early, and that young alumni give either for friends or impact.

Ward, Howard. "The Impact of Collegiate Involvement on African-American Alumni Giving." PhD, Bowling Green State University, 2004. 4.3.

Black alumni of Ohio Northern were surveyed regarding their undergraduate experiences. When combined with institutional data, a relationship was found between satisfaction and donations. Undergraduate student involvement and years away from campus influenced giving at the Sustaining Donor level. Attending alumni activities did not correlate with giving.

Warner, Gary A. "The Development of Public Relations Offices at American Colleges and Universities." *Public Relations Quarterly* 41 no. 2 (1996): 36–39. 7.1.

This article took a historical look at public relations offices, starting in 1868. Some programs started prior to World War II, but there was tremendous growth postwar.

Warren, Alexander Charles. "A Multi-Case Study of Annual Giving and Fund Raising in Texas Gulf Coast Community College Consortium Foundations." PhD, University of Texas at Austin, 2008. 1.6, 8.2.

Case studies of five community colleges examined their annual fund processes. Colleges followed an input-processes-output model, and each of these were discussed.

Wastyn, M. Linda. "Why Alumni Don't Give: A Qualitative Study of What Motivates Non-Donors to Higher Education." PhD, Illinois State University, 2008. 4.3.

Using the Van Slyke and Brooks model of alumni giving and Schervish's supply-side theory of philanthropy, the author used interviews with 12 alumni nondonors to explore why they do not give. Donors and nondonors socially construct their college experiences differently, influencing giving; who makes giving decisions and how they are prioritized matters as well.

Watts, Dennis E. "The History of Institutional Advancement at the University of Mississippi from Chancellor John Davis Williams through Chancellor Robert Conrad Khayat: Forty-Six Years of Growth." PhD, University of Mississippi, 2004. 7.2.

The history of the University of Mississippi's advancement program was traced, beginning with the hiring of the first advancement staff member in 1954. The author divided the history into presidential administrations.

Weaver-Lariscy, Ruth Ann, Glen T. Cameron, and Duane D. Sweep. "Women in Higher Education Public Relations: AnCed Inkling of Change?" *Journal of Public Relations Research* 6 no. 2 (1994): 125–40. 2.

Based on surveys, the authors examined institutional constraints, personal characteristics, and research styles of male and female public relations officers. Regarding constraints, women tended to serve as a "conscience," while men were dominant insiders. No differences were found in research styles.

Wedgworth, R. "Donor Relations as Public Relations: Toward a Philosophy of Fund-Raising." *Library Trends* 48 no. 3 (2000): 530–40. 1.1, 2, 8.7.

The author argued that academic libraries should engage in fundraising and that it should be considered a part of public relations. Goals, potential donors, and possible threats to autonomy were also covered.

Weerts, David J. "Toward an Engagement Model of Institutional Advancement at Public Colleges and Universities." *International Journal of Educational Advancement* 7 no. 2 (2007): 79–103. 1.16.

The author argues that threats to the "publicness" of public higher education can be answered by engaging in institutional advancement that focuses on a public agenda to generate broad-based public support.

Weerts, David J., Alberto F. Cabrera, and Thomas Sanford. "Beyond Giving: Political Advocacy and Volunteer Behaviors of Public University Alumni." *Research in Higher Education* 51 no. 4 (2010): 346–65. 2.5, 4.7.

Focus groups were used to identify nonmonetary forms of alumni support and to generate a survey regarding those behaviors at one university. Confirmatory factor analysis was used on the survey results to classify the behaviors as political advocacy or volunteerism.

Weerts, David J., and J. M. Ronca. "Profiles of Supportive Alumni: Donors, Volunteers, and Those Who 'Do It All.'" *International Journal of Educational Advancement* 7 no. 1 (2007): 20–34. 4.3, 4.5.

Data from an alumni survey at one university was used to predict which alumni gave, volunteered, did both, or did neither. Only four variables had predictive power, those that measured capacity and inclination to give.

Weerts, David J., and Justin M. Ronca. "Characteristics of Alumni Donors Who Volunteer at Their Alma Mater." *Research in Higher Education* 49 no. 3 (2008): 274–92. 4.6.

Data from an alumni survey at one university was used to sort alumni volunteers from nonvolunteers using social exchange theory. Gender, residence, and overall civic engagement were predictive variables; age and employment status were not predictive.

Weerts, David J., and Justin M. Ronca. "Using Classification Trees to Predict Alumni Giving for Higher Education." *Education Economics* 17 no. 1 (2009): 95–122. 4.3.

Based on utility maximization, the authors used data from one university and regression tree methods to predict whether alumni were donors or nondonors. Influential variables were income, religion, degree, how the alumnus stays in touch, beliefs about institutional needs, and number of other institutions soliciting dollars.

Weir, Cathie S. "A Case Study of Fund-Raising Success at Westark College." EdD, University of Arkansas, 2003. 1.6.

Westark College's above-average endowment was the subject of this case study. Interviews, observations, event participation, and documents were used as evidence. Strong presidential and board leadership, expert advice from consultants, a comprehensive program, following best practices, and connecting fundraising to community and institutional needs were seen as key.

Wells, Douglas Eugene. "Factors Related to Annual Fund Raising Contributions from Individual Donors to NCAA-I-A Institutions." EdD, University of Northern Colorado, 2001. 1.3, 8.4.

Directors of development at Division I institutions were surveyed regarding annual athletic fundraising. Survey data was used to build a predictive equation that accounted for 78 percent of the variation; 5 of 15 predictor variables were significant (the director of development's years of experience, how long a full-time position had been established, season football ticket sales, number of living alumni, and size of prospect list).

Wells, Douglas Eugene, Richard M. Southall, David K. Stotlar, and Daniel J. Mundfrom. "Factors Related to Annual Fund-Raising Contributions from Individual Donors to NCAA Division I-A Institutions." *International Journal of Educational Advancement* 6 no. 1 (2005): 3–10. 1.3, 8.4.

This article was based on Wells' dissertation, "Factors Related to Annual Fund Raising Contributions."

Wells, Ronald Austin. "'The Future Is In Our Minds': The American Indian College Fund." *New Directions for Philanthropic Fundraising* 1 (1993): 73–92. 7.2, 8.6.

The author discussed the history of the AICF and its fundraising strategies. AICF was modeled on the UNCF and incorporated in 1987. Strong tribal college support, foundation grants, and special events helped give the fund legitimacy. Funds are divided equally among member colleges.

Wenrich, J. William, and Betheny L. Reid. "It's Not the Race I Signed Up For, but It's the Race I'm In: The Role of Community College Presidents." *New Directions for Community Colleges* 124 (2003): 27–32. doi: 10.1002/cc.130. 6.1, 8.2.

While most community college presidents take the position with little experience with or training in fundraising, it has become an important part of the job. The role of the president and the foundation CEO were discussed.

Wesley, Derek M. "Catholic College and University Presidents: Fundraising Initiatives and Identity Maintenance." EdD, Johnson & Wales University, 2007. 1.1, 6.1, 8.8.

Catholic institution presidents were surveyed and interviewed regarding their role, techniques used in fundraising, best practices, and the impact of Catholic institutional identity. Eighty-one percent of respondents agreed that promoting a strong Catholic identity increased funds raised. Respondents agreed the president's role was important and that presidents need to build strong relationships with constituents.

West, Rachel Cooey. "Philanthropic Motivation Patterns at Florida Community Colleges." PhD, Florida State University, 2012. 1.2, 8.2.

A survey of $1,000-plus donors to three community colleges was used to profile donors. Typical donors were older, white, married men who lived nearby, contributed to other colleges, had a bachelors degree, and were neither first-generation students nor financial aid recipients. Six motivations were developed, with only some demographic characteristics influencing them.

Whitaker, Evans P. "The Linkage of College and University Seniors to Their Institution: A Study of Factors Related to Institutional Loyalty." PhD doctoral dissertation, Vanderbilt University, 1999. 4.6.

College seniors from 20 institutions were surveyed about institutional loyalty. Five composite variables affected loyalty: overall positive experience, extracurricular involvement, understanding that tuition did not cover the entire cost of education, academic involvement, and satisfaction with career services.

Whitaker, Steve D. "The Role of the Private College President in Fundraising: A Comparative Case Study." PhD, University of Louisville, 2005. 1.1, 6.1.

Five case studies explored the role of the private college president in fundraising. The presidents gained support from faculty for their vision, had strong administrative teams, and expected the trustees to be generous donors.

White, Fredrick. "Community College Finance: An Analysis of Resource Development at Mississippi's Community and Junior Colleges." PhD, Mississippi State University, 2007. 1.1.

Fundraising at rural two-year institutions in Mississippi was explored by analyzing data from a survey developed by Burns. Grants and foundation offices worked together. Capital campaigns were less important than cooperative ventures with community organizations.

White, John L. "An Analysis of the Effects of Fund Raising Investment and Practices on Fund Raising Production: A Case Study of Auburn University's College of Business Fund Raising Program from 1991 to 2001." EdD, Auburn University, 2003. 1.6.

Ten years of fundraising at Auburn's business school was evaluated using ROPES; interviews with staff members and volunteers complemented the quantitative analysis. The number of alumni donors decreased over time; several possible explanations were explored.

Willemain, T. R., A. Goyal, M. Van Deven, and I. S. Thukral. "Alumni Giving: The Influences of Reunion, Class, and Year." *Research in Higher Education* 35 (1994): 609–29. 4.3.

Fifty years of data from Princeton's annual giving program were analyzed. Reunion number, class identity, and fiscal year explained most of the variation in average gift size and percentage of class giving.

Wilkins, Stephen, and Jeroen Huisman. "UK Business School Rankings over the Last 30 Years (1980–2010): Trends and Explanations." *Higher Education* 63 no. 3 (2012): 367–82. 3.4, 5.2, 8.7.

Using institutional theory, the authors examined the role of institutional history in UK business school rankings, 1984–2010. Regulations and normative path dependencies played a large role in how institutions were ranked.

Williams, John D. "Factors Related to Fund-Raising Outcomes at United Negro College Fund Member Institutions." EdD, University of Maryland College Park, 1992. 1.3, 8.1.

Thirty-two UNCF member institutions were subject to correlation analysis to explore the effects of institutional characteristics on the three-year average of total gifts. Educational and general revenues, expenditures, enrollment, number of graduates, and expenditures for fundraising explained at least 50 percent of the variation. Institutional wealth, size, fundraising effort, and socio-economic status of students correlated with gifts.

Williams, Julie M. "Reverend Robert Draper Swanson: Funding a Christian Liberal Arts Ethos at Alma College." PhD, Indiana University, 2012. 7.3, 8.8.

Swanson was president of Alma from 1956 to 1980; during his presidency, he transformed the ailing college to a much stronger institution. Archival documents were used to explore Swanson's fundraising strategies.

Williams, Monica G. "Increasing Philanthropic Support through Entrepreneurial Activities at Historically Black Colleges and Universities." *International Journal of Educational Advancement* 10 no. 3 (2010): 216–29. 1.3, 8.1.

Based on surveys of 13 administrative leaders, the author explored the extent to which HBCU presidents used entrepreneurial framework leadership traits based on Clark's theory. Leaders with those traits were found to have raised more money.

Williams, Ross, and Nina Van Dyke. "Reputation and Reality: Ranking Major Disciplines in Australian Universities." *Higher Education* 56 no. 1 (2008): 1–28. 3.4, 5.4.

The authors compared actual performance measures with rankings by senior academics via survey and found a high level of correlation between survey rankings and both research performance and quality of incoming students, but not with satisfaction levels of recent graduates.

Williams, Roger L. *The Origin of Federal Support for Higher Education: George W. Atherton and the Land-Grant College Movement.* University Park: Pennsylvania State University Press, 1991. 1.16, 7.1.

This book explored the factors that led to the passage of the Morrill Act; the author argued that Atherton, president of Penn State, was instrumental in its passage. Atherton was also involved in the campaigns to pass the Hatch Act and the second Morrill Act.

Willmer, Wesley K. "A Longitudinal Assessment of Administrative Satisfaction with Trustee Involvement in Assisting Admissions, Deciding Fund-Raising Policy, Making Financial Contributions, and Soliciting Donors." *CASE International Journal of Educational Advancement* 2 no. 2 (2001a): 166–77. 1.9, 6.2.

Based on three waves of survey data from Council of Independent Colleges survey, the paper tracked administrator satisfaction with trustees in admissions and fundraising over time. The area of greatest satisfaction was in setting fundraising policy; there was less satisfaction with making contributions, assisting with admissions, and soliciting donors.

Willmer, Wesley K., ed. *Advancing Small Colleges (Strategies for Success in Alumni Relations, Communications, Fund Raising, Marketing, and Enrollment Management).* New York: CASE, 2001b. 1.

Based on a survey by CASE and the Council of Independent Colleges, this edited volume provided best practices that arose from the data. Chapter topics included the fundraising process, the role of trustees and presidents, fundraising, marketing, alumni relations, enrollment trends, and survey results.

Willmer, Wesley K. *Advancing Small Colleges: A Benchmarking Survey Update.* New York: CASE, 2008. 1.

This book detailed the results of the most recent CASE/Council of Independent Colleges survey on advancement. Survey topics included fundraising, marketing, communications, alumni relations, and admissions.

Wilson, Barbara Mefford. "An Analysis of Continuing Education and Development Designed for Baby-Boomer Alumni." PhD, University of Illinois at Urbana-Champaign, 1993. 4.7.

A survey of 35 institutions examined their continuing education programs targeted at Baby Boomer alumni. Programs were found not to be targeted that specifically, although Boomers comprised 49 percent of participants. Private institutions offered more programs and had larger subsidies than public institutions. The number of programs was correlated with endowment size, alumni support, and total support.

Winter, Paul A., and Eric W. Wright. "Vice President of Development Recruitment: The Effect of Applicant Institution Type." *International Journal of Educational Advancement* 4 no. 2 (2003). 6.3, 6.5.

This paper was based on Wright's dissertation "Recruiting Vice Presidents of Development," discussed later.

Wood, Jason S. "Rural Community College Fundraising: A Multi-Site Case Study Exploring the Characteristics and Motivations of Alumni Supporters." PhD, Oregon State University, 2012. 4.3, 8.2.

These qualitative case studies explored what motivational factors and characteristics led rural community college alumni to donate.

Wooten, Melissa E. "Soliciting Elites: The Framing Activities of the United Negro College Fund." *Mobilization: An International Quarterly* 15 no. 3 (2010): 369–91. 1.1, 8.1.

The UNCF's annual reports and brochures to solicit support 1945–1954 were examined to see what frames were used. Frames, in order of frequency, were support, leadership, service, responsibility, citizens, traditions, and race relations. These frames were designed to appeal to elites.

Worth, Michael J. *New Strategies for Educational Fundraising.* Westport, CT: Praeger Publishers, 2002. 1.3.

This edited volume has become a standard primer on higher education fundraising. Chapters were a mix of theory, research, best practices, and trends covering all facets of fundraising for higher education and all institutional types.

Worth, Michael J. *Leading the Campaign: Advancing Colleges and Universities*: Rowman & Littlefield Publishers, 2010. 1.3.

While focused on presidents, this book covered the role multiple leaders play in capital campaigns and the strategic decisions that need to be made, covering key decisions and tasks for various campaign phases; the campaign team; campaign goals, priorities and objectives; executing the campaign; and postcampaign evaluation, planning, and stewardship.

Worth, Michael J., and James W. Asp II. *The Development Officer in Higher Education: Toward an Understanding of the Role*. Vol. 4, ASHE-ERIC Higher Education Reports. Washington: George Washington University, 1994. 6.3.

This monograph focused on the fundraiser in colleges and universities, proposing that the role includes four roles: salesman (bringing in funds), catalyst (supporting other fundraisers), manager, and leader (influencing policy, both fundraising and other). It discusses these roles, professional relationships, and the professionalization of fundraising.

Wright, Eric William. "Recruiting Vice Presidents of Development: The Effects of Applicant Institution Type, Vacancy Institution Type, Vacancy Endowment, and Vacancy Alumni Base." EdD, University of Louisville, 2001. 6.3, 6.5.

A total of 144 directors of development rated simulated job descriptions for vice presidential positions. Vacancy public/private status, large/small endowment size, and large/small alumni type were manipulated. Directors at public institutions rated positions higher than directors at private institutions. The three manipulated variables were not significant.

Wright, Karen. "Generosity vs. Altruism: Philanthropy and Charity in the United States and United Kingdom." *Voluntas* 12 no. 4 (2001): 399–416. 5.2.

The author compared giving to charitable and philanthropic causes in the United States and the United Kingdom. US giving is about 2 percent of GDP, while United Kingdom giving is less than 1 percent. The United States prefers the term "philanthropy"; the United Kingdom, "charity." Differences are due to differing expectations of the roles of the public and private sectors, attitudes toward money and wealth, and tax policy.

Wright, Marshal H., and Mihai C. Bocarnea. "Contributions of Unrestricted Funds: The Donor Organization–Public Relationship and Alumni Attitudes and Behaviors." *Nonprofit Management & Leadership* 18 no. 2 (2007): 215–35. 4.3.

Undergraduate alumni who graduated in the 1990s from Azusa Pacific were surveyed regarding organizational connectedness and willingness to donate. Organization-public relationship was found to predict donor attitudes and willingness to donate. It did not predict gift size or frequency.

Wu, Ke, and Melissa S. Brown. "An Examination of Persistence in Charitable Giving to Education through the 2002 Economic Downturn." *International Journal of Educational Advancement* 9 no. 4 (2010): 196–219. 4.2.

The authors used data from the Center on Philanthropy Study (part of the Panel Study on Income Dynamics) to describe donors who gave to education in each of the three years studied. Those who did so had higher incomes and education levels. There was some support consistency being related to the number and age of children in the household and giving to other secular causes as well.

Wunnava, Phinindra V., and Michael A. Lauze. "Alumni Giving at a Small Liberal Arts College: Evidence from Consistent and Occasional Donors." *Economics of Education Review* 20 no. 6 (2001): 533–43. 4.3.

Based on 23 years of data from Middlebury College, factors influencing alumni giving were found to be college volunteering, majoring in social sciences, attending language school, residing in a state with an alumni chapter, being employed in finance, having alumni relative, and being a varsity athlete.

Wunnava, Phanindra V., and Albert A. Okunade. "Do Business Executives Give More to Their Alma Mater? Longitudinal Evidence from a Large University." *American Journal of Economics and Sociology* 72 no. 3 (2013): 761–78. 4.3.

Twenty-six years of data from one university were used to understand variation in giving among business executive alumni. Male fraternity members with higher job titles who knew other alumni donors gave more. Donations were higher in years with a national athletic championship and the subsequent year.

Zeiss, Tony. "Generating New Sources of Revenue." *New Directions for Community Colleges* 124 (2003): 53–61. doi: 10.1002/cc.134. 1.3.

The author discussed sources of revenue to replace appropriations at community colleges, including contracted services, business partnerships, and entrepreneurial activities. The last category includes starting foundations.

Zimmer, Eric Albert. "For to All Those Who Have, More Will Be Given: The Matthew Effect, Nonprofit Organizations, and the Adoption of Internet Technologies." PhD, University of Pennsylvania, 2001. 3.1.

Case studies of Catholic institutions, website content analysis, and a survey of nonprofits explored the adoption of the Internet by nonprofits.

Zuniga, Kelly J. "A Study of Donors Who Have Made Online Contributions to Universities." EdD, University of Houston, 2005. 1.17.

> Online donors to five universities were surveyed. The average respondent was 43 years old, married, had a gross income of $119,023, and accessed the Internet 278 times a month. They rated the ease of online giving and their comfort with online financial transactions as high.

Notes

4 Hidden Research: Dissertations

1. William Ammentorp, University of Minnesota; Roger Baldwin, William and Mary; Louis Bender, Florida State University; Dale Campbell and Barbara Keener (jointly), University of Florida; Katherine Chaddock, University of South Carolina; James Fisher, the Union Institute; Gerard Fowler, St. Louis University; Conrad Glass, North Carolina State University; Louis Hekhuis, Michigan State University; Marybeth Keim, Southern Illinois University–Carbondale; Barbara LaCost, University of Nevada–Lincoln; David Leslie, William and Mary; Larry Leslie, University of Arizona; Sharon McDade, Teachers College and then George Washington University; Christine McPhail, Morgan State University; Norma Mertz, the University of Tennessee; Albert Miles, the University of Alabama; Michael Miller, the University of Alabama; William Moore, University of Texas at Austin; John Roueche, University of Texas at Austin; Edgar Sagan, University of Kentucky; Alan Seagren, University of Nebraska–Lincoln; David Stotlar, University of Northern Colorado; Eugene Tempel, Indiana University; LeVester Tubbs, University of Central Florida; and Robert Wimpelberg and James Pickering (jointly), University of Houston.
2. Our concern here was with dissertations where the researcher's affiliation could have affected data collection or findings. We did not attempt to discover whether, for example, a researcher's PhD institution was included in a dataset of 200 universities downloaded from VSE.
3. We did not track all institutional types. Those not taxonomized had samples ranging from the entire four-year IPEDS universe to public universities within one particular state. Many of these made no explicit claim about why the sample under study was chosen rather than another.

References

This includes all works cited within this book that were not within the scope of our literature review.

Association of Fundraising Professionals. 2007. "Code of Ethical Principles and Standards." Accessed May 6. http://www.afpnet.org/Ethics/Enforcement Detail.cfm?ItemNumber=3261.

Avery, Vida L. 2013. *Philanthropy in Black Higher Education: A Fateful Hour Creating the Atlanta University System*. New York: Palgrave Macmillan.

Ayers, D. Franklin. 2005. "Neoliberal ideology in community college mission statements: A critical discourse analysis." *The Review of Higher Education* 28 (4): 527–49.

Bok, Derek. 2003. *Universities in the Marketplace: The Commercialization of Higher Education*. Princeton, NJ: Princeton University Press.

Brittingham, Barbara E., and Thomas R. Pezzullo. 1990. "*The Campus Green*: Fund Raising in Higher Education." In Jonathan D. Fife (Ed.), *ASHE-ERIC Higher Education Reports*. Washington, DC: School of Education and Human Development, the George Washington University.

Brown II, M. Christopher, Ronyelle Bertrand Ricard, and Saran Donahoo. 2004. "The changing role of historically black colleges and universities: Vistas on dual missions, desegregation, and diversity." In Christopher M. Brown II and Kassie Freeman (Eds.), *Black Colleges: New Perspectives on Policy and Practice* (pp. 3–28). Westport, CT: Praeger Publisher.

Caboni, Timothy C., and Eve Proper. 2009. "Re-envisioning the professional doctorate for educational leadership and higher education leadership: Vanderbilt University's Peabody College Ed.D. program." *Peabody Journal of Education* 84: 61–68.

Carbone, Robert F. 1986. *An Agenda for Research on Fund Raising*. College Park, MD: Clearinghouse for Research on Fund Raising.

Carlson, Scott. 2013. "What's the payoff for the 'country club' college?" *The Chronicle of Higher Education*, January 28, Buildings & Grounds. http://chronicle.com/blogs/buildings/whats-the-payoff-for-the-country-club-college/32477.

CASE Board of Trustees. 2005. "Principles of practice for fundraising professionals at educational institutions." Accessed May 6. http://www.case.org/Samples_Research_and_Tools/Principles_of_Practice/Principles_of_Practice_for_Fundraising_Professionals_at_Educational_Institutions.html.

The Chronicle of Higher Education. 2002. "Lawsuit accuses Princeton of mismanaging gift to Woodrow Wilson School." *The Chronicle of Higher Education*, August 16, A29, Money and Management.
Cox, Bradley E., Kadian McIntosh, Robert D. Reason, and Patrick T. Terenzini. 2014. "Working with missing data in higher education research: A primer and real-world example." *The Review of Higher Education* 37 (3): 377–402.
Curti, Merle, and Roderick Nash. 1965. *Philanthropy in the Shaping of American Higher Education*. New Brunswick, NJ: Rutgers University Press.
Di Mento, Maria. 2007. "Nike chair gives $100-million for university athletic fund." *The Chronicle of Philanthropy*, September 6. http://philanthropy.com/article/Nike-Chair-Gives-100-Million/54639/.
Dillon, R. Mark. 1990. "Advancing advancement: A study of fundraising effectiveness among protestant seminaries in the U.S." doctoral dissertation, Union Institute.
Fischer, Karin. 2010. "As cities seek payments in lieu of taxes, colleges are urged to work out deals." *The Chronicle of Higher Education*, November 29.
Fisk University. 2011. *Fisk Focus*, edited by Office of Institutional Advancement. Nashville, TN: Fisk University.
Flaherty, Colleen. 2014. "So much to do, so little time." *Inside Higher Ed*, April 9.
Friedman, Milton. 2008. "The social responsibility of business is to increase its profits." In Jon Burchell (Ed.), *The Corporate Social Responsibility Reader* (pp. 84–89). New York: Routledge.
Funk, Cary, and Greg Smith. 2012. *"Nones" on the Rise: One-in-Five Adults Have No Religious Affiliation*. Washington: Pew Research Center.
Gallagher, Victoria J. 1997. "University repositioning: A review of four cases." *Journal of College Admission* 154: 12–17.
Gibbons, Michael. 1998. *Higher Education Relevance in the 21st Century*. Washington, DC: World Bank.
Gonzales, Leslie D. 2013. "Faculty sensemaking and mission creep: Interrogating institutionalized ways of knowing and doing legitimacy." *The Review of Higher Education* 36 (2): 179–209.
Hahn, William, Lyle Bowlin, and Margaret Britt. 2007. "The incidence of publishing among business disciplines: An examination of nontraditional and traditional doctoral programs." *Journal of Education for Business* 83 (2): 77–86.
Jaschik, Scott. 2005. "Lost cause at Vanderbilt." *Inside Higher Ed*, July 13. http://www.insidehighered.com/news/2005/07/13/vandy.
———. 2008. "Viewbook diversity vs. real diversity." *Inside Higher Ed*, July 2. http://www.insidehighered.com/news/2008/07/02/viewbooks.
———. 2014. "Art vs. endowment." *Inside Higher Ed*, February 10.
Kelly, K. S. 1991. *Fund Raising and Public Relations: A Critical Analysis*. Hillsdale, NJ: Lawrence Erlbaum Associates.
Kennedy, Randy. 2012. "Battle over art collection held at Fisk is settled." *The New York Times*, August 4, 2, Artsbeat.
Kiley, Kevin. 2013. "Fund-raising the bar." *Inside Higher Ed*, March 26.
Lagemann, Ellen Condliffe. 1999. *Private Power for the Public Good: A History of the Carnegie Foundation for the Advancement of Teaching*. New York: College Board.

Levinthal, Dave. 2014. "Inside the Koch brothers' campus crusade." The Center for Public Integrity, Washington, DC.

McCurdy, H. E., and R. E. Cleary. 1984. "Why can't we resolve the research issue in public administration?" *Public Administration Review* 44 (1): 49–55.

McLendon, Michael K., and Christine G. Mokher. 2009. "The origins and growth of state policies that privatize public higher education." In Christopher Morphew and P. Eckel (Eds.), *Privatizing the Public Research University: Perspectives from Across the Academy* (pp. 7–32). Baltimore, MD: Johns Hopkins University Press.

Milem, Jeffrey F., Joseph B. Berger, and Eric L. Dey. 2000. "Faculty time allocation: A study of change over twenty years." *The Journal of Higher Education* 71 (4): 454–75. doi: 10.2307/2649148.

Morphew, Christopher C. 2002. "'A rose by any other name': Which colleges became universities." *The Review of Higher Education* 25 (2): 207–23.

Morphew, Christopher C., and Matthew Hartley. 2006. "Mission statements: A thematic analysis of rhetoric across institutional type." *The Journal of Higher Education* 77 (3): 456–71.

Nelson, Libby A. 2013. "The struggling seminaries." *Inside Higher Ed*, March 29.

Pascarella, Ernest T., and Patrick T. Terenzini. 2005. *How College Affects Students: A Third Decade of Research*. Vol. 2. San Francisco: Jossey-Bass.

Payton, R. L. 1987. "American values and private philanthropy; Philanthropic values; The philanthropic dialogue." In K. W. Thompson (Ed.), *Philanthropy: Private Means, Public Ends* (pp. 3–46, 123–36). Lanham, MD: University Press of America.

Rivard, Ry. 2013. "A JPMorgan Ph.D.?" *Inside Higher Ed*, October 7.

———. 2014. "Deeper pockets." *Inside Higher Ed*, February 12.

Rogers, Megan. 2013. "Mascot makeover." *Inside Higher Ed*, December 10.

Shulman, Lee S., Chris M. Golde, Andrea Conklin Bueschel, and Kristen J. Garabedian. 2006. "Reclaiming education doctorates: A critique and a proposal." *Educational Researcher* 35 (3): 25–32.

Slaughter, Sheila. 2011. "Academic freedom, professional autonomy, and the state." In Joseph C. Hermanowicz (Ed.), *The American Academic Profession: Transformation in Contemporary Higher Education* (pp. 241–73). Baltimore, MD: Johns Hopkins University Press.

Stripling, Jack. 2012. "'Wonder blunder' put U. of Hawaii's president on the hot seat." *The Chronicle of Higher Education*, October 18.

Tierney, William G. 1987. "The semiotic aspects of leadership: An ethnographic perspective." *The American Journal of Semiotics* 5 (2): 233–50.

Toma, J. D., M. Hartley, and L. Montoto. 2008. "Senior managers in higher education studying their own organizations using qualitative methods." Presented at the American Educational Research Association, 2008.

van der Werf, Martin. 2006. "The college as real-estate tycoon." *The Chronicle of Higher Education*, November 10, A26, Money and Management.

Weinberg, Cory. 2014. "Ugly history on Tobacco Road." *Inside Higher Ed*, May 5. http://www.insidehighered.com/news/2014/05/05/duke-and-unc-debate-changing-names-buildings-honor-racists.

Index

501(c) foundations, 72

advancement literature, taxonomy of, 10–11 (table), 40
advancement research, suggestions for, 67–75
alumni associations, 22, 40–1 (table)
alumni relations
  and alumni satisfaction, 22, 57–8
  in dissertation research classification, 40–1 (table)
  and influences on alumni giving, 31, 49, 50–2, 53
  in institutional advancement research, 17, 21–2, 23, 25
  as integral to institutional advancement, 3, 21–2
  in taxonomy of advancement literature, 11–12 (table)
  technology and, 72
alumni satisfaction, 11–12 (table), 22, 40–1 (table), 57–8
American Indian College Fund, 28
annual fund donations, 6, 25
Association for Biblical Higher Education, 29
Association of Fundraising Professionals, 5, 71
athletics
  criticism of donations to, 6–7
  in dissertation research classification and topics, 36, 40–1 (table), 42 (figure), 42
  research on fundraising and, 25, 30–1

  in taxonomy of advancement literature, 11–12 (table)

benchmarking, 11–12 (table), 17–18, 22, 23, 40–1 (table)
Bok, Derek, 6
Braxton, John, 36–7

The Campus Green: Fund Raising in Higher Education (Brittingham and Pezzullo), 8–9, 13–14, 19–20, 23, 44, 49, 55–60, 67, 69
Carbone, Robert, 37
Carnegie Foundation for the Advancement of Teaching, 6
Carter, Linnie, 43
CFRE, 72
chief development officers, 26, 40–1 (table), 71
Clarke, Rebecca, 56
Cockriel, Irvin, 36
Community College Journal of Research and Practice, 43
community colleges
  alumni giving and, 5, 68
  in dissertation research classification and topics, 40–1 (table), 42, 42 (figure)
  and donor motivation, 49, 50–1
  in fundraising research, 25–6, 28–9, 57
  in research trends, 61, 62–3, 69
  in taxonomy of advancement literature, 11–12 (table)

community relations, 11–12 (table), 18–19, 40–1 (table)
corporate and foundation giving, 3, 5, 6, 11, 13, 40–1 (table), 73–4
Council for Aid to Education. *See* Voluntary Support of Education (VSE) survey
Council for Christian Colleges and Universities, 29
Council for the Advancement and Support of Education, 5, 71
crisis communications, 11–12 (table), 19, 40–1 (table), 71, 72

DAI database, 9–10, 34–5, 36, 42, 43
deans, 11–12 (table), 40–1 (table)
Dickerson, Frank C., 43
Dissertation Abstracts International, 9–10, 34–5, 36, 42, 43. *See* DAI database
dissertations and theses
  analysis of, 13, 34–45, 35 (table), 40–1 (table), 42 (figure)
  categories and topics in, 39–43, 40–1 (table), 42 (figure)
  and DAI database, 9–10, 34–5, 36, 42, 43
  graduate institutions in, 42
  methodology in analysis of, 34–5
  methodology used in, 37–9
  and *International Journal of Educational Advancement*, 10, 23, 33–4, 43, 61, 62
  and research trends, 61–3, 62 (figure)
  and sharing of research findings of, 43–5
  single-institutional studies in, 33, 38, 49, 50
  and suggestions for research, 74–5
donor behavior. *See* motivation and predictors of giving
donor characteristics, 25, 28, 33, 44, 49, 50–4
donor statistics (2013), 3
Dressel, Fred, 36–7
Drezner, Noah, 8–9, 27, 68

electronic communications and social media, 19–20, 40–1 (table)
endowed funds, 5, 6–7, 73–4
ethics, 8, 11, 19, 40–1 (table), 57, 67, 70–1
evaluation as research, 58

faculty
  as donors, 52, 61, 64, 70
  in fundraising leadership, 26, 40–1 (table), 64, 71
  in taxonomy of advancement literature, 11–12 (table)
Fellow Beggars: The History of Fundraising Campaigning in United States Higher Education (Oliver), 38
financial aid to students, 3, 70
Friedman, Milton, 6, 7
fundraising
  and corporate and foundation giving, 3, 5, 6, 11, 13, 73–4
  in dissertation research classification, 40–1 (table)
  effects and research needs, 6–7, 69–70
  factors influencing success of, 25, 28–9, 30–1, 50–2
  and gender, 26, 52, 53, 68, 72
  and motivation and predictors for giving, 13, 25, 27, 44, 49–54, 56–7, 68
  and online giving, 61, 62, 64, 67
  professionalization of, 5, 26, 45–6, 72
  research trends in, 61–4, 62 (figure)
  as revenue source, 5–6
  and spending and effectiveness, 56–7, 59–60
  in taxonomy of advancement literature, 11–12 (table)
  See also alumni relations; athletics; community colleges; leadership, institutional
Fygetakis, Christine, 43–4

Gasman, Marybeth, 27, 36, 62
gender, fundraising and, 26, 52, 53, 68, 72
Gibbons, Michael, 63–4
Gibbs, Annette, 36–7
government relations and policy, 11–12 (table), 18, 40–1 (table)
grants, 11 (table), 40–1 (table)

HBCUs, 6, 11–12 (table), 27–8, 40–1 (table), 42, 42 (figure), 61, 69
Higher Learning in America, 4
Historically Black Colleges and Universities (HBCUs). *See* HBCUs
history
  in dissertation research classification, 40–1 (table)
  of higher education fundraising in research, 8, 25, 27, 29, 70
  in research methodology, 37, 38–9
  and research needs, 67–9, 70, 72
  in taxonomy of fundraising literature, 11–12 (table)
How College Affects Students (Pascarella and Terenzini), 9

image creation and branding, 20–1, 40–1 (table)
institutional advancement
  distrust and criticism of, 3–4, 6–7
  fundraising as integral to, 3
  growth of, 5, 6–7, 72
  role of, 3, 4–5
  scholarship on, 4, 8–11, 13–14, 17–23
  taxonomy of literature on, 11–12 (table)
institutional characteristics in research, 28, 44, 49, 51, 56, 68
institutional predictors of giving, 56–7
institutional types and causes
  in dissertation research classification and topics, 40–1 (table), 42, 42 (table)
  and HBCUs and MSIs, 6, 25, 27–8, 42, 42 (figure), 61, 69
  and religious institutions, 29–30, 42, 42 (table), 50, 69
  and research needs, 69
  in taxonomy of advancement literature, 11–12 (table)
  See also athletics; community colleges
integrated communications management, 20, 40–1 (table)
Integrated Postsecondary Education Data System (IPEDS), 5, 23, 37, 50, 53, 73, 74
international institutions, 11–12 (table), 30, 40–1 (table)
International Journal of Educational Advancement, 10, 23, 33–4, 43, 61, 62
Internet, role of. *See* online giving
IPEDS. *See* Integrated Postsecondary Education Data System (IPEDS)

The Journal of Higher Education, 43, 45

Kelly, Kathleen, 33, 44, 49, 51, 58
Kotler, Phillip, 19

leadership, institutional
  in dissertation research classification, 40–1 (table)
  and fundraising, 25, 26, 29, 52, 57, 64, 67–8, 71–2
  public relations professionals within, 17–18
  and research needs, 71–2
  in taxonomy of advancement literature, 11–12 (table)
Letzring, Timothy, 36–7
lobbyists, 18

marketing
  in dissertation research classification, 40–1 (table)
  growth and development of, 19

marketing—*Continued*
  in institutional advancement
    research, 19–21
  as part of institutional
    advancement, 3
  in taxonomy of advancement
    literature, 11–12 (table)
  and university rankings, 7, 21,
    37, 74
  See also ethics; public relations
media relations, 18
methodology and research needs,
  59–60, 68–9
methodology in research, 9–11
minority-serving institutions.
  See MSIs (minority-serving
  institutions)
mission, consistency of, 55–6, 59–60,
  69–70
motivation and predictors of giving,
  11–12 (table), 13, 25, 27, 44,
  49–54, 56, 68
MSIs (minority-serving institutions),
  11–12 (table), 25, 27–8, 40–1
  (table), 42, 69. *See also* HBCUs

National Collegiate Athletic
  Association, 50
Native Americans, institutions
  serving, 28, 56, 69
Neuman, Lisa K., 56, 59
*New Directions for Community
  Colleges*, 62–3
*New Directions for Philanthropic
  Fundraising*, 36
New Directions in Higher Education,
  43
*New Strategies for Educational
  Fundraising* (Worth), 8
nonalumni donors, 13, 52, 53, 67
*Nonprofit and Voluntary Sector
  Quarterly*, 36, 43
nontraditional donors and research
  needs, 68

online giving, 11–12 (table), 40–1
  (table), 61, 62, 64, 67

Peterson, Marvin, 36, 62
*Philanthropy and Fundraising in
  American Higher Education*
  (Drezner), 8–9
planned giving, 11–12 (table), 40–1
  (table)
presidents, 26, 29, 40–1 (table), 52,
  71
private institutions, 5–6, 45, 57
professional organizations, rise of, 72
public image, 69–70
public relations
  in dissertation research
    classification, 39, 40–1 (table)
  and electronic communications and
    social media, 20
  increasing sophistication of, 7
  in institutional advancement
    research, 17–19, 25
  as part of institutional
    advancement, 3
  and suggestions for research, 67, 73

rankings, university. *See* university
  rankings
religious institutions, 11–12 (table),
  29–30, 40–1 (table), 42, 42
  (figure), 50, 69
Research in Higher Education, 43, 45
restricted giving, 6–7
The Review of Higher Education, 45
Rooney, Margarete, 56

single- v. multi-institutional studies
  in dissertations and theses, 33, 34,
    38, 49, 50, 58
  donor motivation in, 13, 51
  in fundraising research, 28–9
  in institutional advancement
    research, 19, 20, 23
  and suggestions for research, 73
social media, 11–12 (table), 19–20,
  40–1 (table), 72
Southerland, Arthur, 36–7
staff giving, 52, 70
staffing, 4, 11–12 (table), 25, 26, 29,
  40–1 (table), 42 (figure)

state funding for higher education, 5–6, 18
Stein, Ronald, 36
stewardship, 11–12 (table), 40–1 (table)
Strategic Marketing for Education Institutions (Kotler and Fox), 19
student affairs, 25, 31
Sweitzer, Kyle, 43

taxonomy of advancement literature, 10–11, 11–12 (table), 40
Tierney, Bill, 71
time-diary studies, 72–3
tribal colleges, 28, 69
trustees, 26, 29, 52, 55, 57, 71

U.S. News and World Report, 7, 21, 37, 74. *See also* rankings, university

university rankings, 7, 11–12 (table), 21, 37, 40–1 (table), 74
unrestricted gifts, 5–6

Vanderbilt University, 3, 35 (table), 36–7, 69–70
Veblen, Thorstein, 4
venture philanthropy, 32
vice presidents, provosts, and chief development officers, 11–12 (table), 26, 40–1 (table), 71
Voluntary Support of Education (VSE) survey, 6, 23, 37, 50, 51, 53, 73–4
volunteers, 11–12 (table), 26, 40–1 (table)
VSE. *See* Voluntary Support of Education survey (VSE)

GPSR Compliance

The European Union's (EU) General Product Safety Regulation (GPSR) is a set of rules that requires consumer products to be safe and our obligations to ensure this.

If you have any concerns about our products, you can contact us on

ProductSafety@springernature.com

In case Publisher is established outside the EU, the EU authorized representative is:

Springer Nature Customer Service Center GmbH
Europaplatz 3
69115 Heidelberg, Germany

www.ingramcontent.com/pod-product-compliance
Lightning Source LLC
LaVergne TN
LVHW051914060526
838200LV00004B/139